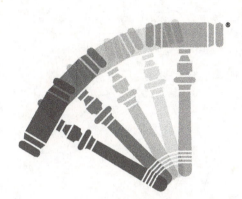

Casenote® Legal Briefs

TORTS

Keyed to Courses Using

Franklin, Rabin, Green, and Geistfeld
Tort Law and Alternatives: Cases and Materials
Tenth Edition

Wolters Kluwer

Copyright © 2017 CCH Incorporated. All Rights Reserved.

Published by Wolters Kluwer in New York.

Wolters Kluwer Legal & Regulatory US serves customers worldwide with CCH, Aspen Publishers, and Kluwer Law International products. (www.WKLegaledu.com)

To contact Customer Service, e-mail customer.service@wolterskluwer.com, call 1-800-234-1660, fax 1-800-901-9075, or mail correspondence to:

Wolters Kluwer
Attn: Order Department
P.O. Box 990
Frederick, MD 21705

Printed in the United States of America.

1 2 3 4 5 6 7 8 9 0

ISBN 978-1-4548-8315-9

About Wolters Kluwer Legal & Regulatory US

Wolters Kluwer Legal & Regulatory US delivers expert content and solutions in the areas of law, corporate compliance, health compliance, reimbursement, and legal education. Its practical solutions help customers successfully navigate the demands of a changing environment to drive their daily activities, enhance decision quality and inspire confident outcomes.

Serving customers worldwide, its legal and regulatory portfolio includes products under the Aspen Publishers, CCH Incorporated, Kluwer Law International, ftwilliam.com and MediRegs names. They are regarded as exceptional and trusted resources for general legal and practice-specific knowledge, compliance and risk management, dynamic workflow solutions, and expert commentary.

Format for the Casenote® Legal Brief

Nature of Case: This section identifies the form of action (e.g., breach of contract, negligence, battery), the type of proceeding (e.g., demurrer, appeal from trial court's jury instructions), or the relief sought (e.g., damages, injunction, criminal sanctions).

Fact Summary: This is included to refresh your memory and can be used as a quick reminder of the facts.

Rule of Law: Summarizes the general principle of law that the case illustrates. It may be used for instant recall of the court's holding and for classroom discussion or home review.

Facts: This section contains all relevant facts of the case, including the contentions of the parties and the lower court holdings. It is written in a logical order to give the student a clear understanding of the case. The plaintiff and defendant are identified by their proper names throughout and are always labeled with a (P) or (D).

Palsgraf v. Long Island R.R. Co.

Injured bystander (P) v. Railroad company (D)

N.Y. Ct. App., 248 N.Y. 339, 162 N.E. 99 (1928).

NATURE OF CASE: Appeal from judgment affirming verdict for plaintiff seeking damages for personal injury.

FACT SUMMARY: Helen Palsgraf (P) was injured on R.R.'s (D) train platform when R.R.'s (D) guard helped a passenger aboard a moving train, causing his package to fall on the tracks. The package contained fireworks which exploded, creating a shock that tipped a scale onto Palsgraf (P).

🏛 RULE OF LAW
The risk reasonably to be perceived defines the duty to be obeyed.

FACTS: Helen Palsgraf (P) purchased a ticket to Rockaway Beach from R.R. (D) and was waiting on the train platform. As she waited, two men ran to catch a train that was pulling out from the platform. The first man jumped aboard, but the second man, who appeared as if he might fall, was helped aboard by the guard on the train who had kept the door open so they could jump aboard. A guard on the platform also helped by pushing him onto the train. The man was carrying a package wrapped in newspaper. In the process, the man dropped his package, which fell on the tracks. The package contained fireworks and exploded. The shock of the explosion was apparently of great enough strength to tip over some scales at the other end of the platform, which fell on Palsgraf (P) and injured her. A jury awarded her damages, and R.R. (D) appealed.

ISSUE: Does the risk reasonably to be perceived define the duty to be obeyed?

HOLDING AND DECISION: (Cardozo, C.J.) Yes. The risk reasonably to be perceived defines the duty to be obeyed. If there is no foreseeable hazard to the injured party as the result of a seemingly innocent act, the act does not become a tort because it happened to be a wrong as to another. If the wrong was not willful, the plaintiff must show that the act as to her had such great and apparent possibilities of danger as to entitle her to protection. Negligence in the abstract is not enough upon which to base liability. Negligence is a relative concept, evolving out of the common law doctrine of trespass on the case. To establish liability, the defendant must owe a legal duty of reasonable care to the injured party. A cause of action in tort will lie where harm,

though unintended, could have been averted or avoided by observance of such a duty. The scope of the duty is limited by the range of danger that a reasonable person could foresee. In this case, there was nothing to suggest from the appearance of the parcel or otherwise that the parcel contained fireworks. The guard could not reasonably have had any warning of a threat to Palsgraf (P), and R.R. (D) therefore cannot be held liable. Judgment is reversed in favor of R.R. (D).

DISSENT: (Andrews, J.) The concept that there is no negligence unless R.R. (D) owes a legal duty to take care as to Palsgraf (P) herself is too narrow. Everyone owes to the world at large the duty of refraining from those acts that may unreasonably threaten the safety of others. If the guard's action was negligent as to those nearby, it was also negligent as to those outside what might be termed the "danger zone." For Palsgraf (P) to recover, R.R.'s (D) negligence must have been the proximate cause of her injury, a question of fact for the jury.

▶ ANALYSIS

The majority defined the limit of the defendant's liability in terms of the danger that a reasonable person in defendant's situation would have perceived. The dissent argued that the limitation should not be placed on liability, but rather on damages. Judge Andrews suggested that only injuries that would not have happened but for R.R.'s (D) negligence should be compensable. Both the majority and dissent recognized the policy-driven need to limit liability for negligent acts, seeking, in the words of Judge Andrews, to define a framework "that will be practical and in keeping with the general understanding of mankind." The Restatement (Second) of Torts has accepted Judge Cardozo's view.

▬▬

Quicknotes

FORESEEABILITY A reasonable expectation that change is the probable result of certain acts or omissions.

NEGLIGENCE Conduct falling below the standard of care that a reasonable person would demonstrate under similar conditions.

PROXIMATE CAUSE The natural sequence of events without which an injury would not have been sustained.

▬▬

Party ID: Quick identification of the relationship between the parties.

Concurrence/Dissent: All concurrences and dissents are briefed whenever they are included by the casebook editor.

Analysis: This last paragraph gives you a broad understanding of where the case "fits in" with other cases in the section of the book and with the entire course. It is a hornbook-style discussion indicating whether the case is a majority or minority opinion and comparing the principal case with other cases in the casebook. It may also provide analysis from restatements, uniform codes, and law review articles. The analysis will prove to be invaluable to classroom discussion.

Issue: The issue is a concise question that brings out the essence of the opinion as it relates to the section of the casebook in which the case appears. Both substantive and procedural issues are included if relevant to the decision.

Holding and Decision: This section offers a clear and in-depth discussion of the rule of the case and the court's rationale. It is written in easy-to-understand language and answers the issue presented by applying the law to the facts of the case. When relevant, it includes a thorough discussion of the exceptions to the case as listed by the court, any major cites to the other cases on point, and the names of the judges who wrote the decisions.

Quicknotes: Conveniently defines legal terms found in the case and summarizes the nature of any statutes, codes, or rules referred to in the text.

Wolters Kluwer Legal & Regulatory US is proud to offer *Casenote®* *Legal Briefs*—continuing thirty years of publishing America's best-selling legal briefs.

Casenote® *Legal Briefs* are designed to help you save time when briefing assigned cases. Organized under convenient headings, they show you how to abstract the basic facts and holdings from the text of the actual opinions handed down by the courts. Used as part of a rigorous study regimen, they can help you spend more time analyzing and critiquing points of law than on copying bits and pieces of judicial opinions into your notebook or outline.

Casenote® *Legal Briefs* should never be used as a substitute for assigned casebook readings. They work best when read as a follow-up to reviewing the underlying opinions themselves. Students who try to avoid reading and digesting the judicial opinions in their casebooks or online sources will end up shortchanging themselves in the long run. The ability to absorb, critique, and restate the dynamic and complex elements of case law decisions is crucial to your success in law school and beyond. It cannot be developed vicariously.

Casenote® *Legal Briefs* represents but one of the many offerings in Legal Education's Study Aid Timeline, which includes:

- *Casenote®* *Legal Briefs*
- *Emanuel®* *Law Outlines*
- *Emanuel®* *Law in a Flash* Flash Cards
- *Emanuel®* *CrunchTime®* Series

Each of these series is designed to provide you with easy-to-understand explanations of complex points of law. Each volume offers guidance on the principles of legal analysis and, consulted regularly, will hone your ability to spot relevant issues. We have titles that will help you prepare for class, prepare for your exams, and enhance your general comprehension of the law along the way.

To find out more about our law school tools for success, visit us at *www.WKLegaledu.com* or email us at *legaledu@wolterskluwer.com*. We'll be happy to assist you.

How to Brief a Case

A. Decide on a Format and Stick to It

Structure is essential to a good brief. It enables you to arrange systematically the related parts that are scattered throughout most cases, thus making manageable and understandable what might otherwise seem to be an endless and unfathomable sea of information. There are, of course, an unlimited number of formats that can be utilized. However, it is best to find one that suits your needs and stick to it. Consistency breeds both efficiency and the security that when called upon you will know where to look in your brief for the information you are asked to give.

Any format, as long as it presents the essential elements of a case in an organized fashion, can be used. Experience, however, has led *Casenote® Legal Briefs* to develop and utilize the following format because of its logical flow and universal applicability.

NATURE OF CASE: This is a brief statement of the legal character and procedural status of the case (e.g., "Appeal of a burglary conviction").

There are many different alternatives open to a litigant dissatisfied with a court ruling. The key to determining which one has been used is to discover *who is asking this court for what*.

This first entry in the brief should be kept as *short as possible*. Use the court's terminology if you understand it. But since jurisdictions vary as to the titles of pleadings, the best entry is the one that addresses who wants what in this proceeding, not the one that sounds most like the court's language.

RULE OF LAW: A statement of the general principle of law that the case illustrates (e.g., "An acceptance that varies any term of the offer is considered a rejection and counteroffer").

Determining the rule of law of a case is a procedure similar to determining the issue of the case. Avoid being fooled by red herrings; there may be a few rules of law mentioned in the case excerpt, but usually only one is *the* rule with which the casebook editor is concerned. The techniques used to locate the issue, described below, may also be utilized to find the rule of law. Generally, your best guide is simply the chapter heading. It is a clue to the point the casebook editor seeks to make and should be kept in mind when reading every case in the respective section.

FACTS: A synopsis of only the essential facts of the case, i.e., those bearing upon or leading up to the issue.

The facts entry should be a short statement of the events and transactions that led one party to initiate legal proceedings against another in the first place. While some cases conveniently state the salient facts at the beginning of the decision, in other instances they will have to be culled from hiding places throughout the text, even from concurring and dissenting opinions. Some of the "facts" will often be in dispute and should be so noted. Conflicting evidence may be briefly pointed up. "Hard" facts must be included. Both must be *relevant* in order to be listed in the facts entry. It is impossible to tell what is relevant until the entire case is read, as the ultimate determination of the rights and liabilities of the parties may turn on something buried deep in the opinion.

Generally, the facts entry should not be longer than three to five *short* sentences.

It is often helpful to identify the role played by a party in a given context. For example, in a construction contract case the identification of a party as the "contractor" or "builder" alleviates the need to tell that that party was the one who was supposed to have built the house.

It is always helpful, and a good general practice, to identify the "plaintiff" and the "defendant." This may seem elementary and uncomplicated, but, especially in view of the creative editing practiced by some casebook editors, it is sometimes a difficult or even impossible task. Bear in mind that the *party presently* seeking something from this court may not be the plaintiff, and that sometimes only the cross-claim of a defendant is treated in the excerpt. Confusing or misaligning the parties can ruin your analysis and understanding of the case.

ISSUE: A statement of the general legal question answered by or illustrated in the case. For clarity, the issue is best put in the form of a question capable of a "yes" or "no" answer. In reality, the issue is simply the Rule of Law put in the form of a question (e.g., "May an offer be accepted by performance?").

The major problem presented in discerning what is *the* issue in the case is that an opinion usually purports to raise and answer several questions. However, except for rare cases, only one such question is really the issue in the case. Collateral issues not necessary to the resolution of the matter in controversy are handled by the court by language known as *"obiter dictum"* or merely *"dictum."* While dicta may be included later in the brief, they have no place under the issue heading.

To find the issue, ask *who wants what* and then go on to ask *why did that party succeed or fail in getting it*. Once this is determined, the "why" should be turned into a question.

The complexity of the issues in the cases will vary, but in all cases a single-sentence question should sum up the issue. *In a few cases,* there will be two, or even more rarely, three issues of equal importance to the resolution of the case. Each should be expressed in a single-sentence question.

Since many issues are resolved by a court in coming to a final disposition of a case, the casebook editor will reproduce the portion of the opinion containing the issue or issues most relevant to the area of law under scrutiny. A noted law professor gave this advice: "Close the book; look at the title on the cover." Chances are, if it is Property, you need not concern yourself with whether, for example, the federal government's treatment of the plaintiff's land really raises a federal question sufficient to support jurisdiction on this ground in federal court.

The same rule applies to chapter headings designating sub-areas within the subjects. They tip you off as to what the text is designed to teach. The cases are arranged in a casebook to show a progression or development of the law, so that the preceding cases may also help.

It is also most important to remember to *read the notes and questions* at the end of a case to determine what the editors wanted you to have gleaned from it.

HOLDING AND DECISION: This section should succinctly explain the rationale of the court in arriving at its decision. In capsulizing the "reasoning" of the court, it should always include an application of the general rule or rules of law to the specific facts of the case. Hidden justifications come to light in this entry: the reasons for the state of the law, the public policies, the biases and prejudices, those considerations that influence the justices' thinking and, ultimately, the outcome of the case. At the end, there should be a short indication of the disposition or procedural resolution of the case (e.g., "Decision of the trial court for Mr. Smith (P) reversed").

The foregoing format is designed to help you "digest" the reams of case material with which you will be faced in your law school career. Once mastered by practice, it will place at your fingertips the information the authors of your casebooks have sought to impart to you in case-by-case illustration and analysis.

B. Be as Economical as Possible in Briefing Cases

Once armed with a format that encourages succinctness, it is as important to be economical with regard to the time spent on the actual reading of the case as it is to be economical in the writing of the brief itself. This does not mean "skimming" a case. Rather, it means reading the case with an "eye" trained to recognize into which "section" of your brief a particular passage or line fits and having a system for quickly and precisely marking the case so that the passages fitting any one particular part of

the brief can be easily identified and brought together in a concise and accurate manner when the brief is actually written.

It is of no use to simply repeat everything in the opinion of the court; record only enough information to trigger your recollection of what the court said. Nevertheless, an accurate statement of the "law of the case," i.e., the legal principle applied to the facts, is absolutely essential to class preparation and to learning the law under the case method.

To that end, it is important to develop a "shorthand" that you can use to make marginal notations. These notations will tell you at a glance in which section of the brief you will be placing that particular passage or portion of the opinion.

Some students prefer to underline all the salient portions of the opinion (with a pencil or colored underliner marker), making marginal notations as they go along. Others prefer the color-coded method of underlining, utilizing different colors of markers to underline the salient portions of the case, each separate color being used to represent a different section of the brief. For example, blue underlining could be used for passages relating to the rule of law, yellow for those relating to the issue, and green for those relating to the holding and decision, etc. While it has its advocates, the color-coded method can be confusing and time-consuming (all that time spent on changing colored markers). Furthermore, it can interfere with the continuity and concentration many students deem essential to the reading of a case for maximum comprehension. In the end, however, it is a matter of personal preference and style. Just remember, whatever method you use, underlining must be used sparingly or its value is lost.

If you take the marginal notation route, an efficient and easy method is to go along underlining the key portions of the case and placing in the margin alongside them the following "markers" to indicate where a particular passage or line "belongs" in the brief you will write:

N	(NATURE OF CASE)
RL	(RULE OF LAW)
I	(ISSUE)
HL	(HOLDING AND DECISION, relates to the RULE OF LAW behind the decision)
HR	(HOLDING AND DECISION, gives the RATIONALE or reasoning behind the decision)
HA	(HOLDING AND DECISION, applies the general principle(s) of law to the facts of the case to arrive at the decision)

Remember that a particular passage may well contain information necessary to more than one part of your brief, in which case you simply note that in the margin. If you are using the color-coded underlining method instead of marginal notation, simply make asterisks or checks in the margin next to the passage in question in the colors that indicate the additional sections of the brief where it might be utilized.

The economy of utilizing "shorthand" in marking cases for briefing can be maintained in the actual brief writing process itself by utilizing "law student shorthand" within the brief. There are many commonly used words and phrases for which abbreviations can be substituted in your briefs (and in your class notes also). You can develop abbreviations that are personal to you and which will save you a lot of time. A reference list of briefing abbreviations can be found on page x of this book.

C. Use Both the Briefing Process and the Brief as a Learning Tool

Now that you have a format and the tools for briefing cases efficiently, the most important thing is to make the time spent in briefing profitable to you and to make the most advantageous use of the briefs you create. Of course, the briefs are invaluable for classroom reference when you are called upon to explain or analyze a particular

case. However, they are also useful in reviewing for exams. A quick glance at the fact summary should bring the case to mind, and a rereading of the rule of law should enable you to go over the underlying legal concept in your mind, how it was applied in that particular case, and how it might apply in other factual settings.

As to the value to be derived from engaging in the briefing process itself, there is an immediate benefit that arises from being forced to sift through the essential facts and reasoning from the court's opinion and to succinctly express them in your own words in your brief. The process ensures that you understand the case and the point that it illustrates, and that means you will be ready to absorb further analysis and information brought forth in class. It also ensures you will have something to say when called upon in class. The briefing process helps develop a mental agility for getting to the *gist* of a case and for identifying, expounding on, and applying the legal concepts and issues found there. The briefing process is the mental process on which you must rely in taking law school examinations; it is also the mental process upon which a lawyer relies in serving his clients and in making his living.

Abbreviations for Briefs

acceptance	acp		offer	O
affirmed	aff		offeree	OE
answer	ans		offeror	OR
assumption of risk	a/r		ordinance	ord
attorney	atty		pain and suffering	p/s
beyond a reasonable doubt	b/r/d		parol evidence	p/e
bona fide purchaser	BFP		plaintiff	P
breach of contract	br/k		prima facie	p/f
cause of action	c/a		probable cause	p/c
common law	c/l		proximate cause	px/c
Constitution	Con		real property	r/p
constitutional	con		reasonable doubt	r/d
contract	K		reasonable man	r/m
contributory negligence	c/n		rebuttable presumption	rb/p
cross	x		remanded	rem
cross-complaint	x/c		res ipsa loquitur	RIL
cross-examination	x/ex		respondeat superior	r/s
cruel and unusual punishment	c/u/p		Restatement	RS
defendant	D		reversed	rev
dismissed	dis		Rule Against Perpetuities	RAP
double jeopardy	d/j		search and seizure	s/s
due process	d/p		search warrant	s/w
equal protection	e/p		self-defense	s/d
equity	eq		specific performance	s/p
evidence	ev		statute	S
exclude	exc		statute of frauds	S/F
exclusionary rule	exc/r		statute of limitations	S/L
felony	f/n		summary judgment	s/j
freedom of speech	f/s		tenancy at will	t/w
good faith	g/f		tenancy in common	t/c
habeas corpus	h/c		tenant	t
hearsay	hr		third party	TP
husband	H		third party beneficiary	TPB
injunction	inj		transferred intent	TI
in loco parentis	ILP		unconscionable	uncon
inter vivos	I/v		unconstitutional	unconst
joint tenancy	j/t		undue influence	u/e
judgment	judgt		Uniform Commercial Code	UCC
jurisdiction	jur		unilateral	uni
last clear chance	LCC		vendee	VE
long-arm statute	LAS		vendor	VR
majority view	maj		versus	v
meeting of minds	MOM		void for vagueness	VFV
minority view	min		weight of authority	w/a
Miranda rule	Mir/r		weight of the evidence	w/e
Miranda warnings	Mir/w		wife	W
negligence	neg		with	w/
notice	ntc		within	w/i
nuisance	nus		without	w/o
obligation	ob		without prejudice	w/o/p
obscene	obs		wrongful death	wr/d

Table of Cases

Introduction to Tort Liability

Quick Reference Rules of Law

Hammontree v. Jenner

Injured plaintiff (P) v. Epileptic driver (D)

Cal. Ct. App., 20 Cal. App. 3d 528, 97 Cal. Rptr. 739 (1971).

NATURE OF CASE: Action for damages based on negligence and strict liability.

FACT SUMMARY: Jenner (D) had an epileptic fit while driving and injured Hammontree (P).

🏛 RULE OF LAW
A sudden illness that renders a driver unconscious will not be grounds for an action in negligence or strict liability.

FACTS: Jenner (D) had a history of epileptic seizures. Jenner (D) had been under doctor's care and medication since 1951. Jenner's (D) last seizure was in 1953. In 1967, Jenner (D) apparently had a seizure while driving and while unconscious he crashed into Hammontree's (P) store causing personal injuries and property damage. Hammontree (P) brought suit for negligence and strict liability in tort. The judge refused to instruct the jury on strict liability on the ground that the theory was not applicable to sudden illnesses which strike a driver rendering him unconscious. The jury found no negligence.

ISSUE: Is strict liability in tort a proper theory to apply to sudden illnesses that renders a driver unconscious?

HOLDING AND DECISION: (Lillie, J.) No. A sudden illness that renders a driver unconscious will not be grounds for an action in negligence or strict liabilitiy. We decline to superimpose absolute liability in such situations. This is not akin to a products liability case where a manufacturer put out a defective product. Here, Jenner (D) had not had a seizure for 14 years, was under doctor's care, and was receiving medication to control his condition. The jury properly found he had no notice of the onset of the seizure, nor any grounds to suspect it was likely to occur. Since there were no grounds for a finding of negligence, Hammontree (P) could not recover. Affirmed.

▶ANALYSIS

Where the driver has constructive or actual notice of the onset of a serious illness that might make driving dangerous, negligence may be found. Where an outside force beyond the driver's control, e.g., a swarm of bees enters the car, causes the accident, no liability will normally be found. These cases are all decided on a fault/negligence issue. Sudden heart attack is not grounds for liability. *Tannyhill v. Pacific Motor Transport Co.*, 227 Cal. App. 2d 512.

Quicknotes

ACTUAL NOTICE Direct communication of information that would cause an ordinary person of average prudence to inquire as to its truth.

CONSTRUCTIVE NOTICE Knowledge of a fact imputed to an individual who was under a duty to inquire and who could have learned of the fact through the exercise of reasonable prudence.

NEGLIGENCE Conduct falling below the standard of care that a reasonable person would demonstrate under similar conditions.

STRICT LIABILITY Liability for all injuries proximately caused by a party's conducting of certain inherently dangerous activities without regard to negligence or fault.

■■■

Christensen v. Swenson

Injured (P) v. Tortfeasor-employee (D)

Utah Sup. Ct., 874 P.2d 125 (1994).

NATURE OF CASE: Appeal from summary judgment for employer.

FACT SUMMARY: Christensen (P) alleged that Swenson's (D) employer was vicariously liable for damages.

🏛 RULE OF LAW
For an employer to be vicariously liable for the torts committed by an employee, the employee must have been acting within the scope of his employment.

FACTS: Swenson (D), a security guard, was taking a short lunch break when his car was involved in an accident. Christensen (P) sued Swenson (D) and his employer (D). The trial court granted the employer's motion for summary judgment, holding that Swenson (D) was not within the ordinary spatial boundaries of her employment when the accident occurred. Christensen (P) appealed, alleging that reasonable minds could differ as to whether Swenson (D) was acting within or outside the scope of her employment when she collided with Christensen's (P) motorcycle.

ISSUE: For an employer to be vicariously liable for the torts committed by an employee, must the employee have been acting within the scope of his employment?

HOLDING AND DECISION: (Durham, J.) Yes. For an employer to be vicariously liable for the torts committed by an employee, the employee must have been acting within the scope of his employment. Three criteria, stated in *Birkner v. Salt Lake County*, 771 P.2d 1053, 1057 (Utah 1989), are helpful in determining whether an employee is acting within the scope of her employment. First, the employee's conduct must be of the general kind the employee is hired to perform. Second, the employee's conduct must occur substantially within the hours and ordinary spatial boundaries of the employment. Third, the employee's conduct must be motivated, at least in part, by the purpose of serving the employer's interest. This court's review of the record reveals that reasonable minds could differ on all three criteria. Reversed and remanded.

▶ ANALYSIS

The Restatement (Second) of Agency § 229(2) lists ten factors to be considered in determining whether an employee was acting within the scope of his employment. Under the doctrine of respondeat superior, employers are vicariously liable for torts committed by their employees while acting within the scope of their employment. In this case, the plaintiff was alleging that the defendant was driving negligently when she hit the motorcycle.

Quicknotes

NEGLIGENCE Conduct falling below the standard of care that a reasonable person would demonstrate under similar conditions.

RESPONDEAT SUPERIOR Rule that the principal is responsible for tortious acts committed by its agents in the scope of their agency or authority.

VICARIOUS LIABILITY The imputed liability of one party for the unlawful acts of another.

Roessler v. Novak

Patient (P) v. Hospital (D)

Fla. Dist. Ct. App., 858 So. 2d 1158 (2003).

NATURE OF CASE: Appeal from the granting of a defense motion for a summary judgment in a medical malpractice suit.

FACT SUMMARY: When Klaus Roessler (P) sued Sarasota Memorial Hospital (the Hospital) (D) at which he received emergency treatment, the Hospital (D) argued that the allegedly negligent radiologist, although part of a radiology group located within the Hospital (D), was an independent contractor, hence there was no agency relationship between the Hospital (D) and the radiology physicians.

RULE OF LAW

A hospital may be held vicariously liable for acts of independent contractor physicians if the latter act with the apparent authority of the hospital.

FACTS: Klaus Roessler (P) entered the emergency room of Sarasota Memorial Hospital (the Hospital) (D) where he was evaluated and admitted. Diagnostic radiological scans of his abdomen were taken by Dr. Richard Lichtenstein, the radiologist on duty. After surgery, Roessler (P) suffered serious complications that had to be surgically treated. Roessler (P) sued the Hospital (D), alleging that Dr. Lichtenstein misinterpreted the scans taken at the Hospital (D) and was also negligent in failing to make a proper differential diagnosis. The Hospital (D) filed a motion for a summary judgment, contending that it was not liable for the acts of Dr. Lichtenstein on the grounds that the radiology physicians at the Hospital (D) were independent contractors, thus no agency relationship existed between them and the Hospital (D). The trial court granted the motion, and Roessler (P) appealed.

ISSUE: May a hospital be held vicariously liable for acts of independent contractor physicians if the latter act with the apparent authority of the hospital?

HOLDING AND DECISION: (Salcines, J.) Yes. A hospital may be held vicariously liable for acts of independent contractor physicians if the latter act with the apparent authority of the hospital. Here, the evidence fulfilled all three elements to constitute an apparent authority between Dr. Lichtenstein and the Hospital (D), namely, (1) a representation by the purported principal (the Hospital); (2) a reliance on that representation by a third party (Roessler); and (3) a change in position by the third party (Roessler) in reliance on the representation. Roessler (D) was reasonably led by the Hospital (D) to rely upon it to provide radiological services. Specifically, the Hospital (D) maintained a radiology department that was physically located within the Hospital's (D) grounds. The Hospital (D) contracted with a radiology group, of which Dr. Lichtenstein was a member, for it to be the exclusive provider of radiology services for the Hospital (D). The radiology group provided all radiology services to the Hospital (D) twenty-four hours a day, seven days a week. When Roessler (P) was admitted to the Hospital (D) for emergency care, he was sent directly to the radiology department. Roessler (P) did not attempt to secure an outside specialist but rather accepted the radiologist provided to him by the Hospital (D). It would have been reasonably apparent to Roessler (P) that this was "the Hospital's" radiology department. On the facts presented, there was at the least a jury question concerning this issue. Reversed and remanded.

CONCURRENCE: (Altenbernd, C.J.) While the theory of apparent authority works reasonably well to create vicarious liability for some types of cases, it has not generally worked well to establish responsibility for torts in the context of a complex institution like a hospital that has many interrelated independent contractors working side by side for the same customers.

▶ ANALYSIS

Some hospitals employ their own staff physicians while others enter into contractual arrangements with legal entities made up of an association of physicians to provide medical services as independent contractors with the expectation that vicarious liability will not attach to the hospital for negligence of those physicians. Under certain circumstances, however, such an arrangement may still give rise to vicarious liability of the hospital (under the doctrine of apparent authority), particularly where emergency treatment is involved.

■■◄■

Quicknotes

APPARENT AUTHORITY The authority granted to an agent to act on behalf of the principal in order to effectuate the principal's objective, which may not be expressly granted, but which is inferred from the conduct of the principal and the agent.

NEGLIGENCE Conduct falling below the standard of care that a reasonable person would demonstrate under similar conditions.

VICARIOUS LIABILITY The imputed liability of one party for the unlawful acts of another.

■■◄■

The Negligence Principle

Quick Reference Rules of Law

13. *Byrne v. Boadle*. There are circumstances in which the mere fact an accident has occurred give rise to a presumption of negligence that must then be rebutted by the defendant.

14. *McDougald v. Perry*. The doctrine of res ipsa loquitur provides an injured plaintiff with an inference of negligence where direct proof is not available, if the plaintiff establishes that the instrumentality causing his injury was under the exclusive control of the defendant and the accident is one that would not, in the ordinary course of events, have occurred in the absence of negligence on the part of the one in control of the instrumentality.

15. *Ybarra v. Spangard*. Where a medical patient suffers unexplained injuries to a part of his body not under treatment and not within the area being operated on, res ipsa loquitur applies and gives rise to a presumption of negligence covering all those defendants who had any control over his body or the instrumentalities that might have caused the injuries.

16. *Sheeley v. Memorial Hospital*. A physician is under a duty to use the degree of caution and skill that is expected of a reasonably competent practitioner in the same class, acting in the same or similar circumstances.

17. *Matthies v. Mastromonaco*. To obtain a patient's informed consent to one of several alternative courses of treatment, the physician should explain medically reasonable invasive and noninvasive alternatives, even when the chosen course is noninvasive.

Brown v. Kendall

Injured (P) v. Dog owner (D)

Mass. Sup. Jud. Ct., 60 Mass. (6 Cush.) 292 (1850).

NATURE OF CASE: Trespass for assault and battery.

FACT SUMMARY: Kendall (D), while attempting to separate his dog from Brown's (P) dog when the two dogs were fighting, accidentally struck Brown (P) with a stick.

🏛 RULE OF LAW
If in the prosecution of a lawful act, a casualty purely accidental arises, i.e., the injury was unavoidable, and the conduct of the defendant was free from blame, no action can be supported for an injury arising therefrom.

FACTS: Two dogs, owned by Brown (P) and Kendall (D), respectively, were fighting. Kendall (D) attempted to separate the dogs with a stick. When Kendall (D) raised the stick to strike the dogs, Kendall (D) stepped back to avoid the dogs as they approached him, and he accidentally struck Brown (P), who was behind him, in the eye, inflicting a serious injury. Brown (P) brought an action in trespass for assault and battery. The trial court instructed the jury that if it was not a necessary act and Kendall (D) was not in duty bound to part the dogs, he was responsible for the consequences of the blow, unless it appeared he exercised extraordinary care, so the accident was inevitable. It further instructed that if Kendall (D) had no duty to separate the dogs, then the burden of proving extraordinary care was on him, as well as showing alternatively a lack of ordinary care on the part of Brown (P). Following Kendall's (D) death, his executrix (D) was summoned in.

ISSUE: If in the prosecution of a lawful act, a casualty purely accidental arises, i.e., the injury was unavoidable, and the conduct of the defendant was free from blame, can an action be supported for an injury arising therefrom?

HOLDING AND DECISION: (Shaw, C.J.) No. If in the prosecution of a lawful act, a casualty purely accidental arises, i.e., the injury was unavoidable, and the conduct of the defendant was free from blame, no action can be supported for an injury arising therefrom. The instructions that should have been given are to the effect that Brown (P) could not recover (1) if at the time of the accident both Kendall (D) and he were using ordinary care; or (2) if Kendall (D) was using ordinary care and Brown (P) was not; or (3) if neither were using ordinary care. What constitutes ordinary care will vary with the circumstances, but, generally, it means that kind and degree of care, which prudent and cautious people would use, such as required under the circumstances and as necessary to guard against probable danger. An inevitable accident is one the defendant could not avoid by the use of the kind and degree of care necessary under the circumstances. Because the instructions to the jury placed the burden on Kendall (D) to show that he used extraordinary care or that Brown (P) failed to use ordinary care, rather than having placed the burden of proof on Brown (P) to prove his case, a new trial must be ordered.

▶ ANALYSIS

This case established that some form of fault, negligent or intentional, must form the basis of liability. Consequently, the loss from an unavoidable accident will stay where it falls. This case is also interesting because its discussion includes the concept of contributory negligence, which was fully accepted by the Massachusetts court, but which is losing favor to the concept of comparative negligence today.

Quicknotes

ASSAULT AND BATTERY Any unlawful touching of another person without justification or excuse.

COMPARATIVE NEGLIGENCE Doctrine whereby the court in assessing the appropriate measure of damages compares the relative fault of the parties and reduces the amount of damages to be collected by the plaintiff in proportion to his degree of fault.

CONTRIBUTORY NEGLIGENCE Behavior on the part of an injured plaintiff falling below the standard of ordinary care that contributes to the defendant's negligence, resulting in the plaintiff's injury.

DUTY An obligation owed by one individual to another.

Adams v. Bullock

Injured (P) v. Trolley operator (D)

N.Y. Ct. App., 227 N.Y. 208, 125 N.E. 93 (1919).

NATURE OF CASE: Suit for damages.

FACT SUMMARY: Bullock (D) operated a trolley line, the wires for which ran under a bridge. Adams (P) received a shock while crossing the bridge when a wire he was carrying made contact with the trolley wires.

🏛 RULE OF LAW
A party will not be deemed negligent if he has taken reasonable precautions to avoid predictable dangers.

FACTS: Bullock (D) ran a trolley system that utilized an overhead wire system. At one point, a railroad bridge passed over the trolley lines. An eighteen-inch wide parapet protected the side of the bridge, and the trolley lines passed more than four and a half feet beneath the parapet. Adams (P), a twelve-year-old boy, was crossing the bridge carrying a wire approximately eight feet long. The wire extended below the bridge and made contact with the trolley lines, causing a shock that burned Adams (P). Alleging negligence on the part of Bullock (D), Adams (P) sued to recover damages. Adams (P) had judgment at trial and the appellate court affirmed, whereupon Bullock (D) again appealed, contending that he had not been negligent.

ISSUE: Should a party be considered negligent it he has taken every possible measure to prevent accidents?

HOLDING AND DECISION: (Cardozo, J.) No. A party will not be deemed negligent if he has taken reasonable precautions to avoid predictable dangers. The trolley wires were deliberately placed out of reach of persons on the bridge. Bullock (D) could not have known where an unforeseeable accident such as befell Adams (P) would occur. Special safety measures might have been utilized, but Bullock (D) could not have known where to place them. Unlike electrical wires, trolley wires cannot be insulated. Bullock (D) could only have avoided this extraordinary accident by running his wires underground, but he had no duty to do so. Reversed.

▶ ANALYSIS

It is probably impossible to formulate any quantitative description of the amount of care that a party must exercise in order to absolve himself of liability for negligence. Of course, different standards of care may be imposed according to the activity involved. This case illustrates the fact that a party will not ordinarily be held to be the insurer of all persons with whom his actions bring him into contact. The law recognizes that some accidents are unavoidable, and that the mere fact that an accident has occurred does not require a finding that one party or the other has been negligent.

Quicknotes

DUTY An obligation owed by one individual to another.

NEGLIGENCE Conduct falling below the standard of care that a reasonable person would demonstrate under similar conditions.

United States v. Carroll Towing Co.

Federal government (P) v. Towing company (D)

159 F.2d 169 (2d Cir. 1947).

NATURE OF CASE: Action to recover damages in admiralty for the sinking of a barge.

FACT SUMMARY: The attendant of the Conners Co. (P) barge left the vessel unwatched for 21 hours. During that period, the barge broke loose and was sunk.

🏛 RULE OF LAW
There is a duty of care to protect others from harm when the burden of taking adequate precautions is less than the product of the probability of the resulting harm and the magnitude of the harm.

FACTS: A deckhand aboard a tug (the Carroll) readjusted the lines holding the Anna C, a barge owned by Connors, in the course of his efforts to drill out another barge in the vicinity. Because of his negligence in securing the Anna C, it broke loose, ramming against a tanker, whose propeller broke a hole in the bottom of the barge. The Anna C sank, losing boat and cargo. Connors attempted to recover the value of its barge from Carroll Towing Co, (Carroll) (D), while Carroll sought to reduce damages because the plaintiff's barge was absent from the Anna C. Siphoning efforts by other boats in the area would have kept the barge afloat if the bargee had been aboard to sound a warning. The trial judge found no negligence on the part of the bargee, and Carroll (D) appealed.

ISSUE: Is the duty of care breached when defendant's conduct incurred a risk which could be avoided with very few precautions and which if it inflicts injury will cause a great amount of damage?

HOLDING AND DECISION: (Hand, J.) Yes. If the burden of preventing the injury is lower than the product of the probability of its occurring and the amount of harm which it will cause, then there is a breach of the duty of care and liability for negligence. In this case, the burden of preventing the accident was low; it only involved the watchmen staying in the vicinity of the barge or recruiting someone else to stand by and watch it. The probability of the barge getting untied and striking another barge is undoubtedly a variable that changes with conditions as is the amount of injury which will result. The existing conditions, the crowded harbor with barges constantly being moved about, made the probability of injury more than a negligible factor and made the magnitude of resulting injury an enormous figure. Thus, since the burden of preventing the collision was low and the product of the probability and the amount of injury projected is high, the fact that it occurred was a breach of duty. Reversed and remanded.

▶ ANALYSIS

This effort to formulate negligence, this "calculus of the risk," is an acceptable method of determining negligence. Behind this formula, however, is always the recognition that the measure of the reasonableness of the risk revolves around the specific circumstances of the situation. Conduct is relative to the particular occasion and need.

Quicknotes

ADMIRALTY That area of law pertaining to navigable waters.

DUTY OF CARE A principle of negligence requiring an individual to act in such a manner as to avoid injury to a person to whom he or she owes an obligatory duty.

Bethel v. New York City Transit Authority

Injured passenger (P) v. Bus company (D)

N.Y. Ct. App., 92 N.Y.2d 348, 703 N.E.2d 1214 (1998).

NATURE OF CASE: Appeal from judgment for plaintiff.

FACT SUMMARY: Bethel (P) alleged that the New York City Transit Authority was negligent when it failed to repair a wheelchair-accessible seat on one of its buses and that common carriers such as public buses were to be held to a higher standard of care.

🏛 RULE OF LAW

A common carrier is subject to the same duty of care as any other potential tortfeasor.

FACTS: Bethel (P) was hurt when a wheelchair-accessible chair on a New York City Transit Authority (NYCTA) (D) bus collapsed under him. Bethel (P) sued NYCTA (D) for negligence and the judge charged the jury that, as a common carrier, the bus company had a duty to use the highest degree of care that human prudence and foresight could suggest in the maintenance of its vehicles and equipment for safety of its passengers. The jury found for Bethel (P) and NYCTA (D) appealed, claiming that the carrier's duty of extraordinary care conflicted with the fundamental concept of negligence in tort doctrine.

ISSUE: Is a common carrier subject to the same duty of care as any other potential tortfeasor?

HOLDING AND DECISION: (Levine, J.) Yes. A common carrier is subject to the same duty of care as any other potential tortfeasor. The single duty of care is for reasonable care under all of the circumstances of the particular case. The rule of a common carrier's duty of extraordinary care is no longer viable. Because the jury was specifically charged to exercise the highest degree of care, there was reversible error. Reversed and remanded.

▶ *ANALYSIS*

The court did away with the nineteenth-century rule for common carriers. That rule coincided with the advent of steam railroad accidents. Technological advances and governmental regulation in the twentieth century have eliminated the need for such a rule today.

◼◼

Quicknotes

NEGLIGENCE Conduct falling below the standard of care that a reasonable person would demonstrate under similar conditions.

STANDARD OF CARE A uniform degree of behavior against which a person's conduct can be measured when determining liability in negligence cases.

Baltimore & Ohio Railroad Co. v. Goodman

Railroad (D) v. Estate (P)

275 U.S. 66 (1927).

NATURE OF CASE: Suit seeking damages for wrongful death.

FACT SUMMARY: Goodman was killed when his truck was struck by a B & O (D) train. Goodman's view obscured, he slowed down before crossing the tracks, but did not seen the train until it was too late for him to stop.

🏛 RULE OF LAW
A person who has failed to exercise reasonable care to avoid an accident is not entitled to recover damages from the other party.

FACTS: Goodman was killed when his truck was struck by a Baltimore & Ohio Railroad Co. (B & O) (D) train. A section house 243 feet north of the railroad crossing had obscured Goodman's view, so he had slowed to a speed of five or six miles per hour as he approached the tracks. The train that struck Goodman was travelling at not less than 60 miles per hour. Goodman's widow (P), the administratrix of his estate, sued to recover damages from B & O (D). Although B & O (D) moved for a directed verdict, the jury ruled in favor of Mrs. Goodman (P) and an appellate court affirmed. On appeal, B & O (D) argued that Goodman had been contributorily negligent.

ISSUE: May a party to an accident recover damages despite the fact that he did not use reasonable care?

HOLDING AND DECISION: (Holmes, J.) No. A person who has failed to exercise reasonable care to avoid an accident is not entitled to recover damages from the other party. This accident occurred during the daylight hours at a crossing with which Goodman was apparently familiar. Goodman should have stopped and should even have stepped down to look up the track for trains if necessary. He knew the train would not stop for him, and he should therefore have taken every reasonable precaution to protect himself. Instead, he proceeded onto the tracks despite awareness that his view of oncoming trains was obscured. Ordinarily the negligence of the parties should be assessed by the jury, but Goodman's failure to exercise due care is so evident that it is appropriate for the Court to reverse the judgment in favor of Mrs. Goodman (P). Reversed.

▸ ANALYSIS

According to the traditional view, the contributory negligence of a plaintiff or a plaintiff's decedent bars recovery despite negligence on the part of the defendant. Recently, many jurisdictions have adopted the comparative negligence standard, which permits even a contributorily negligent plaintiff to recover as long as his negligence was less extensive than the defendant's. Whether the common-law approach of the comparative negligence test is applied, the issue of negligence is ordinarily resolved by the trier of fact, with its finding accepted by the appellate court except where manifest error has occurred. The result of the *Goodman* case may be best explained by the fact that rail travel was still a burgeoning industry in 1927, and railroads often prevailed before appellate tribunals simply because they were railroads.

Quicknotes

COMPARATIVE NEGLIGENCE Doctrine whereby the court in assessing the appropriate measure of damages compares the relative fault of the parties and reduces the amount of damages to be collected by the plaintiff in proportion to his degree of fault.

CONTRIBUTORY NEGLIGENCE Behavior on the part of an injured plaintiff falling below the standard of ordinary care that contributes to the defendant's negligence, resulting in the plaintiff's injury.

REASONABLE CARE The degree of care observed by a reasonably prudent person under similar circumstances; synonymous with due care or ordinary care.

WRONGFUL DEATH An action brought by the beneficiaries of a deceased person, claiming that the deceased's death was the result of wrongful conduct by the defendant.

Pokora v. Wabash Railway Co.

Car driver (P) v. Railroad company (D)

292 U.S. 98 (1934).

NATURE OF CASE: Action to recover damages for personal injury from negligence.

FACT SUMMARY: Pokora (P) drove a truck across a railroad crossing and was hit by a train.

🏛 **RULE OF LAW**
Unless reasonable minds could not differ on the point, the standard by which negligence is measured is for the jury to decide. Failure to get out of a vehicle and look before crossing a railroad track is not contributory negligence as a matter of law.

FACTS: Pokora (P) drove a truck up to a railroad crossing at which Wabash Railway Co. (D) had four tracks. Because of boxcars on the first track, Pokora (P) could not see the tracks to the north. He stopped, looked, and listened, but heard nothing. He did not get out of his truck to walk forward and look down the tracks. As he drove slowly onto the main track, he was struck by a train coming from the north. The trial court took the case from the jury and granted a directed verdict for the defendant railroad on the ground that Pokora's (P) conduct was contributory negligence as a matter of law. The case was affirmed by the circuit court of appeals; the United States Supreme Court then granted certiorari.

ISSUE: Was Pokora's (P) failure to get out of the vehicle and walk forward to look down the track before driving forward contributory negligence as a matter of law?

HOLDING AND DECISION: (Cardozo, J.) No. It is for the jury to decide whether a plaintiff's conduct is contributory negligence, unless the conduct is so obviously negligent that reasonable minds could not differ on the point. Whether one must stop, look, and listen, or whether one must get out of the vehicle and reconnoiter, depends on the situation. What is safe varies, and it is up to the jury to decide whether a particular conduct is safe for the particular situation. Reversed and remanded.

▶ *ANALYSIS*

Pokora reaffirms the proposition that, unless reasonable minds could not differ, it is up to the jury to decide whether a particular conduct is safe or negligent. Justice Cardozo, writing for the Court, warns about the danger of framing inflexible standards of behavior that amount to rules of law applied by the judge. The Court then limits the stop, look, listen, and/or get out rule enunciated by Justice Holmes in *Baltimore & Ohio R.R. Co. v. Goodman*, 275 U.S. 66 (1927).

Quicknotes

CONTRIBUTORY NEGLIGENCE Behavior on the part of an injured plaintiff falling below the standard of ordinary care that contributes to the defendant's negligence, resulting in the plaintiff's injury.

NEGLIGENCE Conduct falling below the standard of care that a reasonable person would demonstrate under similar conditions.

Andrews v. United Airlines, Inc.

Injured passenger (P) v. Airlines (D)

24 F.3d 39 (9th Cir. 1994).

NATURE OF CASE: Appeal from summary judgment dismissing action in negligence.

FACT SUMMARY: Andrews (P), a passenger injured on a United Airlines, Inc. (United) (D) flight, when a briefcase fell out of an overhead compartment and hit her, alleged that United (D) was liable for negligence because it breached its duty of care to her.

🏛 RULE OF LAW
Even a small risk of serious injury to passengers may form the basis of a common carrier's liability if that risk could be eliminated consistent with the practical operation of airline travel.

FACTS: Andrews (P) was a passenger aboard a United Airlines, Inc. (United) (D) flight when a briefcase fell out of an overhead compartment and hit her in the head, causing serious injuries. Andrews (P) alleged that United (D), as a common carrier, owed Andrews (P) an utmost duty of care and that United (D) breached that duty by not doing more to prevent objects from falling out of overhead compartments. United (D) moved for summary judgment, arguing that Andrews (P) showed too little proof of United's (D) breach to be allowed to go to a jury on the issue. The district court granted summary judgment for United (D) and Andrews (P) appealed.

ISSUE: May even a small risk of serious injury form the basis of a common carrier's liability if that risk could be eliminated consistent with the practical operation of airline travel?

HOLDING AND DECISION: (Kozinski, J.) Yes. Even a small risk of serious injury to passengers may form the basis of a common carrier's liability if that risk could be eliminated consistent with the practical operation of airline travel. Andrews (P) demonstrated that United (D) was aware of the problem of items falling out of overhead bins; however, its solution was to merely warn passengers of the danger. Here, United (D) as a common carrier owed an utmost duty of care to passenger Andrews (P). Andrews (P) presented enough proof that United (D) breached its duty to defeat summary judgment and have a jury decide the issue of breach. A reasonable jury might find that United (D) should have done more to prevent items from falling out of the overhead compartments, or it might find that United (D) did do enough. The district court, therefore, incorrectly granted summary judgment for United (D). Reversed and remanded.

▶ ANALYSIS

Common carriers owe a higher duty to passengers than the ordinary standard of care. The ordinary standard is that of reasonable care under the circumstances. Common carriers, as this case demonstrates, are responsible for even the slightest negligence. Regardless of the standard applied, the issues of duty and breach are ones to be decided by the jury, if a reasonable jury could decide the issues either way.

Quicknotes

COMMON CARRIER An entity whose business is the transport of persons or property.

DUTY OF CARE A principle of negligence requiring an individual to act in such a manner as to avoid injury to a person to whom he or she owes an obligatory duty.

NEGLIGENCE Conduct falling below the standard of care that a reasonable person would demonstrate under similar conditions.

Trimarco v. Klein

Tenant (P) v. Landlord (D)

N.Y. Ct. App., 56 N.Y.2d 98, 436 N.E.2d 502 (1982).

NATURE OF CASE: Appeal from reversal of award of damages for negligence.

FACT SUMMARY: Klein's (D) tenant, Trimarco (P), attempted to show that use of shatterproof glass for tub enclosures had become common over the years and that the regular glass enclosure on which he was injured therefore no longer met accepted safety standards.

🏛 RULE OF LAW
Evidence of custom and usage by others engaged in the same business is admissible as bearing on what is reasonable conduct under all the circumstances, which is the quintessential test of negligence.

FACTS: Trimarco (P), a tenant in Klein's (D) building, was injured when he fell through the glass door enclosing his tub. The glass looked like tempered glass but was just ordinary thin glass. In his negligence action, Trimarco (P) offered expert evidence that it had become common practice to use shatterproof glass in such enclosures so that by the date of his accident the glass door in his bathroom no longer conformed to accepted safety standards. The appellate division reversed a decision awarding Trimarco (P) damages, holding that even if the aforementioned evidence established a custom of using shatterproof glass in such enclosures, Klein (D) was nonetheless under no common-law duty to replace the glass, unless he had prior notice of the danger (either from Trimarco (P) or from a similar accident in the building).

ISSUE: Does evidence of custom and usage have a bearing on what constitutes reasonable conduct under the circumstances of a particular case?

HOLDING AND DECISION: (Fuchsberg, J.) Yes. The quintessential test of negligence is whether a party's conduct was reasonable under all the circumstances of a particular case. Because evidence of custom and usage by others engaged in the same business bears on what is reasonable conduct, it is admissible, although it is not necessarily a conclusive or even compelling test of negligence. Customs and usages run the gamut, like everything else. As Holmes put it, "[w]hat usually is done may be evidence of what ought to be done, but what ought to be done is fixed by a standard of reasonable prudence, whether it usually is complied with or not." The trial court followed these principles in admitting the evidence of custom and usage, and it should not have been reversed. However, a new trial must be had here because the trial judge erroneously admitted certain other evidence.

▶ **ANALYSIS**

There is only one area in which the courts have been willing to let prevailing custom serve to define the standard of care that must be met to avoid a charge of negligence, and that area is malpractice. Even where the standard of care is not set by prevailing custom in a particular field of endeavor, custom may still be important in deciding whether the actor behaved as would a reasonable man.

◼━━━◼

Quicknotes

NEGLIGENCE Conduct falling below the standard of care that a reasonable person would demonstrate under similar conditions.

REASONABLE MAN STANDARD A hypothetical person whose judgment represents the standard to which society requires its members to act in their private affairs and in their dealings with others.

STANDARD OF CARE A uniform degree of behavior against which a person's conduct can be measured when determining liability in negligence cases.

◼━━━◼

Martin v. Herzog

Intestate (P) v. Driver (D)

N.Y. Ct. App., 228 N.Y. 164, 126 N.E. 814 (1920).

NATURE OF CASE: Action to recover damages for injuries resulting in the death of Martin's (P) intestate.

FACT SUMMARY: Mrs. Martin's (P) husband was killed when the buggy he was driving at night without lights, in violation of a statute requiring same, collided with the car Herzog (D) was driving somewhat over the center line.

🏛 RULE OF LAW
Failure to perform a statutory duty constitutes negligence per se, which can be prima facie evidence of contributory negligence (which must be overcome by proof in the opposite direction).

FACTS: On the night of August 21, 1915, Mrs. Martin (P) was a passenger in the buggy her husband was driving into Tarrytown. The buggy was traveling without lights. By statute, lights were required. A collision with Herzog's (D) car, which was allegedly traveling over the center line of the highway, occurred at a curve in the road, whose confirmation caused Martin's buggy to be outside the area illuminated by the car's headlights. At the trial of Mrs. Martin's (P) damage suit, the court refused to give Herzog's (D) requested instruction that Mr. Martin's failure to have the statutorily required lights was prima facie evidence of contributory negligence. Rather, the jury was instructed that lack of lights could be considered some evidence of negligence, but not conclusive evidence of such. Furthermore, Mrs. Martin's (P) request for an instruction that driving without the lights was not negligence in itself was granted. Following a verdict for Mrs. Martin (P), Herzog (D) was successful in having the appellate division reverse the decision. Mrs. Martin (P) now appeals from said reversal of the trial court judgment.

ISSUE: Does failure to perform a statutory duty, absent some excuse, constitute negligence per se?

HOLDING AND DECISION: (Cardozo, J.) Yes. Purposeful omission of a statutory duty designed to safeguard others necessarily means that one has fallen short of the standard of diligence to which it is one's duty to conform, and the result amounts not to just some evidence of negligence but negligence itself. For this reason, the jurors in this case should not have been given the power to relax the duty that a statute says one highway traveler owes another, i.e., the use of lights for protection of travelers. However, the bare facts of negligence "in the air" is insufficient to support an assertion of contributory negligence absent some proof of a causal connection between the negligence and the injury. In this case, such a connection may be inferred from evidence that the collision occurred after dark between a car and on an unseen, unlighted buggy. This prima facie case for contributory negligence may only be overcome by contrary evidence breaking the causal connection. As the instructions to the jury did not reflect those basic principles, the appellate division's reversal is affirmed.

▶ ANALYSIS

The majority of courts follow the general principles set forth in this case. Those principles, according to Justice Traynor, are applicable even where the statute involved never became effective for lack of proper publishing—meaning a violator cannot be punished criminally for his action, but the statute provides a viable standard by which negligence can be judged. The courts accept the fact that the legislature has, regardless of the legal technicalities involved, generalized a standard from community experience, and that is not altered. *Clinkscales v. Carver*, 22 Cal. 2d 72, 136 P.2d 777 (1943).

━━

Quicknotes

CONTRIBUTORY NEGLIGENCE Behavior on the part of an injured plaintiff falling below the standard of ordinary care that contributes to the defendant's negligence, resulting in the plaintiff's injury.

NEGLIGENCE PER SE Conduct amounting to negligence as a matter of law because it is either so contrary to ordinary prudence or it is in violation of statute.

PRIMA FACIE An action in which the plaintiff introduces sufficient evidence to submit an issue to the judge or jury for determination.

STATUTORY DUTY An obligation owed by one individual to another pursuant to a particular statute.

━━

Tedla v. Ellman

Injured (P) v. Driver (D)

N.Y. Ct. App., 280 N.Y. 124, 19 N.E.2d 987 (1939).

NATURE OF CASE: Appeal in action for damages based on negligence.

FACT SUMMARY: Ellman (D), the driver of a car that injured Tedla (P) and killed Bachek, defended a suit against him by asserting the fact that the victims were struck while walking on the right side of the roadway, which was a violation of a statute.

🏛 RULE OF LAW
Where a statutory general rule of conduct fixes no definite standard of care, but merely codifies or supplements a common-law rule, which has been subject to exceptions; or where the statute is intended to promote public convenience or safety, then in the absence of clear language to the contrary, it is not negligence as a matter of law for one to violate the statute, if by so doing he is likely to prevent—rather than cause—the accident which it is the purpose of the statute to avoid.

FACTS: Tedla (P) was injured—and her brother, Bachek, was killed—when they were struck by a car driven by Ellman (D). The incident occurred as they were wheeling a junk-laden baby carriage at night along a public highway. Bachek was reportedly carrying a lighted lantern. The highway consisted of two roadways separated by a soft grass plot. There were no footpaths and the two victims were walking on the right (eastbound) side of the roadway in the same direction as the oncoming traffic. Ellman (D) cited the vehicle and traffic statute requiring pedestrians to walk on the left side of the roadway and moved to dismiss the complaint on the grounds that a violation of the statutory rule constitutes contributory negligence as a matter of law. Tedla (P) produced the testimony of a state policeman that there were few cars going eastbound but that the westbound roadway had heavy traffic. The jury found the accident due solely to Ellman's (D) negligence.

ISSUE: Is a violation of a statute always regarded as negligence per se?

HOLDING AND DECISION: (Lehman, J.) No. The argument of the defendant is that the statute automatically makes the plaintiffs guilty of contributory negligence when they used the safer of the two roadways. This argument holds that disregard of the statute is negligence per se which as a matter of law is the proximate cause of the accident, even though, had the plaintiffs observed the statute they might—due to the heavy traffic they would have been subjected to—have been exposed to serious danger. Were this argument valid it would mean that the legislature

had dictated that pedestrians must observe safety rules even under such circumstances that to do so would expose them to unusual risk. But the rule is that a pedestrian is bound to exercise such care for his safety as a reasonably prudent person would use; and it would be unreasonable to ascribe to the legislature the intention to charge a pedestrian with negligence as a matter of law when he is acting as prudence dictates. Now it is true that in some instances the legislature feels it necessary to prescribe safety standards for preservation of life and limb in rigid and inflexible terms which will admit to no variation in terms of what a reasonably prudent man would do. Failure to comply with such a statute is negligence as a matter of law. But the statute here in question is not of this nature. While this statute, directing pedestrians to face oncoming traffic, better enables them to care for their safety, we cannot assume that the legislature intended it to be observed when to do so would subject the observers to a more imminent danger. The Restatement of Torts § 286, states the generally accepted rule that it is not wrongful for persons when, due to an emergency, circumstances justify disobedience to a statute or ordinance, to deviate from the statute, if by so doing his action is likely to prevent—rather than cause—the accident which it is the purpose of the ordinance to prevent. Affirmed.

▌ ANALYSIS

Torts Professor Prosser remarks that a statute may impose an absolute duty with no recognized excuse for its violation. This is really a matter of strict liability rather than negligence and is imposed on those able to control their causes rather than on those helpless in that respect. Examples are found in cases regulating interstate train equipment, prohibiting child labor, and pure food cases. However, normally no such strict interpretation will be placed on a statute unless it is seen as the clear purpose of the legislature. Ordinarily, all that is required is reasonable diligence in observing the statute.

Quicknotes

CONTRIBUTORY NEGLIGENCE Behavior on the part of an injured plaintiff falling below the standard of ordinary care that contributes to the defendant's negligence, resulting in the plaintiff's injury.

Continued on next page.

NEGLIGENCE PER SE Conduct amounting to negligence as a matter of law because it is either so contrary to ordinary prudence or it is in violation of statute.

PROXIMATE CAUSE The natural sequence of events without which an injury would not have been sustained.

STANDARD OF CARE A uniform degree of behavior against which a person's conduct can be measured when determining liability in negligence cases.

STRICT LIABILITY Liability for all injuries proximately caused by a party's conducting of certain inherently dangerous activities without regard to negligence or fault.

Negri v. Stop and Shop, Inc.

Customer (P) v. Store (D)

N.Y. Ct. App., 65 N.Y.2d 625, 480 N.E.2d 740 (1985).

NATURE OF CASE: Appeal from reversal of award of damages for negligence.

FACT SUMMARY: In Negri's (P) action against Stop and Shop, Inc. (D), Negri (P) alleged Stop and Shop (D) was negligent because it had constructive notice of a dangerous condition that caused injuries to its customers and did not remedy the condition.

> ### 🏛 RULE OF LAW
> A plaintiff may make out a prima facie case of negligence by presenting circumstantial evidence that defendant had constructive notice of a dangerous condition that allegedly caused injury to its customers and did not remedy the condition.

FACTS: Negri (P), while shopping at Stop and Shop, Inc. (D), fell backward in the store aisle, did not come into contact with shelves, but hit her head directly on the floor where many broken jars of baby food lay. Negri (P) alleged that the baby food was dirty and messy, and a witness in the immediate vicinity stated that she had not heard any jars falling from shelves or otherwise breaking during the 15-20 minutes before the accident happened. Evidence was also presented showing that the aisle had not been cleaned or inspected for at least 50 minutes to two hours prior to the accident. Negri (P) asserted that Stop and Shop (D) was negligent, and that the evidence which she presented was sufficient to prove that Stop and Shop (D) had constructive notice of a dangerous condition which caused injury to its customers and did nothing to remedy the condition. The trial court found for Negri (P), the appellate division reversed, and Negri (P) appealed.

ISSUE: May a plaintiff make out a prima facie case of negligence by presenting circumstantial evidence that defendant had constructive notice of a dangerous condition that allegedly caused injury to its customers and did nothing to remedy the condition?

HOLDING AND DECISION: (Memorandum) Yes. The record contains some evidence tending to show that defendant had constructive notice of a dangerous condition that allegedly caused injuries to its customers. The circumstantial evidence was sufficient to permit the jury to draw the inference that a slippery condition was created by jars of baby food which had fallen and broken a sufficient length of time prior to the accident to permit Stop and Shop's (D) employees to discover and remedy the condition. Viewing the evidence in a light most favorable to Negri (P) and according Negri (P) the benefit of every reasonable inference, it is clear that Negri (P) has made out a prima facie case of negligence. The order of the Appellate Division should be reversed.

▶ ANALYSIS

In civil suits, unlike criminal prosecution, the burden of proof requires only that the jury be persuaded that a preponderance of the evidence is in favor of the party sustaining the burden. This is true as to the issue of negligence, although the act to be proved may also be a crime. The burden of proof of defendant's negligence is quite clearly upon the plaintiff, since he is asking the court for relief and must lose if his case does not outweigh that of his adversary.

━■━

Quicknotes

CIRCUMSTANTIAL EVIDENCE Evidence that, though not directly observed, supports the inference of principal facts.

CONSTRUCTIVE NOTICE Knowledge of a fact imputed to an individual who was under a duty to inquire and who could have learned of the fact through the exercise of reasonable prudence.

NEGLIGENCE Conduct falling below the standard of care that a reasonable person would demonstrate under similar conditions.

PREPONDERANCE OF THE EVIDENCE A standard of proof requiring the trier of fact to determine whether the fact sought to be established is more probable than not.

PRIMA FACIE CASE Action, where the plaintiff introduces sufficient evidence to submit the issue to the judge or jury for determination.

━■━

Gordon v. American Museum of Natural History

Injured (P) v. Museum (D)

N.Y. Ct. App., 67 N.Y.2d 836, 492 N.E.2d 774 (1986).

NATURE OF CASE: Appeal from award of damages for negligence.

FACT SUMMARY: Gordon (P), who alleged he fell on a piece of paper on the front entrance steps of the American Museum of Natural History (Museum) (D), argued that the Museum (D) was negligent because its employees failed to discover and remove the paper before Gordon (P) fell on it, and that the Museum (D) had constructive notice of the dangerous condition.

🏛 RULE OF LAW
To constitute constructive notice, a defect must be visible and apparent and it must exist for a sufficient length of time prior to the accident to permit defendant to discover and remedy it.

FACTS: Gordon (P) was injured when he fell on the front entrance steps of the American Museum of Natural History (Museum) (D). Gordon (P) alleged that he slipped as he was descending the upper level of the Museum's (D) steps and that while he was in midair, he saw a piece of white, waxy paper near his left foot. Gordon (P) further alleged that the paper came from a nearby concession stand which the Museum (D) contracted to have present, and that the Museum (D) was negligent because its employees failed to discover and remove the paper before he fell on it. The case was submitted to the jury on the theory that the Museum (D) had either actual or constructive notice of the dangerous condition presented by the paper on the steps. The jury found against the Museum (D) on the issue of liability. The appellate division affirmed, and the Museum (D) appealed.

ISSUE: To constitute constructive notice, must a defect be visible and apparent and must it exist for a sufficient length of time prior to the accident to permit defendant to discover and remedy it?

HOLDING AND DECISION: (Memorandum) Yes. To constitute constructive notice, a defect must be visible and apparent and it must exist for a sufficient length of time prior to the accident to discover and remedy it. There is no evidence here that anyone, including Gordon (P), observed the piece of white paper prior to the accident. Nor did Gordon (P) describe the paper as being dirty and worn, which would indicate that it had been present for a period of time. Here, neither general awareness that litter may be present nor the fact that Gordon (P) observed other papers on another portion of the steps approximately 10 minutes before his fall is legally sufficient to charge the Museum (D) with constructive

notice of the paper Gordon (P) fell on. Also, there is no evidence in the record that the Museum (D) had actual notice of the paper. The order of the Appellate Division should be reversed.

▶ ANALYSIS

Since it is impossible to delineate definite rules in advance for every combination of circumstances that may arise, the details of the standard of conduct must be filled in in each particular case. The question becomes what the reasonable person would have done under the circumstances. This question is to be determined, in all doubtful cases, by the jury, because the public insists that its conduct be judged in part by the person in the street rather than by lawyers.

Quicknotes

ACTUAL NOTICE Direct communication of information that would cause an ordinary person of average prudence to inquire as to its truth.

CONSTRUCTIVE NOTICE Knowledge of a fact imputed to an individual who was under a duty to inquire and who could have learned of the fact through the exercise of reasonable prudence.

NEGLIGENCE Conduct falling below the standard of care that a reasonable person would demonstrate under similar conditions.

REASONABLE PERSON STANDARD The standard of care exercised by a hypothetical person who possesses the intelligence, education, knowledge, attention, and judgment required by society of its members when governing behavior; the standard applies to a person's judgment when determining breach of a duty under the theory of negligence.

Byrne v. Boadle

Injured (P) v. Shop owner (D)

Ex., 2 H & C. 722, 159 Eng. Rep. 299 (1863).

NATURE OF CASE: Action in negligence to recover damages for personal injuries.

FACT SUMMARY: Although he did not see what had hit him, Byrne (P) produced witnesses who testified that Byrne (P) was struck by a barrel of flour that fell from a window in Boadle's (D) shop as Byrne (P) passed by on the street below.

🏛 RULE OF LAW
There are circumstances in which the mere fact an accident has occurred give rise to a presumption of negligence that must then be rebutted by the defendant.

FACTS: As he walked on the street in front of Boadle's (D) flour shop, Byrne (P) was struck by a barrel of flour that fell out of a window in Boadle's (D) shop. Byrne (P) sued to recover for his injuries. At trial, Boadle (D) successfully argued there was no evidence introduced to show Boadle's (D) negligence. The trial court, therefore, nonsuited Byrne (P). Byrne (P) appealed, arguing that there existed circumstances that gave rise to a presumption of negligence that had to be rebutted by Boadle (D).

ISSUE: Are there circumstances in which the mere fact an accident has occurred give rise to a presumption of negligence that must then be rebutted by the defendant?

HOLDING AND DECISION: (Pollock, C.B.) Yes. There are circumstances in which the mere fact an accident has occurred give rise to a presumption of negligence that must then be rebutted by the defendant. Where a party has control of an object, as Boadle (D) had control of the flour barrel, and it injures another under circumstances that would not occur absent some negligence, he must then suffer the imposition of a presumption of negligence, which he can rebut. Here, the mere fact that the barrel of flour under Boadle's (D) control fell is prima facie evidence of negligence, for a barrel does not fall out of a window but for some negligence. Boadle (D), of course, has the opportunity to rebut this presumption. Reversed.

▶ ANALYSIS

This case is one of the earliest examples of the doctrine of res ipsa loquitur, literally, "the thing speaks for itself." When the doctrine is applied, the burden of persuasion is not affected; the plaintiff must still convince the factfinder that his version of what happened is more probable than not. Res ipsa loquitur does not force the jury to find for the plaintiff; it merely allows them to do so in situations when the plaintiff cannot prove exactly how the alleged negligence occurred.

Quicknotes

NEGLIGENCE Conduct falling below the standard of care that a reasonable person would demonstrate under similar conditions.

PRIMA FACIE EVIDENCE Evidence presented by a party sufficient, in the absence of contradictory evidence, to support the fact or issue for which it is offered.

RES IPSA LOQUITUR A rule of law giving rise to an inference of negligence where the instrument inflicting the injury is in the exclusive control of the defendant and where such harm could not ordinarily result in the absence of negligence.

McDougald v. Perry

Injured (P) v. Driver (D)

Fl. Sup. Ct., 716 So. 2d 783 (1998).

NATURE OF CASE: Personal injury action.

FACT SUMMARY: McDougald (P) sued Perry (D) for personal injuries sustained when a tire chained to the underside of Perry's (D) tractor-trailer struck McDougald's (P) windshield.

RULE OF LAW

The doctrine of res ipsa loquitur provides an injured plaintiff with an inference of negligence where direct proof is not available, if the plaintiff establishes that the instrumentality causing his injury was under the exclusive control of the defendant and the accident is one that would not, in the ordinary course of events, have occurred in the absence of negligence on the part of the one in control of the instrumentality.

FACTS: McDougald (P) sued Perry (D) for injuries sustained in an accident that occurred when McDougald (P) was driving behind a tractor-trailer driven by Perry (D). As Perry (D) drove over some railroad tracks, a 130-pound spare tire fell out of its cradle underneath the trailer and fell to the ground. The trailer's rear tires ran over the spare, which flew up into McDougald's windshield. Perry (D) testified that the tire had been held in place by the original chain that came with the trailer in 1969. He also stated that he conducted a pretrip inspection including an inspection of the chain; however, he stated that he did not check every link of the chain. After the accident the chain was dragging under the trailer. The judge instructed the jury on the doctrine of res ipsa loquitur and the jury returned a verdict for McDougald (P). The district court reversed on the basis that the trial court erred in instructing the jury on res ipsa loquitur. McDougald (P) appealed.

ISSUE: Does the doctrine of res ipsa loquitur provide an injured plaintiff with an inference of negligence where direct proof is not available?

HOLDING AND DECISION: (Wells, J.) Yes. The doctrine of res ipsa loquitur provides an injured plaintiff with an inference of negligence where direct proof is not available, if the plaintiff establishes the instrumentality causing his injury was under the exclusive control of the defendant and the accident is one that would not, in the ordinary course of events, have occurred in the absence of negligence on the part of the one in control of the instrumentality. Res ipsa loquitur means "the thing speaks for itself." The doctrine compels a finding of negligence under certain circumstances. The district court concluded that McDougald (P) failed to show that this accident would not have occurred without negligence on the part of Perry (D). A plaintiff at trial must still present sufficient evidence, beyond the mere happening of the accident, allowing the jury to infer that the accident would not have occurred but for the defendant's breach of care. An injury alone does not indicate negligence unless it is accompanied by a sufficient showing of an immediate, precipitating cause. The doctrine only applies in rare instances. Here the accident is of the type that would not normally occur without the failure to exercise ordinary care by the person in control of the instrumentality. Reversed and remanded.

CONCURRENCE: (Anstead, J.) We can hardly improve upon the court's opinion in *Byrne v. Boadle*, Ex., 2 H & C. 722, 159 Eng. Rep. 299 (1863), for our decision today.

ANALYSIS

The Restatement (Second) of Torts § 328D elaborates on the doctrine of res ipsa loquitur. The comments to that section set forth certain types of accidents that do not usually occur in the absence of someone's negligence. This conclusion is based on past experience and common sense.

Quicknotes

NEGLIGENCE Conduct falling below the standard of care that a reasonable person would demonstrate under similar conditions.

RES IPSA LOQUITUR A rule of law giving rise to an inference of negligence where the instrument inflicting the injury is in the exclusive control of the defendant and where such harm could not ordinarily result in the absence of negligence.

Ybarra v. Spangard

Paralyzed patient (P) v. Physicians (D)

Cal. Sup. Ct., 25 Cal. 2d 486, 154 P.2d 687 (1944).

NATURE OF CASE: Medical malpractice action to recover for personal injuries.

FACT SUMMARY: During surgery to remove his appendix, Ybarra (P) apparently suffered an unexplained injury to his right arm and shoulder during the time he was unconscious.

🏛 RULE OF LAW
Where a medical patient suffers unexplained injuries to a part of his body not under treatment and not within the area being operated on, res ipsa loquitur applies and gives rise to a presumption of negligence covering all those defendants who had any control over his body or the instrumentalities that might have caused the injuries.

FACTS: A number of doctors, nurses, and other hospital employees took part in the appendectomy that Ybarra (P) underwent, Dr. Spangard (D) having been the surgeon. Ybarra (P), who had been anesthetized and was unconscious during the procedure, discovered upon regaining consciousness that his right arm and shoulder had been injured. After his release from the hospital, the injury developed paralysis, and the muscles around his shoulder atrophied. Alleging that this type of injury did not normally occur during an appendix operation in the absence of some negligence by somebody, Ybarra (P) brought suit to recover for his personal injuries and claimed that the doctrine of res ipsa loquitur applied so as to give rise to a presumption of negligence against all of those who had participated in his operation. Dr. Spangard (D) and the other defendants argued that the doctrine of res ipsa loquitur could not be applied because Ybarra (P) could not specify which particular instrumentality caused his injury, could not therefore say whose exclusive control it was in, and could point to no specific person whose negligence had caused the injury. From a decision nonsuiting him, Ybarra (P) appealed.

ISSUE: If, in the course of medical treatment, a patient suffers injury to a part of the body not under treatment or being operated on, does the doctrine of res ipsa loquitur apply so as to raise a presumption of negligence with regard to any and all persons who had any control over his body or the instrumentalities that might have caused the injuries?

HOLDING AND DECISION: (Gibson, C.J.) Yes. The doctrine of res ipsa loquitur applies when, in the course of medical treatment, a patient suffers unexplained injury to a part of the body not under treatment or being operated on, and the result is a presumption of negligence that covers any and all persons who had any control over his body or the instrumentalities that might have caused the injuries. It simply does not make sense to require an unconscious patient to identify precisely which of a number of persons charged with exercising ordinary care for his safety failed to fulfill his duty. The climate that exists in medicine is not one facilitating voluntary disclosures by one hospital employee that another was negligent in treating a patient. Thus, a patient who suffered injury would be precluded from recovery if res ipsa loquitur did not apply to place the burden of proving individual non-negligence on hospital employees so that they have an incentive to reveal whatever knowledge they might have about who was responsible for the injury. The only other alternative would be to resort to a doctrine of absolute liability regardless of negligence in such cases, and that should be avoided. For these reasons, res ipsa loquitur will be applied under circumstances like those in this case. Reversed.

▶ ANALYSIS
On remand, each defendant testified he had not seen anything that could have caused Ybarra's (P) injury, which had been found to be traumatic and not the result of infection. Nonetheless, a decision against the defendants was rendered and affirmed on appeal. The appellate court specifically noted that the court can quite properly decide to believe the inferences to be reasonably drawn from circumstantial evidence over contrary direct testimony.

▄▬▄

Quicknotes

NEGLIGENCE Conduct falling below the standard of care that a reasonable person would demonstrate under similar conditions.

RES IPSA LOQUITUR A rule of law giving rise to an inference of negligence where the instrument inflicting the injury is in the exclusive control of the defendant and where such harm could not ordinarily result in the absence of negligence.

▄▬▄

Sheeley v. Memorial Hospital

Injured patient (P) v. Hospital and physician (D)

R.I. Sup. Ct., 710 A.2d 161 (1998).

NATURE OF CASE: Appeal from directed verdict for defendant in medical malpractice suit.

FACT SUMMARY: Sheeley (P) alleged that Memorial Hospital (D) and the second-year family practice resident (D) who performed an episiotomy on her were negligent, but her expert witness was not allowed to testify.

🏛 RULE OF LAW
A physician is under a duty to use the degree of caution and skill that is expected of a reasonably competent practitioner in the same class, acting in the same or similar circumstances.

FACTS: Sheeley (P) developed complications following an episiotomy performed by a second-year family practice resident (D) at Memorial Hospital (Hospital) (D). Sheeley (P) sued the Hospital (D) and the resident (D) for medical malpractice. Sheeley (P) sought to introduce the expert testimony of a board-certified obstetrician/gynecologist about the medical malpractice and the applicable standard of care. The trial court ruled that the expert witness could not testify because he was not in family practice. The Hospital's (D) motion for a directed verdict was granted. Sheeley (P) appealed, claiming that the court had erred in excluding the expert medical testimony. The Hospital (P) alleged that, pursuant to the similar locality rule, the expert witness was properly disqualified because he lacked any direct knowledge about the applicable standard of care for a family practice resident providing obstetric care in Rhode Island, or in a similar locality.

ISSUE: Is a physician under a duty to use the degree of caution and skill that is expected of a reasonably competent practitioner in the same class, acting in the same or similar circumstances?

HOLDING AND DECISION: (Goldberg, J.) Yes. A physician is under a duty to use the degree of caution and skill that is expected of a reasonably competent practitioner in the same class, acting in the same or similar circumstances. The traditional locality rules no longer fit the present-day medical malpractice case. The same or similar communities test is repudiated, in favor of a national standard. Even though he does not practice in the same specialty as the defendant, an expert who has the prerequisite knowledge, skill, experience, training or education in the field of the alleged malpractice may serve as an expert medical witness. Except in extreme cases, a witness who has obtained board certification in a particular specialty should be presumptively qualified to render an opinion. Reversed and remanded.

▶ ANALYSIS

The court here adopted a new, national standard to be applied in medical malpractice cases. Many states have similarly changed their rules. Even in states that have not switched to a national standard, physicians holding themselves out as specialists are held to the general standard of care expected of all physicians in the same specialty.

Quicknotes

DIRECTED VERDICT A verdict ordered by the court in a jury trial.

EXPERT WITNESS A witness providing testimony at trial who is specially qualified regarding the particular subject matter involved.

MEDICAL MALPRACTICE Conduct on the part of a doctor falling below that demonstrated by other doctors of ordinary skill and competency under the circumstances, resulting in damages.

NEGLIGENCE Conduct falling below the standard of care that a reasonable person would demonstrate under similar conditions.

Matthies v. Mastromonaco

Patient (P) v. Physician (D)

N.J. Sup. Ct., 160 N.J. 26, 733 A.2d 456 (1999).

NATURE OF CASE: Appeal from reversal of judgment for defendant.

FACT SUMMARY: Matthies (P) sued her physician, Mastromonaco (D), for medical malpractice when he failed to discuss with her the possibility of operating on her hip after a fall.

RULE OF LAW
To obtain a patient's informed consent to one of several alternative courses of treatment, the physician should explain medically reasonable invasive and noninvasive alternatives, even when the chosen course is noninvasive.

FACTS: Matthies (P) was eighty-three years old when she fell and broke her hip. Mastromonaco (D), her doctor, reviewed her medical history and decided against surgery to pin her hip. As a result, Matthies (P) lost the ability to walk and was confined to a nursing home. Matthies (P) alleged that Mastromonaco (D) negligently failed to consult with her or her family about the possibility of surgery, and that she would not have consented to bed rest if Mastromonaco (D) had informed her of the probable effect of the treatment on her quality of life. The jury found that Mastromonaco (D) had not committed malpractice by failing to perform surgery. The appellate division reversed because of the failure to charge on informed consent. Mastromonaco (D) appealed, claiming that the informed consent doctrine did not apply where the recommendation was noninvasive.

ISSUE: To obtain a patient's informed consent to one of several alternative courses of treatment, should the physician explain medically reasonable invasive and noninvasive alternatives, even when the chosen course is noninvasive?

HOLDING AND DECISION: (Pollock, J.) Yes. To obtain a patient's informed consent to one of several alternative courses of treatment, the physician should explain medically reasonable invasive and noninvasive alternatives, even when the chosen course is noninvasive. To assure that a patient's consent is informed, the physician should describe the material risks inherent in the procedure or course of treatment. The test for materiality of a risk is whether a reasonable patient in the patient's position would have considered the risk material. Physicians may not impose their values on their patients. Since the issues of informed consent and medical malpractice are intertwined in this case, the jury should consider both issues on retrial. Affirmed.

ANALYSIS

In some states, a plaintiff needs to introduce an expert witness to establish inadequate information when alleging lack of informed consent. In other states, the essence of a medical malpractice claim is a battery. Here, the court said that the physician's deviation from a standard of care was the main focus in analyzing informed consent claims.

━━━

Quicknotes

BATTERY Unlawful contact with the body of another person.

INFORMED CONSENT An individual's consent to a particular occurrence following full disclosure of the consequences of that decision.

MEDICAL MALPRACTICE Conduct on the part of a doctor falling below that demonstrated by other doctors of ordinary skill and competency under the circumstances, resulting in damages.

NEGLIGENCE Conduct falling below the standard of care that a reasonable person would demonstrate under similar conditions.

━━━

The Duty Requirement: Physical Injuries

Quick Reference Rules of Law

Harper v. Herman

Impromptu diver (P) v. Boat owner (D)

Minn. Sup. Ct., 499 N.W.2d 472 (1993).

NATURE OF CASE: Appeal of a reversal of summary judgment in defendant's favor.

FACT SUMMARY: Harper (P), who was injured while diving off Herman's (D) boat, sued Herman (D), alleging that Herman (D) owed him a duty of care to warn him about the shallowness of the water.

🏛 RULE OF LAW
A boat owner who is a social host does not owe a duty of care to warn a guest that the water is too shallow for diving if the guest is neither particularly vulnerable nor lacks the ability to protect himself.

FACTS: Harper (P), a twenty-year-old male, was one of four guests on Herman's (D) boat for a sailing outing. Herman (D) set anchor in an area he knew was shallow so that the guests could swim toward a nearby island. Harper (P), without warning, dove from the side of the boat, hitting his head on the lake bottom and severely injuring himself. Harper (P) then sued, alleging that Herman (D) owed him a duty to warn him about the shallowness of the water. The trial court granted summary judgment for Herman (D), on the ground that Herman (D) did not owe any duty to warn. The court of appeals reversed, holding that Herman (D) voluntarily assumed such a duty when he allowed Harper (P) on his boat.

ISSUE: Does a boat owner who is a social host owe a duty of care to warn a guest that the water is too shallow for diving if the guest is neither particularly vulnerable nor lacks the ability to protect himself?

HOLDING AND DECISION: (Page, J.) No. A boat owner who is a social host does not owe a duty of care to warn a guest that the water is too shallow for diving, where the guest is neither particularly vulnerable nor lacks the ability to protect himself. Generally, a duty in such a situation will only be imposed if the guest was deprived of the opportunity to protect himself. Here, Harper (P) was a twenty-year-old adult, well able to protect himself. Also, Herman (D) did not hold considerable power over Harper's (P) welfare and did not receive any financial gain from him. Thus, Herman (D) did not owe Harper (P) a duty to warn him about the shallow water. Reversed and judgment in favor of Herman (D) reinstated.

▶ ANALYSIS

This case demonstrates the common-law principle that an individual generally owes no duty toward another person unless a special relationship exists. However, a duty will be imposed even toward a stranger when an individual begins aiding the stranger, or the individual actually put the stranger in peril. In this case, Harper (P) unsuccessfully tried to establish that because Herman (D) was a host with special knowledge of the water, the general common-law lack of duty rule should be ignored.

Quicknotes

AFFIRMATIVE DUTY An obligation to undertake an affirmative action for the benefit of another.

DUTY OF CARE A principle of negligence requiring an individual to act in such a manner as to avoid injury to a person to whom he or she owes an obligatory duty.

Farwell v. Keaton

Decedent's father (P) v. Ineffective rescuer (D)

Mich. Sup. Ct., 396 Mich. 281, 240 N.W.2d 217 (1976).

NATURE OF CASE: Appeal from reversal of award of damages for wrongful death.

FACT SUMMARY: In Farwell's (P) action against Siegrist for the wrongful death of Farwell's (P) son, Farwell (P) contended that Siegrist failed to exercise reasonable care after voluntarily coming to the son's aid and that his negligence was the proximate cause of the son's death.

🏛 RULE OF LAW
When companions are engaged in a common undertaking, there is a special relationship between them and implicit in this relationship is the understanding that one will render assistance to the other when he is in peril if he can do so without endangering himself.

FACTS: Farwell's (P) son, Richard, and Siegrist followed some girls to a drive-in restaurant. The girls complained to their friends that they were being followed, and six boys chased Richard and Siegrist to a parking lot. Siegrist escaped unharmed, but Richard was badly beaten. Ice was applied to Richard's head, and Siegrist then drove Richard around in Richard's car for about two hours. Richard fell asleep in the back seat of the car. Siegrist drove Richard to the home of Richard's grandparents, parked in the driveway, and after being unable to rouse Richard, left. Richard's grandparents found him the next morning and took him to the hospital, where he died three days later from an epidural hematoma. Farwell (P) sued Siegrist in a wrongful death action, contending that Siegrist failed to exercise reasonable care after voluntarily coming to Richard's aid and that his negligence was the proximate cause of Richard's death. A jury returned a verdict for Farwell (P), but the court of appeals reversed, stating that Siegrist had not assumed the duty of obtaining aid for Richard. Farwell (P) appealed.

ISSUE: When companions are engaged in a common undertaking is there a special relationship between them and is the understanding implicit in this relationship that one will render assistance to the other when he is in peril, if he can do so without endangering himself?

HOLDING AND DECISION: (Levin, J.) Yes. Where companions are engaged in a common undertaking, there is a special relationship between them, and implicit in this relationship is the understanding that one will render assistance to the other when the other is in peril if he can do so without endangering himself. Richard and Siegrist were companions engaged in a social venture, a common

undertaking; there was a special relationship between them. Siegrist knew or should have known of the peril Richard was in and could have rendered assistance without endangering himself. Siegrist had an affirmative duty to come to Richard's aid. Reversed.

DISSENT: (Fitzgerald, J.) Siegrist's nonfeasance is urged as being the proximate cause of Richard's death. We must reject Farwell's (P) proposition which elevates a moral obligation to a legal duty where, as here, the facts within Siegrist's knowledge in no way indicated medical attention was necessary and the relationship between the parties imposed no affirmative duty to render assistance.

▶ ANALYSIS

Concerning motor vehicles, a common reaction to the traditional no-duty view in such situations has been the adoption of criminal statutes. California provides that "the driver of any vehicle involved in an accident causing injury shall render to the person injured in the accident reasonable assistance . . . if it is apparent that treatment is necessary or is requested by the injured person." Cal. Vehicle Code § 20003. This statute has been held applicable regardless of whose negligence, if any, caused the accident.

■■■

Quicknotes

AFFIRMATIVE DUTY An obligation to undertake an affirmative action for the benefit of another.

DUTY OF CARE A principle of negligence requiring an individual to act in such a manner as to avoid injury to a person to whom he or she owes an obligatory duty.

PROXIMATE CAUSE The natural sequence of events without which an injury would not have been sustained.

WRONGFUL DEATH An action brought by the beneficiaries of a deceased person, claiming that the deceased's death was the result of wrongful conduct by the defendant.

■■■

Randi W. v. Muroc Joint Unified School District

Student (P) v. School district (D)

Cal. Sup. Ct., 14 Cal. 4th 1066, 929 P.2d 582 (1997).

NATURE OF CASE: Review of reversal of demurrer.

FACT SUMMARY: Randi W. (P) alleged that Muroc Joint Unified School District (D) and three other school districts (D) had negligently recommended a teacher for a new teaching position.

🏛 RULE OF LAW
The writer of a letter of recommendation owes to third parties a duty not to misrepresent the facts in describing the qualifications and character of a former employee, if making those misrepresentations would present a substantial, foreseeable risk of physical injury to the third persons.

FACTS: Randi W. (P) claimed that Muroc and the other school districts (D) fraudulently and negligently misrepresented facts when they placed unreservedly affirmative references in a placement file for a teacher despite knowing that prior charges or complaints of sexual misconduct and impropriety had been leveled against that teacher. As a result, that same teacher later sexually assaulted Randi W. (D). The lower court granted demurrers on all claims. The court of appeal reversed. The state Supreme Court granted review.

ISSUE: Does the writer of a letter of recommendation owe to third parties a duty not to misrepresent the facts in describing the qualifications and character of a former employee, if making those misrepresentations would present a substantial, foreseeable risk of physical injury to the third persons?

HOLDING AND DECISION: (Chin, J.) Yes. The writer of a letter of recommendation owes to third parties a duty not to misrepresent the facts in describing the qualifications and character of a former employee, if making those misrepresentations would present a substantial, foreseeable risk of physical injury to the third persons. The recommendation letters constituted affirmative misrepresentations and were false and misleading in light of the School Districts' (D) alleged knowledge of the charges previously made against the teacher. The negligent misrepresentation and fraud claims are affirmed. Since the recommending school districts were never the custodians of Randi W. (P), Randi (P) was not a member of the class for whose protection the child abuse reporting statute was enacted and therefore had no standing to sue for negligence per se under that statute. Affirmed in part, reversed in part.

▶ ANALYSIS

Three judges dissented. They would have found negligence per se as well. In their view, the court should have construed the intended protected class broadly to include all children who foreseeably could be protected from abuse by compliance with the Reporting Act.

Quicknotes

DEMURRER The assertion that the opposing party's pleadings are insufficient and that the demurring party should not be made to answer.

FRAUD A false representation of facts with the intent that another will rely on the misrepresentation to his detriment.

NEGLIGENCE PER SE Conduct amounting to negligence as a matter of law because it is either so contrary to ordinary prudence or it is in violation of statute.

NEGLIGENT MISREPRESENTATION A misrepresentation that is made pursuant to a business relationship, in violation of an obligation owed, upon which the plaintiff relies to his detriment.

STANDING Whether a party possesses the right to commence suit against another party by having a personal stake in the resolution of the controversy.

Tarasoff v. The Regents of the University of California

Parents of murder victim (P) v. Psychologist and university (D)

Cal. Sup. Ct., 551 P.2d 334 (1976).

NATURE OF CASE: Appeal from dismissal of action for wrongful death based on failure to warn.

FACT SUMMARY: Moore (D), a psychologist, failed to notify the Tarasoffs' (P) daughter Tatiana or others who could have warned her, that one of his patients, Poddar, had threatened to kill her.

🏛 RULE OF LAW
Where a person bears a special relationship to a party or others who may be the victim of violent conduct and such conduct is reasonably foreseeable, a legally cognizable duty arises to protect or control the third party.

FACTS: Poddar was a patient of Dr. Moore (D), a psychologist employed by the University of California at Berkeley (University) (D). During a therapy session, Poddar told Moore (D) he was going to kill Tatiana, the plaintiffs' daughter. Moore (D) informed the campus police who finally released Poddar because he appeared rational. Poddar killed Tatiana several days later. The Tarasoffs (P), Tatiana's parents, brought a wrongful death action against Powelson (D), Moore's superior, Moore (D) and the University (D) on the ground they negligently failed to either warn Tatiana or to restrain Poddar. The lower court dismissed the action because it determined that the defendants did not owe a duty to Tatiana. The Tarasoffs (P) argued that the special relationship of doctor to patient created a duty to protect their daughter. The Tarasoffs (P) appealed. The state's highest court granted review.

ISSUE: Where a person bears a special relationship to a party or others who may be the victim of violent conduct and such conduct is reasonably foreseeable, does a legally cognizable duty arise to protect or control the third party?

HOLDING AND DECISION: (Tobriner, J.) Yes. Where a person bears a special relationship to a party or others who may be the victim of violent conduct and such conduct is reasonably foreseeable, a legally cognizable duty arises to protect or control the third party. As a general rule, a person is not liable for the conduct of another. An exception is created where a special relationship exists between the person and the actor or the person and a third party. These types of special relationships impose duties to prevent injury that may be caused by the actor or to protect a third party from injury. A doctor/patient relationship gives rise to this duty. Moore (D) had a duty to protect Tatiana from Poddar, Moore's (D) patient. The law recognizes that certain conduct must be prevented or certain interests protected. The overriding issue is whether there is a reasonably foreseeable likelihood of an unwarranted risk. Here, the relationship exists and the risk was readily foreseeable. While the doctor/patient relationship requires the keeping of confidences, this privilege is outweighed by the need to protect human life. Reversed as to this issue. [The court permitted the Tarasoffs (P) to amend their complaint to state a cause of action against Moore (D) by asserting that Moore (D) in fact determined that Poddar presented a serious danger of violence to Tatiana, or should have so determined pursuant to the standards of the profession, but nevertheless failed to exercise reasonable care to protect her from that danger.]

CONCURRENCE AND DISSENT: (Mosk, J.) The result reached by the majority is correct only because Moore (D) had predicted that Poddar would kill a specific person. However, the majority's rule that a therapist may be held liable for failing to predict a patient's tendency to violence if other therapists, pursuant to the "standards of the profession," would have done so. Seemingly, there is no agreement on such a standard, and persuasive evidence has demonstrated that psychiatric predictions of violence are unreliable.

DISSENT: (Clark, J.) Until today's majority opinion, both legal and medical authorities have agreed that confidentiality is essential to effectively treat the mentally ill, and that imposing a duty on doctors to disclose patient threats to potential victims would greatly impair treatment. Further, recognizing that effective treatment and society's safety are necessarily intertwined, the Legislature has already decided effective and confidential treatment is preferred over imposition of a duty to warn. The issue whether effective treatment for the mentally ill should be sacrificed to a system of warnings is, in my opinion, properly one for the Legislature, and we are bound by its judgment. Moreover, even in the absence of clear legislative direction, we must reach the same conclusion because imposing the majority's new duty is certain to result in a net increase in violence. The majority rejects the balance achieved by the Legislature's Lanterman-Petris-Short Act (Welf. & Inst. Code, § 5000 et seq.). In addition, the majority fails to recognize that, even absent the act, overwhelming policy considerations mandate against sacrificing fundamental patient interests without gaining a corresponding increase in public benefit.

▶ ANALYSIS

In *Bellah v. Greenson*, C.A. 1st, 1 Civ. 39770 (1977), the parents of a suicidal teenager who died from a

Continued on next page.

self-inflicted overdose of sleeping pills relied on the above case in a wrongful death action against the girl's psychiatrist. The parents claimed the psychiatrist had failed to warn others of her proclivity towards sleeping pills. They also alleged the psychiatrist had failed to warn them their daughter was consorting with heroin addicts. The appellate court declined to extend the holding of *Tarasoff* to the case. Instead, the court distinguished it by holding that in *Bellah v. Greenson*, there was a danger of self-inflicted harm rather than harm to others.

◼▬◼

Quicknotes

PSYCHOTHERAPIST/PATIENT PRIVILEGE The right of a patient to refuse to reveal confidential information given during the course of a relationship with a physician entered into for the purpose of treatment.

◼▬◼

Uhr v. East Greenbush Central School District

Parents (P) v. School district (D)

N.Y. Ct. App., 94 N.Y.2d 32, 720 N.E.2d 886 (1999).

NATURE OF CASE: Appeal from summary judgment for defendant in negligence case.

FACT SUMMARY: The Uhrs (P) alleged that East Greenbush Central School District (EGCSD) (D) was negligent when it failed to test their daughter for scoliosis as required by state statute.

🏛 RULE OF LAW
A private right of action cannot be fairly implied where it would be inconsistent with the statute's legislative scheme.

FACTS: Education Law § 905(1) required testing of all students between 8 and 16 for scoliosis at least once each school year. The Uhrs (P) claimed that the EGCSD (D) failed to test their daughter in the 1993-1994 school year and, as a result, the ailment was allowed to progress undetected, to her detriment. The court granted EGCSD's (D) motion for summary judgment, holding that Education Law § 905(1) did not create a private cause of action, and that the Uhrs (P) had not stated a valid claim for common-law negligence. The Uhrs (P) appealed, claiming a private cause of action may be fairly implied when the statute is silent.

ISSUE: May a private right of action be fairly implied where it would be inconsistent with the statute's legislative scheme?

HOLDING AND DECISION: (Rosenblatt, J.) No. A private right of action cannot be fairly implied where it would be inconsistent with the statute's legislative scheme. Here, the Legislature has vested the Commissioner of Education with the duty to implement Education Law and to adopt rules and regulations for that purpose. Education Law § 905(1) provides that school authorities shall not suffer any liability that would not have existed in the absence of that section. When creating the statutory duty for school districts to test students for scoliosis, the Legislature clearly precluded any private cause of action based on that statutory duty. Affirmed.

▶ ANALYSIS

The court found that the school district did have a statutory duty to test the students. It also found that the Legislature had clearly contemplated administrative enforcement of the statute. The language of the statute clearly sought to immunize the school districts from any liability that might arise out of the scoliosis-screening program.

Quicknotes

BREACH The violation of an obligation imposed pursuant to contract or law, by acting or failing to act.

DUTY An obligation owed by one individual to another.

IMMUNITY Exemption from a legal obligation.

NEGLIGENCE Conduct falling below the standard of care that a reasonable person would demonstrate under similar conditions.

■■■

Strauss v. Belle Realty Co.

Tenant (P) v. Landlord (D)

N.Y. Ct. App., 65 N.Y.2d 399, 482 N.E.2d 34 (1985).

NATURE OF CASE: Plaintiff's appeal from dismissal of action.

FACT SUMMARY: In Strauss's (P) action against Belle Realty Co. (D) and Consolidated Edison (D), Strauss (P) alleged that Con Edison (D) owed a duty of care to Strauss (P) as a tenant who suffered personal injuries in a common area of an apartment building where Strauss's (P) landlord, Belle Realty (D), had a contractual relation with Con Edison (D).

🏛 RULE OF LAW
A defendant may be liable for negligence only when it breaches a duty owed to the plaintiff.

FACTS: A failure of Consolidated Edison's (D) power system left most of New York City in darkness. During the blackout, Strauss (P) fell on darkened, defective basement stairs in his apartment building, and he sustained injury. Con Edison (D) provided electricity to Strauss's (P) apartment pursuant to an agreement with Strauss (P) but provided power to the common areas of the building under a separate agreement with Belle Realty Co. (D), Strauss's (P) landlord. Strauss (P) fell in a common area of the building and maintained that not only Belle Realty (D) owed him a duty of care to maintain the stairs in good condition, but that Con Edison (D) owed him a duty to provide electricity. Con Edison (D) maintained that it owed no duty to a noncustomer. The trial court found for Strauss (P) on the duty of care issue, the appellate division reversed, and Strauss (P) appealed.

ISSUE: May a defendant be liable in negligence only when it breaches a duty owed to the plaintiff?

HOLDING AND DECISION: (Kaye, J.) Yes. A defendant may be held liable for negligence only when it breaches a duty owed to the plaintiff. Strauss (P) did not have a contract with Con Edison (D) for lighting in the apartment building's common areas. In determining the liability of utilities for consequential damages for failure to provide service, courts have declined to extend the duty of care to noncustomers. Central to these decisions was the ability to extend the defendant's duty to cover foreseeable parties but, at the same time, to contain liability to manageable levels. Permitting recovery to those in Strauss's (P) circumstances would violate the court's responsibility to define an orbit of duty that places controllable limits on liability. "Con Edison (D) is not answerable to the tenant of an apartment building injured in a common area because of Con Edison's (D) negligent failure to provide electric service as required by its agreement with the building owner." Affirmed.

DISSENT: (Meyer, J.) Con Ed (D) may well be able to do so, but before its motion is granted at the expense of an unknown number of victims who have suffered injuries, the extent and effects of which are unknown, it should be required to establish that the catastrophic probabilities are great enough to warrant the limitation of duty it seeks.

▌ ANALYSIS

A duty, in negligence cases, may be defined as an obligation, to which the law will give recognition and effect, to conform to a particular standard of conduct to another. In early English law, there was virtually no consideration of duty. Liability was imposed with no great regard even for the fault of the defendant. The requirements as to conduct were absolute, and once the act was found to be wrongful, the actor was liable for any damage which might result.

■━■

Quicknotes

CONSEQUENTIAL DAMAGES Monetary compensation that may be recovered in order to compensate for injuries or losses sustained as a result of damages that are not the direct or foreseeable result of the act of a party, but that nevertheless are the consequence of such act and which must be specifically pled and demonstrated.

DUTY OF CARE A principle of negligence requiring an individual to act in such a manner as to avoid injury to a person to whom he or she owes an obligatory duty.

NEGLIGENCE Conduct falling below the standard of care that a reasonable person would demonstrate under similar conditions.

UTILITY A private business that provides a service to the public which is of need.

■━■

Reynolds v. Hicks

Accident victim (P) v. Social hosts (D)

Wash. Sup. Ct., 134 Wash. 2d 491, 951 P.2d 761 (1998).

NATURE OF CASE: Appeal from summary judgment for defendants in social host liability suit.

FACT SUMMARY: Reynolds (P) alleged that the Hickses (D) were liable when an underage guest at their wedding party consumed alcohol and then was involved in an accident in which Reynolds (P) was injured.

⚖ RULE OF LAW

The statute making it unlawful for any person to supply liquor to any person under the age of twenty-one does not allow a third person injured by an intoxicated minor to sue the social hosts providing the liquor.

FACTS: The Hickses' (D) under-age nephew consumed alcohol at their wedding party and later injured Reynolds (P) in an auto accident. Reynolds (P) sued the Hickses (D), claiming they had been negligent in serving liquor to a minor. The court granted the Hickses' (D) motion for summary judgment because Washington law did not extend social host liability for furnishing alcohol to a minor to third persons injured by the intoxicated minor. Reynolds (P) appealed.

ISSUE: Does the statute making it unlawful for any person to supply liquor to any person under the age of twenty-one allow a third person injured by an intoxicated minor to sue the social hosts providing the liquor?

HOLDING AND DECISION: (Madsen, J.) No. The statute making it unlawful for any person to supply liquor to any person under the age of twenty-one does not allow a third person injured by an intoxicated minor to sue the social hosts providing the liquor. Only the minor who was injured has a cause of action against the social hosts who supplied the alcohol. Social hosts are ill equipped to monitor the alcohol consumption of their social guests and adults also do not have a cause of action against social hosts. Adults do have a cause of action against a commercial vendor in the same situation, however. Affirmed.

CONCURRENCE: (Durham, C.J.) The judiciary is ill equipped to impose social host liability. There should be no liability on commercial vendors or social hosts without legislative mandate.

DISSENT: (Johnson, J.) The majority made an insupportable distinction between social hosts and commercial vendors by ignoring that both are committing criminal acts.

▶ **ANALYSIS**

Parents are exempt from the general prohibition against furnishing alcohol to minors. Commercial vendors who hold a proprietary interest and profit motive are expected to exercise greater supervision. The court here found that there was no duty owed by the social hosts to their minor guests regarding the consumption of alcohol.

■■■

Quicknotes

BREACH The violation of an obligation imposed pursuant to contract or law, by acting or failing to act.

DUTY An obligation owed by one individual to another.

NEGLIGENCE Conduct falling below the standard of care that a reasonable person would demonstrate under similar conditions.

SOCIAL GUEST STATUTE A state statute requiring a specified level of culpability, usually more than mere negligence, on the part of the driver of an automobile in order to be liable for injuries resulting to a gratuitous passenger.

■■■

Vince v. Wilson

Accident victim (P) v. Grandparent of driver (D)

Vt. Sup. Ct., 151 Vt. 425, 561 A.2d 103 (1989).

NATURE OF CASE: Cross-appeals from award of damages for negligent entrustment.

FACT SUMMARY: Vince (P) sued Wilson (D) and Gardner (D) for enabling an incompetent driver to purchase a vehicle in which he eventually had an accident.

RULE OF LAW
A person who enables an incompetent driver to purchase a vehicle may be liable for negligent entrustment.

FACTS: Wilson (D) provided funding for her grand-nephew to purchase a vehicle, which he did from Ace Auto Sales (D). Gardner (D) owned Ace Auto Sales (D). The grandnephew was not licensed, had failed a driver's test several times, and had an alcohol problem. Wilson (D) and Gardner (D) knew these facts. The grandnephew was involved in an accident with Vince (P), who sued Wilson (D), Ace (D), and Gardner (D) for negligent entrustment. The trial court directed verdicts for Ace (D) and Gardner (D), holding no duty to exist, but allowed the claim against Wilson (D) to go to the jury, which awarded damages. Vince (P) and Wilson (D) cross-appealed.

ISSUE: May a person who enables an incompetent driver to purchase a vehicle be liable for negligent entrustment?

HOLDING AND DECISION: (Mahady, J.) Yes. A person who enables an incompetent driver to purchase a vehicle may be liable for negligent entrustment. One who provides an instrumentality to a person not competent to use that instrumentality, with knowledge of such incompetence, is liable to third parties for injuries caused by incompetent use of the instrumentality. Whether the provider loans, gives, or in some other manner enables is an irrelevant distinction; it is the enabling, not the form of enabling, that matters. Here, both Wilson (D) and Gardner (D) enabled the grandnephew to take possession of the car, knowing he was unqualified to be a driver. How they did it is of no import. Consequently, both may be liable to Vince (P) for his injuries. Affirmed as to Wilson (D), reversed as to Ace (D) and Gardner (D), and remanded.

ANALYSIS

Negligent entrustment can take numerous forms. Probably the classic example is a parent or friend who loans a car to an intoxicated person. The situation involved here is a bit less usual. Unintentional negligent entrustment, such as keys left in the ignition followed by a theft, has also been a source of liability.

Quicknotes

DUTY OF CARE A principle of negligence requiring an individual to act in such a manner as to avoid injury to a person to whom he or she owes an obligatory duty.

NEGLIGENCE Conduct falling below the standard of care that a reasonable person would demonstrate under similar conditions.

Carter v. Kinney

Slip and fall victim (P) v. Driveway owner (D)

Mo. Sup. Ct., 896 S.W.2d 926 (1995).

NATURE OF CASE: Appeal from summary judgment.

FACT SUMMARY: Carter (P), who slipped and broke his leg on the Kinneys' (D) icy driveway while arriving for a church-related study group, sued for damages.

RULE OF LAW

A social guest is a licensee, and a homeowner has the duty to protect him only from known dangerous conditions.

FACTS: Ronald and Mary Kinney (D) hosted a Bible study group at their home for members of their church. Jonathon Carter (P), attending an early morning session in winter, slipped on a patch of ice on the Kinneys' driveway and broke his leg. Ronald Kinney (D) had shoveled snow from the driveway the night before and was not aware that ice had formed overnight. Carter (P) filed suit against the Kinneys (D) claiming that he was an invitee in their home. Carter (P) argued that the Kinneys (D) owed the duty of care to protect him against both known hazards and those that would be revealed by reasonable inspection. Carter (P) conceded that the Kinneys (D) received no financial or other tangible benefit from hosting the study groups. The Kinneys (D) were granted summary judgment by the trial court on the ground that Carter (P) was a licensee and therefore not owed a duty with respect to an unknown dangerous condition. Carter (P) appealed.

ISSUE: Does a homeowner owe a social guest the duty of care owed to invitees, protection against both known dangers and those that would be revealed by a reasonable inspection?

HOLDING AND DECISION: (Robertson, J.) No. Carter's (P) purpose in visiting the Kinneys' (D) home fits the traditional definition of a licensee, not an invitee. The definition of an invitee is an individual who is invited onto the premises for the purpose of conducting business with the possessor of the land. Carter (P) stipulates that the Kinneys (D) received no financial or other tangible benefits from his presence at the study group. Just because Carter (P) was not close social friends with the Kinneys (D), and the reason for being at their home was for a church study group, does not mean that for the purpose of premise liability law he was an invitee. Affirmed.

ANALYSIS

The court points out that Carter (P) significantly hurt his own cause by attempting show that the Kinneys (D)

received an intangible benefit, rather than a tangible one, from hosting the study group. Carter (P) might have been more successful if he had argued that the ice on the driveway was a danger the Kinneys knew or should have known about, even without an inspection. The accident occurred in the middle of winter, and Mr. Kinney had shoveled snow from the driveway the night before. It seems a logical conclusion that the Kinneys would know that ice would form on the driveway by the following morning under those weather conditions.

Quicknotes

DUTY OF CARE A principle of negligence requiring an individual to act in such a manner as to avoid injury to a person to whom he or she owes an obligatory duty.

INVITEE A person who enters upon another's property by an express or implied invitation and to whom the owner of the property owes a duty of care to guard against injury from those hazards which are discoverable through the exercise of reasonable care.

LICENSEES Persons known to an owner or occupier of land, who come onto the premises voluntarily and for a specific purpose, although not necessarily with the consent of the owner.

Heins v. Webster County

Injured visitor v. Hospital (D)

Neb. Sup. Ct., 250 Neb. 750, 552 N.W.2d 51 (1996).

NATURE OF CASE: Appeal from summary judgment for defendant in negligence action.

FACT SUMMARY: Heins (P) alleged that Webster County (D) was negligent in failing to inspect or to warn of the existence of a dangerous condition at the entrance to its hospital, but the court ruled that Heins (P) was a licensee and the hospital (D) therefore did not owe him a duty of ordinary reasonable care.

🏛 RULE OF LAW
Owners and occupiers have the duty to exercise reasonable care in the maintenance of their premises for the protection of lawful visitors.

FACTS: Heins (P) went to visit his daughter who worked at Webster County hospital (D) and was injured when he fell on some ice and snow at the hospital (D) entrance. When Heins (P) sued the hospital (D) for negligence, the court ruled that Heins (P) had been a licensee at the time and the hospital (D) therefore owed him a duty not to act willfully or wantonly or to fail to warn of known hidden dangers. The court concluded that the hospital (D) had not acted willfully and had not failed to warn of any hidden danger. Heins (P) appealed, claiming that the court had erred in not holding the hospital to a duty of reasonable care.

ISSUE: Do owners and occupiers have the duty to exercise reasonable care in the maintenance of their premises for the protection of lawful visitors?

HOLDING AND DECISION: (Connolly, J.) Yes. Owners and occupiers have the duty to exercise reasonable care in the maintenance of their premises for the protection of lawful visitors. The common-law status distinction between licensees and invitees is eliminated. A standard of reasonable care is required for all non-trespassers. This new rule should be applied to the instant case. Reversed and remanded.

DISSENT: (Fahrnbruch, J.) The court should not enact public policy which imposes a duty upon a landowner to provide the same care to all who enter his land, expect trespassers.

▶ *ANALYSIS*

The court found that modern commercial society has created relationships between persons not contemplated by the traditional classifications. It was patently unfair to hold the hospital faultless for its negligence merely because Heins (P) was visiting his daughter rather than entering the hospital as a patient. England statutorily abolished the common-law distinction in 1957. Several states have followed suit.

Quicknotes

INVITEES A person who enters upon another's property by an express or implied invitation and to whom the owner of the property owes a duty of care to guard against injury from those hazards that are discoverable through the exercise of reasonable care.

LICENSEES Persons known to an owner or occupier of land, who come onto the premises voluntarily and for a specific purpose, although not necessarily with the consent of the owner.

NEGLIGENCE Conduct falling below the standard of care that a reasonable person would demonstrate under similar conditions.

STANDARD OF CARE A uniform degree of behavior against which a person's conduct can be measured when determining liability in negligence cases.

TRESPASSERS Persons present on the land of another without the knowledge or express permission of the owner, and to whom only a minimum duty of care is owed for injuries incurred while on the premises.

Posecai v. Wal-Mart Stores, Inc.

Injured customer (P) v. Store (D)

La. Sup. Ct., 752 So. 2d 762 (1999).

NATURE OF CASE: Review of judgment for plaintiff in negligence action.

FACT SUMMARY: Mrs. Posecai (P) alleged that Wal-Mart Stores, Inc. (D) was negligent in failing to provide adequate security in its parking lot.

🏛 RULE OF LAW

Business owners do have a duty to implement reasonable measures to protect their patrons from criminal acts when those acts are foreseeable.

FACTS: Mrs. Posecai (P) was leaving a Wal-Mart store after shopping when she was robbed. Posecai (P) alleged that Wal-Mart Stores, Inc. (D) was negligent in failing to provide security in the parking lot. A judgment was entered in favor of Posecai (P). Wal-Mart (D) appealed, alleging that it did not owe Posecai (P) a duty to protect her from criminal acts of third parties.

ISSUE: Do business owners have a duty to implement reasonable measures to protect their patrons from criminal acts when those acts are foreseeable?

HOLDING AND DECISION: (Marcus, J.) Yes. Business owners do have a duty to implement reasonable measures to protect their patrons from criminal acts when those acts are foreseeable. Generally, there is no duty to protect customers from criminal acts of third parties. The duty arises only in the limited circumstances where the criminal act in question was reasonably foreseeable to the owner of the business. A balancing test is the best method for determining whether the crime was foreseeable and the business owner owed such a duty to provide security. Here the foreseeability and gravity of harm in the parking lot was slight since there had been only one other similar incident in the parking lot. The degree of foreseeability was not sufficient for the imposition of a duty to provide security. Reversed.

CONCURRENCE: (Johnson, J.) The majority's use of the balancing test is flawed. I would adopt the totality of Circumstances test.

▶ ANALYSIS

The court discussed various tests that may be applied to determine whether a crime is foreseeable. Some jurisdictions apply a specific harm rule. Other jurisdictions have adopted a prior similar incidents test.

Quicknotes

DUTY OF CARE A principle of negligence requiring an individual to act in such a manner as to avoid injury to a person to whom he or she owes an obligatory duty.

FORESEEABILITY A reasonable expectation that an act or omission would result in injury.

NEGLIGENCE Conduct falling below the standard of care that a reasonable person would demonstrate under similar conditions.

A.W. v. Lancaster County School District 0001

Mother (P) v. School system (D)

Neb. Sup. Ct., 784 N.W.2d 907 (2010).

NATURE OF CASE: Appeal of summary judgment.

FACT SUMMARY: After a kindergarten student was sexually assaulted in a school restroom during the school day, the child's mother, A.W. (P), sued the Lincoln Public School District 0001 (LPS) (D) on the child's behalf, alleging negligence. The district court entered summary judgment for LPS (D), on the grounds that the assault was unforeseeable.

🏛 **RULE OF LAW**
The duty of due care is a legal standard that does not depend on foreseeability of harm.

FACTS: Joseph Siems entered Arnold Elementary School in Lincoln, Nebraska, during lunchtime, and walked past the main office without signing in as visitors are required to do, without being noticed by the office workers. A teacher noticed he was out-of-place, and after he ignored her inquiry about whether he needed help, she went to the office to see that he had signed in. Then, two other teachers who were monitoring some first graders also saw Siems in the hallway, and one went to talk to Siems while the other stayed with the students. Siems told her he needed to use the restroom, and the teacher pointed it out and told Siems that he had to return to the main office after using the restroom. The teacher knew there were no students in that restroom at the time. But while one of the teachers saw him go into the empty restroom, no one saw him come out of it and go into another restroom down the hallway that was closer to the school's main entrance. In the meantime, the teachers went to the office to report the incident. While the administrator was being informed, C.B. (P), who was 5 years old, returned from a trip to the restroom and told his teacher that there was a "bad man" in the restroom, and that Siems had briefly performed oral sex on C.B. (P). The administrator went to the restroom and saw Siems sitting in a stall, and at the time, there were no children in the restroom. She then called the office to initiate a "Code Red" lockdown of the school, and called 911. The custodian then detained Siems while police arrived. The district court granted summary judgment for the school (D), and A.W. (P), C.B.'s (P) mother, appealed. A.W. (P) argued that the district court erred in finding that (1) the Lincoln Public School District 0001 (LPS) (D) did not owe a duty to protect C.B. (P) from the danger of sexual assault, (2) the sexual assault of C.B. was not reasonably foreseeable, and (3) LPS took reasonable steps to protect against foreseeable acts of violence on school grounds.

ISSUE: Is the duty of due-care a legal standard that does not depend on foreseeability of harm?

HOLDING AND DECISION: (Gerrard, J.) Yes. The duty of due care is a legal standard that does not depend on foreseeability of harm. In order to win a negligence case, a plaintiff has to show legal duty owed by the defendant to the plaintiff, a breach of that duty, causation, and damages. A.W.'s (P) arguments are basically three ways of saying the same thing: Was Siems's assault of C.B. (P) reasonably foreseeable? Many courts, have tied the question of whether a duty exists to the question of foreseeability. If risk of harm was foreseeable by a reasonable person, the theory goes, then the duty of due care exists. Because the existence of a legal duty is a question of law, courts treat the foreseeability of a particular injury as a question of law. But while the duty is to conform to the legal standard of reasonable conduct in light of the apparent risk, and whether a duty exists is a question of law, whether a breach of that duty occurred is a question of fact for the fact finder, and the existence of the duty and the breach of the duty should not be conflated. This court has erroneously done so in the past: The court has reasoned that a university's legal duty to protect students on its campus from criminal activity existed because violent altercations were not unknown at the location on campus, and such attacks were therefore foreseeable. But the reasoning is flawed. Foreseeability depends on the circumstances and is therefore a question of fact. Therefore, foreseeability is not the determinant of duty; by incorporating foreseeability into the analysis of duty, a court transforms a factual question into a legal issue and expands the authority of judges at the expense of the fact finder.

The Restatement (Third) of Torts echoes that view, stating that foreseeable risk is an element in the determination of negligence, not legal duty. To determine what appropriate care is necessary—that is, what duty is owed—one should look to the law. To determine whether appropriate care was exercised, the one must look to the fact finder to assess the foreseeable risk at the time of the alleged negligence. The extent of foreseeable risk depends on the specific facts of the case and cannot be assessed for a category of cases. If the court removes from the jury the question of negligence because reasonable minds could not differ about whether an actor exercised reasonable care, then the court's decision reflects that the case is clear, and that should not be misinterpreted as involving exemption from the ordinary duty of due care.

Continued on next page.

In this case, it is clear and undisputed that LPS (D) owed C.B. (P) a duty of reasonable care. The duty to protect students is a well-established legal standard under the Restatement (Second) of Torts, the Restatement (Third) of Torts, and case law. But what is in dispute is whether Siems's assault of C.B. (P) was reasonably foreseeable, and that is a question of fact related to what LPS (D) employees knew, when they knew it, and whether a reasonable person would infer from those facts that there was a danger. But A. W.'s (P) evidence of past criminal behavior in the area of the school is inadequate to present a jury question that the security plan was inadequate. But after Siems entered the building, reasonable minds could differ about whether LPS's (D) initial failure to take notice of his presence, and response to his presence, satisfied its duty of reasonable care. Several employees spotted him, all thought he was out of place and responded to the threat, but none made sure that he did not make contact with a student. Reasonable minds could differ as to whether Siems's assault of C.B. (P) was foreseeable, and therefore, A.W. (P) is entitled to a full trial. Reversed and remanded.

▶ **ANALYSIS**

Carefully consider the court's distinction between the duty of due care, which is a legal standard of acceptable behavior, and foreseeability, which is a factual question about whether the risk of harm was foreseeable by a reasonable person, which is a question of fact. In this case, the court carefully drew the line between the two: there was no question about whether the school owed a duty of reasonable care to C.B., so that element of the negligence case was satisfied. The question then becomes whether Siems's assault of C.B. was reasonably foreseeable, which is a factual question. If the jury decides it was foreseeable, then that element of the negligence case will also be proved, because a breach of the legal duty would be shown. If on the other hand the jury decides it was not foreseeable, then the school did not breach its duty, and the negligence case fails. The question of foreseeability is a question of breach of the duty of due care, not a question of whether a duty exists.

◼━◼

Quicknotes

DUTY OF CARE A principle of negligence requiring an individual to act in such a manner as to avoid injury to a person to whom he or she owes a duty.

DUTY TO PROTECT/AID A moral duty and not one imposed by law; no liability attaches to those persons who fail to undertake a rescue or otherwise aid a person in need, absent a special relationship between them.

NEGLIGENCE Conduct falling below the standard of care that a reasonable person would demonstrate under similar conditions.

◼━◼

Broadbent v. Broadbent

Injured son (P) v. Mother (D)

Ariz. Sup. Ct., 184 Ariz. 74, 907 P.2d 43 (1995).

NATURE OF CASE: Appeal from dismissal of case alleging parental negligence.

FACT SUMMARY: Mr. Broadbent, representing his disabled son (P), alleged that Mrs. Broadbent (D) was liable for injuries the son (P) sustained when Mrs. Broadbent (D) left him near the pool while she answered a phone call.

🏛 RULE OF LAW
Parental immunity is abolished and a parent's conduct is judged by whether that parent's conduct comported with that of a reasonable and prudent parent in a similar situation.

FACTS: Mrs. Broadbent (D) left her two-and-a-half year-old son alone near the pool while she answered a phone call. He fell into the pool and suffered severe permanent brain damage as a result. Mr. Broadbent, as the son's conservator (P), sued Mrs. Broadbent (D) for negligence. The trial court dismissed the claim on the basis of parental immunity. Broadbent (P) appealed, claiming that the doctrine of parental immunity did not apply.

ISSUE: Is parental immunity abolished and is a parent's conduct judged by whether that parent's conduct comported with that of a reasonable and prudent parent in a similar situation?

HOLDING AND DECISION: (Corcoran, J.) Yes. Parental immunity is abolished and a parent's conduct is judged by whether that parent's conduct comported with that of a reasonable and prudent parent in a similar situation. A parent is not immune from liability for tortious conduct toward his child solely by reason of that relationship. In this case, a trier of fact may find that Mrs. Broadbent (D) did not act as a reasonable and prudent parent would under the circumstances. Vacated and remanded.

CONCURRENCE: (Feldman, C.J.) In those areas of broad discretion in which only parents have authority to make decisions the parent's conduct must be palpably unreasonable in order to impose liability.

▶ ANALYSIS

The court traced the history of the doctrine of parental tort immunity. There was no such immunity under English common law. Almost all states adopted such immunity but carved exceptions in certain circumstances.

Quicknotes

DUTY OF CARE A principle of negligence requiring an individual to act in such a manner as to avoid injury to a person to whom he or she owes an obligatory duty.

NEGLIGENCE Conduct falling below the standard of care that a reasonable person would demonstrate under similar conditions.

REASONABLE PERSON STANDARD The standard of care exercised by a hypothetical person who possesses the intelligence, education, knowledge, attention, and judgment required by society of its members when governing behavior; the standard applies to a person's judgment when determining breach of a duty under the theory of negligence.

Riss v. City of New York

Girlfriend (P) v. City (D)

N.Y. Ct. App., 22 N.Y.2d 579, 240 N.E.2d 860 (1968).

NATURE OF CASE: Appeal from denial of damages for negligence.

FACT SUMMARY: In Riss's (P) action against the City of New York (D), Riss (P) contended that she was repeatedly threatened with personal harm and eventually suffered dire injuries because of failure of the City (D) to provide special police protection for her, and that the City (D) is liable for negligently failing to provide her with protection.

🏛 **RULE OF LAW**
A municipality is not liable for failure to provide special protection to a member of the public who has repeatedly been threatened with personal harm.

FACTS: Riss (P) was terrorized for six months by a former boyfriend. She sought police protection unsuccessfully. When she became engaged to another man, she received a call threatening her safety. Riss (P) again sought police help but was refused. The next day, a thug hired by the former boyfriend threw lye in Riss's (P) face, leaving her permanently scarred, blind in one eye, and with little vision in the other. Riss (P) sued the City of New York (D) for negligent failure to provide her with special police protection. The lower court dismissed Riss's (P) complaint, and Riss (P) appealed.

ISSUE: Is a municipality liable for failure to provide special protection to a member of the public who has repeatedly been threatened with personal harm?

HOLDING AND DECISION: (Breitel, J.) No. A municipality is not liable for failure to provide special protection to a member of the public who has been repeatedly threatened with personal harm. The amount of protection that may be provided is limited by the resources of the community and by a considered legislative executive decision as to how those resources may be deployed. Before such extension of responsibilities should be dictated by the indirect imposition of tort liabilities, there should be a legislative determination that that should be the scope of public responsibility. Although this appeal presents a very sympathetic framework, in the absence of legislation this court cannot carve out an area of tort liability for police protection to members of the public such as Riss (P). Affirmed.

DISSENT: (Keating, J.) No one is contending that the police must be at the scene of every potential crime or must provide a personal bodyguard to every person who walks into a police station and claims to have been threatened. The police only need act as a reasonable person would

under the circumstances. At first, there would be a duty to inquire. If the inquiry indicates nothing to substantiate the alleged threat, the matter may be put aside and other matters attended to. If, however, the claims prove to have some basis, appropriate steps would be necessary.

▶ **ANALYSIS**

Protecting the personal security of the community is, of course, a traditional function of government. *Riss* has been an important case because it raises fundamental issues about police responsibility to the public at large. For a discussion of a variety of scenarios involving requests for police protection and a proposal that the courts recognize a general duty to meet "professional standards governing law enforcement crime prevention activity," see Note, "Police Liability for Negligent Failure to Prevent Crime," 94 *Harv. L. Rev.* 821 (1981).

Quicknotes

NEGLIGENCE Conduct falling below the standard of care that a reasonable person would demonstrate under similar conditions.

Lauer v. City of New York

Murder suspect (P) v. City (D)

N.Y. Ct. App., 95 N.Y.2d 95, 733 N.E.2d 184 (2000).

NATURE OF CASE: Appeal from reinstatement of claim for negligent infliction of emotional distress.

FACT SUMMARY: Lauer (P) alleged that the City of New York (D) was negligent when the Medical Examiner (D) failed to correct incorrect information on an autopsy report and death certificate.

🏛 **RULE OF LAW**
To sustain liability against a municipality, the duty breached must be more than that owed the public generally.

FACTS: When Lauer's (P) three-year-old son died, the New York City Medical Examiner (D) performed an autopsy and prepared a report stating that the death was a homicide. The police began an investigation focusing on Lauer (P) as the prime suspect. When the Medical Examiner (D) later determined that the true cause of death was a ruptured brain aneurysm, he failed to correct the autopsy report or death certificate and failed to inform law enforcement authorities. Lauer (P) sued for negligent infliction of emotional distress he suffered as a result of the City's (D) negligent ministerial acts. The trial court dismissed all claims based on governmental tort immunity, but on appeal the court reinstated the claim for negligent infliction of emotional distress.

ISSUE: To sustain liability against a municipality, must the duty breached be more than that owed the public generally?

HOLDING AND DECISION: (Kaye, C.J.) Yes. To sustain liability against a municipality, the duty breached must be more than that owed the public generally. Lauer (P) was not a person for whose benefit the statute requiring accurate record keeping was enacted. Members of the general public do not have a cause of action against municipalities performing public functions absent a duty to use due care for the benefit of particular persons or classes of persons. Here Lauer's (P) claim must fail because the Chief Medical Officer (D) did not owe him any specific duty of care. Reversed.

DISSENT: (Smith, J.) I believe that Lauer (P) has pleaded a prima facie case for negligent infliction of emotional distress.

DISSENT: (Bellacosa, J.) To immunize the kind of alleged misconduct described herein would reward government agents who hide the truth and sweep wrongdoings under a rug of tort impunity.

▶ **ANALYSIS**

Lauer (P) did not have standing to sue since he was not a member of the class protected by the statute. Nor did Lauer (P) establish that the Medical Examiner (D) owed him any duty of care based on any special relationship. The Medical Examiner (D) had not undertaken to act on Lauer's (P) behalf.

Quicknotes

DUTY OF CARE A principle of negligence requiring an individual to act in such a manner as to avoid injury to a person to whom he or she owes an obligatory duty.

IMMUNITY Exemption from a legal obligation.

MINISTERIAL ACT An action performed by a public official at the direction of a superior officer or pursuant to statute.

NEGLIGENCE Conduct falling below the standard of care that a reasonable person would demonstrate under similar conditions.

NEGLIGENT INFLICTION OF EMOTIONAL DISTRESS Violation of the duty of care owed to another that occurs when an individual creates a foreseeable risk of injury to the other person, which causes emotional distress resulting in some physical harm to that person.

Friedman v. State of New York

Injured (P) v. State (D)

N.Y. Ct. App., 67 N.Y.2d 271, 493 N.E.2d 893 (1986).

NATURE OF CASE: Consolidated appeal in personal injury actions involving crossover collisions.

FACT SUMMARY: In Friedman's (P) action against the State of New York (D), Friedman (P) claimed that her car was sideswiped on a viaduct, causing her to swerve into the oncoming traffic where she was hit head-on, and that the State (D) was negligent in failing to construct a median barrier.

▦ **RULE OF LAW**
When the State is made aware of a dangerous highway condition and does not take action to remedy it, the State can be held liable for resulting injuries.

FACTS: Friedman's (P) car was sideswiped on a viaduct, causing her to swerve into oncoming traffic, where she was hit head-on. Friedman (P) claimed that the State of New York (D) was negligent in not constructing a median barrier on the viaduct. The State Department of Transportation had studied the question five years earlier and decided that a median barrier should be constructed, but at the time of the accident, no action had been taken. The State (D) attempted to justify its nonaction by pointing to funding priorities and project revisions but did not offer concrete evidence in support of its claims. The appellate division affirmed a judgment for Friedman (P), and the State (D) appealed on the grounds of qualified immunity.

ISSUE: When the State is made aware of a dangerous highway condition and does not take action to remedy it, can the State be held liable for resulting injuries?

HOLDING AND DECISION: (Alexander, J.) Yes. Once a decision has been reached by the State to go forward with a plan intended to remedy a dangerous condition, liability may result from a failure to effectuate the plan within a reasonable period of time. When the State is made aware of a dangerous highway condition and does not take action to remedy it, the State can be held liable for resulting injuries. Here, the State of New York (D) argued that the doctrine of qualified immunity applied, and, thus, that State (D) or municipal highway planning and decision-making functions should not be subject to intrusions by the courts. However, even under the doctrine, a governmental body may be held liable when its study of a traffic condition is plainly inadequate or where it has unreasonably delayed remedial action. Here, the State (D) failed to show that the five-year delay between the Department of Transportation's recognition of the hazardous condition on the viaduct and its project proposal and the Friedman (P) accident was necessary to study and formulate a reasonable safety plan. Affirmed.

▶ **ANALYSIS**

Until very recently, the chief breach in the governmental immunity of a state arose out of constitutional provisions against the taking or sometimes also the damaging of private property for public purposes without compensation. Such provisions have usually been held to be self-executing. Thus, even though the legislature has not provided any procedure for prosecuting such claims against the state, resort to the court is open only if it can be found that there has been a taking, or damaging, within the terms of the Constitution.

■━■

Quicknotes

NEGLIGENCE Conduct falling below the standard of care that a reasonable person would demonstrate under similar conditions.

QUALIFIED IMMUNITY An affirmative defense relieving officials from civil liability for the performance of activities within their discretion so long as such conduct is not in violation of an individual's rights pursuant to law as determined by a reasonable person standard.

■━■

Cope v. Scott

Injured motorist (P) v. Federal government (D)

45 F.3d 445 (D.C. Cir. 1995).

NATURE OF CASE: Appeal from summary judgment for defendant.

FACT SUMMARY: Cope (P) alleged that the National Park Service (D) negligently maintained the road surface and acted negligently in failing to adequately sign a curve on a road.

🏛 RULE OF LAW
Discretionary judgments regarding where and what types of signs to post are not fraught with public policy considerations and such judgments are therefore not necessarily protected from suit.

FACTS: Cope (P) suffered injuries following an accident that occurred on a busy road that transverses an urban park in Washington D.C. and is maintained by the National Park Service (D). The road was worn and slick because of rain the day of the accident. Cope (P) alleged that the National Park Service (D) was liable for his injuries because it had been negligent in its road maintenance and in its failure to post adequate safety warnings along the road. The district court found that the Government's (D) allegedly negligent actions were discretionary functions and were therefore immune from suit. Cope (P) appealed.

ISSUE: Are discretionary judgments regarding where and what types of signs to post fraught with public policy considerations and are such judgments therefore necessarily protected from suit?

HOLDING AND DECISION: (Tatel, J.) No. Discretionary judgments regarding where and what types of signs to post are not fraught with public policy considerations and such judgments are therefore not necessarily protected from suit. The discretionary function exception applies only to judgments implicating economic, social, or political concerns. Cope (P) was entitled to attempt and convince a finder of fact that the government acted negligently by failing to provide adequate warning signs on the road. Affirmed in part, reversed in part, and remanded.

▶ ANALYSIS

The aesthetic considerations that allegedly prevented the National Park Service (D) from posting more signs were not political. Only those policy decisions fraught with political considerations are considered discretionary acts. Discretionary acts are immune from suit, but ministerial functions are not immune from suit since failure to follow explicit directives may be considered negligence.

Quicknotes

DISCRETIONARY FUNCTIONS Those acts left to an individual's judgment and are not subject to a defined rule or course of conduct.

GOVERNMENTAL IMMUNITY Implied immunity of state and federal governments from taxation by the other.

MINISTERIAL ACT An action performed by a public official at the direction of a superior officer or pursuant to statute.

NEGLIGENCE Conduct falling below the standard of care that a reasonable person would demonstrate under similar conditions.

◼◼◼

The Duty Requirement: Nonphysical Harm

Quick Reference Rules of Law

Falzone v. Busch

Injured (P) v. Tortfeasor (D)

N.J. Sup. Ct., 45 N.J. 559, 214 A.2d 12 (1965).

NATURE OF CASE: Appeal from dismissal of claims of negligent emotional distress.

FACT SUMMARY: Falzone (P) alleged that she had been emotionally distressed as a result of fear for her safety occasioned by Busch's (D) negligence.

🏛 RULE OF LAW
A physical injury may be directly traceable to fright, and so may be caused by it.

FACTS: Busch (D) negligently caused an accident in which Falzone's (P) husband was injured. Falzone (P) was on the scene of the accident and had feared for her personal safety as a result. When Falzone (P) sued for negligent infliction of emotional distress, the court dismissed the claim, holding that there could be no recovery where there had been no physical impact. Falzone (P) appealed.

ISSUE: May a physical injury be directly traceable to fright, and therefore be caused by it?

HOLDING AND DECISION: (Proctor, J.) Yes. A physical injury may be directly traceable to fright, and so may be caused by it. Case precedents that a physical impact is necessary to sustain a negligence action are no longer tenable. The court cannot determine as a matter of law that it is not probable or natural for persons of normal health to suffer physical injuries when subjected to fright. The issue is to be determined on the basis of medical evidence. Medical knowledge on the relationship between emotional disturbance and physical injury has expanded and such relationship no longer seems open to serious challenge. Where negligence causes fright from a reasonable fear of immediate personal injury, which fright is shown to have resulted in substantial bodily injury or sickness, the injured person may recover if such bodily injury or sickness would be regarded as proper elements of damage had they occurred as a consequence of direct physical injury rather than fright. Reversed.

▶ ANALYSIS

This was a case of first impression. Earlier New Jersey cases had consistently held that fright could not be the proximate cause of substantial physical injury. Modern legal scholars were virtually unanimous in condemning the rule denying recovery in the absence of impact.

━━■

Quicknotes

DAMAGES Monetary compensation that may be awarded by the court to a party who has sustained injury or loss to his or her person, property or rights due to another party's unlawful act, omission or negligence.

NEGLIGENCE Conduct falling below the standard of care that a reasonable person would demonstrate under similar conditions.

NEGLIGENT INFLICTION OF EMOTIONAL DISTRESS Violation of the duty of care owed to another that occurs when an individual creates a foreseeable risk of injury to the other person, which causes emotional distress resulting in some physical harm to that person.

PHYSICAL IMPACT Contact with another's body.

PROXIMATE CAUSE The natural sequence of events without which an injury would not have been sustained.

━━■

Metro-North Commuter Railroad Company v. Buckley

Employer (D) v. Employee (P)

521 U.S. 424 (1997).

NATURE OF CASE: Review of dismissal of action brought under the Federal Employers' Liability Act.

FACT SUMMARY: Buckley (P) alleged that Metro-North Commuter Railroad Company (D), his employer, negligently had exposed him to asbestos at work and should pay damages for his resulting emotional distress.

🏛 **RULE OF LAW**
A worker cannot recover for negligently inflicted emotional distress unless, and until, he manifests symptoms of a disease.

FACTS: Buckley (P) was exposed to asbestos while working for Metro-North Commuter Railroad Company (Metro-North) (D). Since attending an asbestos awareness class, Buckley (P) has allegedly suffered emotional distress. When Buckley (P) sued Metro-North (D) for damages to cover the cost of future medical checkups and emotional distress, the court dismissed the claims, holding that the Federal Employers' Liability Act (FELA) did not permit recovery in cases where no physical impact occurred. Buckley (P) appealed, claiming that the physical impact with insulation dust that accompanied his emotional distress amounted to a physical impact as required by the statute. The court of appeals reversed. Metro-North (D) appealed.

ISSUE: Can a worker recover for negligently inflicted emotional distress if he does not manifest symptoms of a disease?

HOLDING AND DECISION: (Breyer, J.) No. A worker cannot recover for negligently inflicted emotional distress unless, and until, he manifests symptoms of a disease. Only those who have sustained a physical impact or who were placed in immediate risk of physical harm by the allegedly negligent conduct can recover for emotional injury. Here Buckley's (P) contact with asbestos amounted to no more than an exposure to a substance that poses some future risk of disease. Common-law courts also have denied recovery to those who, like Buckley (P), are disease and symptom free. Reversed and remanded.

CONCURRENCE AND DISSENT: (Ginsburg, J.) Buckley's (P) emotional distress claim failed because he failed to present objective evidence of severe emotional distress.

▶ **ANALYSIS**

The case was based on FELA, but the court discussed common-law principles as well. The "zone of danger" test applied in such cases usually requires an immediate risk of physical harm to be present. Some courts have awarded damages for emotional distress during the window of time between the event that created the anxiety or concern and the results of negative tests.

Quicknotes

NEGLIGENCE Conduct falling below the standard of care that a reasonable person would demonstrate under similar conditions.

NEGLIGENT INFLICTION OF EMOTIONAL DISTRESS Violation of the duty of care owed to another that occurs when an individual creates a foreseeable risk of injury to the other person, which causes emotional distress resulting in some physical harm to that person.

Gammon v. Osteopathic Hospital of Maine, Inc.

Son (P) v. Hospital (D)

Me. Sup. Jud. Ct., 534 A.2d 1282 (1987).

NATURE OF CASE: Appeal of dismissal of claim for negligent infliction of emotional distress.

FACT SUMMARY: Gammon (P) sought to sue for negligently inflicted psychic distress not accompanied by physical impact.

🏛 RULE OF LAW
One may recover for negligently inflicted psychic distress not accompanied by physical injury.

FACTS: Gammon's (P) father died while at Osteopathic Hospital of Maine, Inc. (D). Gammon (P) requested that the Hospital (D) return his father's personal effects. The Hospital (D) instead mistakenly sent a bag of severed body parts taken from the pathology lab. Gammon (P), believing that the parts were his father's, became hysterical. He suffered a temporary condition of emotional disturbance. He sued the Hospital (D) for, among other things, negligent infliction of emotional distress. The court dismissed this claim as no physical injury occurred. Gammon (P) appealed.

ISSUE: May one recover for negligently inflicted psychic distress not accompanied by physical injuries?

HOLDING AND DECISION: (Roberts, J.) Yes. One may recover for negligently inflicted psychic distress not accompanied by physical injuries. A person's psychic well-being is no less entitled to protection than his physical well-being. The rules that require some form of physical injury for psychic injury to be considered basically arise out of a fear of fabrication and place an undue burden on defendants. However, these concerns are better addressed by confidence in the trial process, not by arbitrary rules of demarcation. Consequently, if a person has a valid and provable psychic injury, he should be compensated even absent a physical manifestation. Here, Gammon (P) made out a credible claim, and the jury should have been allowed to decide the issue. Reversed and remanded.

▶ ANALYSIS

The main problem with emotional distress claims is proof. It is impossible to prove that someone is not psychologically injured, so a defendant can have a difficult time. However, most jurisdictions, such as Maine here, impose an objective standard in this area. This presents unduly sensitive individuals from prevailing on claims based on objectively reasonable behavior.

Quicknotes

NEGLIGENT INFLICTION OF EMOTIONAL DISTRESS Violation of the duty of care owed to another that occurs when an individual creates a foreseeable risk of injury to the other person, which causes emotional distress resulting in some physical harm to that person.

OBJECTIVE STANDARD A standard that is not personal to an individual but is dependent on some external source.

Johnson v. Jamaica Hospital

Mother of abducted child (P) v. Hospital (D)

N.Y. Ct. App., 62 N.Y.2d 523, 467 N.E.2d 502 (1984).

NATURE OF CASE: Appeal from denial of motion to dismiss for failure to state a claim.

FACT SUMMARY: Johnson (P) sued Jamaica Hospital (D) for emotional distress brought on by negligence when her daughter was abducted from the hospital and not recovered until four and a half months later.

🏛 RULE OF LAW
There is no cause of action for indirect "psychic injuries" unless the plaintiff was within the zone of danger, and their injuries resulted from the contemporaneous observation of serious physical injury or death caused by the defendant's negligence.

FACTS: Johnson (P) gave birth to daughter Kawana at Jamaica Hospital (D) and was discharged several days later. Kawana remained in the Hospital (D) for further treatment. When Johnson (P) returned a week later to visit Kawana, she could not be found. On that same day the hospital had received two bomb threats, and Kawana had apparently been abducted. Johnson (P) filed a suit for emotional distress resulting from the Hospital's (D) negligence. Kawana was found by police and returned to Johnson (P) four and a half months later. The trial court denied the Hospital's (D) motion to dismiss for failure to state a claim, and the appellate division affirmed by a divided vote. The court of appeals granted review. A suit was also brought on Kawana's behalf, which is a separate matter.

ISSUE: Does a cause of action for emotional distress resulting from defendant's negligence exist if the plaintiff was not within the zone of danger at the time that the injury causing the emotional distress occurred?

HOLDING AND DECISION: (Kaye, J.) No. There is no basis for recovery on the grounds stated by Johnson (P). The standard for recovery requires that Johnson (P) had been within the zone of danger at the time of the abduction, and that her injuries were caused by the contemporaneous observation of the incident resulting from the Hospital's (D) negligence. Neither of these requirements was met. There is no duty owed to Johnson (P), and to impose one would invite boundless liability for indirect emotional injuries, contrary to public policy. Although the Hospital (D) may have been negligent in caring for Kawana, and directly liable to her, it is not liable for emotional distress suffered by Johnson (P). Reversed and complaint dismissed.

DISSENT: (Meyer, J.) The Hospital (D) interfered with the custodial rights of parents. Hospitals have checkout procedures already in place, and they have a duty to exercise reasonable care so that a newborn baby is not removed from the hospital by someone not authorized to do so. For the majority to deny recovery by Johnson (P) for fear of opening the floodgates of litigation is ridiculous.

▶ ANALYSIS

The majority points out that their decision reflects the prevailing view of courts in other states. Although the verdict may seem like a harsh one, it is important to remember that the Hospital (D) was not completely absolved of its negligence, as Kawana has a separate cause of action. Nonetheless, there seems little doubt that Johnson's (P) emotional distress was sincere, or that any parent in this situation would feel similar emotional harm. Undoubtedly, most parents would expect a more concrete assurance of their child's safety while in a hospital, and allowing recovery would probably not cause the rash of lawsuits that the majority fears.

━━■■■■■━━

Quicknotes

NEGLIGENCE Conduct falling below the standard of care that a reasonable person would demonstrate under similar conditions.

NEGLIGENT INFLICTION OF EMOTIONAL DISTRESS Violation of the duty of care owed to another that occurs when an individual creates a foreseeable risk of injury to the other person, which causes emotional distress resulting in some physical harm to that person.

ZONE OF DANGER For purposes of tort liability, the requirement plaintiff be within the area of risk of injury from the defendant's conduct in order to recover for negligence.

━━■■■■■━━

Portee v. Jaffee

Father of decedent (P) v. Elevator company (D)

N.J. Sup. Ct., 84 N.J. 88, 417 A.2d 521 (1980).

NATURE OF CASE: Appeal of dismissal of action for damages for emotional injuries.

FACT SUMMARY: Portee (P), who witnessed the prolonged and violent death of her son in a malfunctioning elevator, sued for emotional distress.

🏛 RULE OF LAW
A person may sue for emotional distress caused by injuries to another person.

FACTS: Portee's (P) son was caught between an elevator door and the wall of the elevator shaft. The elevator went into operation and her son became jammed in the shaft. He suffered severe injuries from which he later died. Portee (P) witnessed the incident. Subsequent to this, Portee (P) suffered profound psychological problems, including an attempted suicide. She brought a suit seeking damages for emotional distress. The trial court granted summary judgment dismissing the case, and Portee (P) appealed.

ISSUE: May a person sue for emotional distress caused by injuries to another person?

HOLDING AND DECISION: (Pashman, J.) Yes. A person may sue for emotional distress caused by injuries sustained by another person. The legal concept of duty is essentially a policy judgment that only if risk of injury to another by one's conduct is sufficiently foreseeable should one be expected to mold his conduct to avoid a risk of harm to that other person. Prior law in this state, requiring physical impact for a person to recover, was based on the assumption that, absent physical impact, injury to a person is not foreseeable. This is clearly incorrect. It cannot be seriously argued that a parent witnessing the violent death of a child could not foreseeably suffer psychological injury. Consequently, the physical impact rule should be jettisoned. In ruling whether a party may recover for injuries sustained by another, a court should look to the relationship of the plaintiff to the injured party, the contemporaneousness of the viewing, the physical proximity of the viewing, and the severity of the injury. Here, all these factors clearly indicate that injury to Portee (P) was foreseeable, and so she may proceed with this suit. Reversed.

▶ ANALYSIS

The seminal case in this area was *Dillon v. Legg*, 441 P.2d 912 (Cal. 1968). In that case, a woman was allowed to recover for emotional distress caused by an accident occurring to her child. The factors outlined by the court here were largely borrowed from *Dillon*, although the *Dillon* court did not discuss severity of injury.

Quicknotes

DUTY An obligation owed by one individual to another.

FORESEEABILITY A reasonable expectation that an act or omission would result in injury.

Nycal Corporation v. KPMG Peat Marwick LLP

Investor (P) v. Auditor (D)

Mass. Sup. Jud. Ct., 426 Mass. 491, 688 N.E.2d 1368 (1998).

NATURE OF CASE: Appeal from summary judgment for defendant.

FACT SUMMARY: Nycal Corporation (P) alleged that KPMG Peat Marwick LLP (D) materially misrepresented the financial condition of a company in which Nycal (P) had invested, to its detriment.

RULE OF LAW
The potential liability of an accountant to noncontractual third parties is limited to those who can demonstrate actual knowledge on the part of the accountant that the third parties would rely on the accountant's report.

FACTS: Nycal Corporation (P) allegedly relied on an auditors' report prepared by KPMG Peat Marwick LLP (KPMG) (D) in deciding to enter into a stock purchase agreement. When the company became insolvent, Nycal (P) sought damages and costs resulting from its alleged reliance on KPMG's (D) report. The court granted KPMG's (D) motion for summary judgment. Nycal (P) appealed.

ISSUE: Is the potential liability of an accountant to noncontractual third parties limited to those who can demonstrate actual knowledge on the part of the accountant that the third parties would rely on the accountant's report?

HOLDING AND DECISION: (Greaney, J.) Yes. The potential liability of an accountant to noncontractual third parties is limited to those who can demonstrate actual knowledge on the part of the accountant that the third parties would rely on the accountant's report. The undisputed facts show that KPMG (D) did not know or intend that Nycal (P) would rely on the audit report in connection with an investment in the company. The test set forth in the Restatement (Second) of Torts § 552 comports most closely with the liability standard applied in other professional contexts. Section 552 describes the tort of negligent misrepresentation committed in the process of supplying information for the guidance of others, namely, that a person who, in the course of their business or employment, or in any other transaction in which he or she has a pecuniary interest, supplies false information for guidance of others in their business, is liable for pecuniary loss caused to them by their justifiable reliance on such information, for failing to exercise reasonable care or competence in obtaining or communicating the information. However, under § 552(2), such liability is limited to losses suffered by the person for whose benefit the guidance

is intended to be supplied. KPMG (D) did not even learn of the stock purchase agreement until after it had been signed. Affirmed.

ANALYSIS

The court refused to extend the scope of liability to include all possible plaintiffs. In cases involving personal injury, traditional tort principles apply. In cases involving economic harm alone, a professional's liability is limited.

Quicknotes

ACTUAL KNOWLEDGE Knowledge that presently and objectively exists.

DUTY OF CARE A principle of negligence requiring an individual to act in such a manner as to avoid injury to a person to whom he or she owes an obligatory duty.

NEGLIGENCE Conduct falling below the standard of care that a reasonable person would demonstrate under similar conditions.

LAN/STV v. Martin K. Eby Construction Co., Inc.

Architect firm (D) v. General contractor (P)

Tex. Sup. Ct., 435 S.W.3d 234 (2014).

NATURE OF CASE: Appeal from affirmance of jury verdict awarding plaintiff damages in action for negligence and negligent misrepresentation.

FACT SUMMARY: LAN/STV (D), an architecture firm, made significant mistakes in its plans and specifications for a project, which had the effect of greatly increasing the costs of the general contractor, Martin K. Eby Construction Co., Inc. (Eby) (P). LAN/STV (D) contended that the economic loss rule barred damages for those mistakes.

RULE OF LAW

An action for negligent misrepresentation that asserts damages based on economic loss against an architect in a construction project is barred by the economic loss rule where the parties do not have a contractual relationship.

FACTS: The Dallas Area Rapid Transportation Authority (DART) contracted with LAN/STV (D) to prepare plans, drawings, and specifications for the construction of a light rail transit line. DART incorporated LAN/STV's (D) plans into a solicitation for competitive bids to construct the project. Martin K. Eby Construction Co., Inc. (Eby) (P) was awarded the contract, which provided procedure for Eby (P) to assert contract disputes with DART, including complaints about design problems. Eby (P) and LAN/STV (D) had no contract with each other. Thus, LAN/STV (D) was contractually responsible to DART for the accuracy of the plans, as was DART to Eby (P), but LAN/STV (D) owed Eby (P) no contractual obligation. Eby (P) discovered numerous errors in the plans, which required 80 percent of the plans to be changed. This disrupted Eby's (P) construction schedule and required additional labor and materials. Elby (P) calculated it lost nearly $14 million on the project. Elby (P) settled with DART on a breach of contract action for $4.7 million, but also brought an action for negligence and negligent misrepresentation against LAN/STV (D). The jury awarded Elby (P) $5 million, and the state's intermediate appellate court affirmed. The state's highest court granted review.

ISSUE: Is an action for negligent misrepresentation that asserts damages based on economic loss against an architect in a construction project barred by the economic loss rule where the parties do not have a contractual relationship?

HOLDING AND DECISION: (Hecht, C.J.) Yes. An action for negligent misrepresentation that asserts damages based on economic loss against an architect in a construction project is barred by the economic loss rule where the parties do not have a contractual relationship. The recovery of purely economic damages has long been limited in actions for negligence and has not been granted to third parties unless they are third-party beneficiaries of a contract to which the tortfeasor is a party. This development occurred in the law to create a boundary between the law of torts and the law of contracts. One of the rationales for such limitation is that the extent of economic losses may be hard to predict, and might be indeterminate, as compared with physical injuries. Defendants in such cases thus might face liabilities that are indeterminate and out of proportion to their culpability, and might unnecessarily limit certain activities. Additionally, risks of economic loss are especially well suited to allocation by contract, and money is a complete remedy for such losses, making the management and assignment of such risks through contract preferable to managing other risks, such as those of physical damage. As a result, courts generally do not recognize tort liability for economic losses caused by the breach of a contract between the parties, and often restrict the role of tort law in other circumstances in which protection by contract is available. Courts in this state have uniformly applied the economic loss rule to deny recovery of purely economic losses in actions for negligent services not involving professionals, but there is precedent for allowing recovery of such losses in an action for negligent misrepresentation. However, these cases should not be read to suggest that recovery of economic loss is broader for negligent misrepresentation than for negligent performance of services. Instead, the application of the rule depends on an analysis of its rationales in a particular situation. The situation at bar is typical of construction projects, which operate by agreements among the parties, and where the agreements are vertical. Usually, as in this case, the architect does not contract with the general contractor. It is well settled that one participant on a construction project cannot recover from another in negligence, so the issue becomes whether that should also be the rule in instances of negligent misrepresentation, or whether there should be an exception for architects. There is no need to distinguish between the two types of actions, since both torts are based on the same logic and the general theory of liability is the same. And, although the plans drawn by an architect are intended to serve as a basis for reliance by the contractor, the contractor's principal reliance must be on the presentation of the plans by the owner (here, DART). The plans are not an invitation to contractors to rely on them. The risks of errors in the plans can be assigned by contract. If

Continued on next page.

the architect is contractually liable to the owner for defects in the plans, and the owner in turn has the same liability to the contractor, the contractor is protected. A contractor will more likely assume that it must look to its agreements with the owner for damages if the project is not as represented. Therefore, the availability of contractual remedies must preclude tort recovery in the construction setting generally, and there is no reason not to apply the economic loss rule. Here, DART was contractually responsible to Eby (P) for providing accurate plans for the job. Eby (P) agreed to specified-remedies for disputes, pursued those remedies, and settled its claims for $4.7 million. Had DART chosen to do so, it could have sued LAN/STV (D) for breach of their contract to provide accurate plans. But Eby (P) had no agreement with LAN/STV (D) and was not party to LAN/STV's (D) agreement with DART. Clearly, the economic loss rule barred Eby's (P) subcontractors from recovering their own delay damages in negligence claims against LAN/STV (D), and Eby (P) should be treated no differently. Reversed. Judgment is rendered that Eby (P) take nothing from LAN/STV (D).

▌**ANALYSIS**

The courts are split on the issue presented by this case. Also, the Restatement (Third) of Torts permits torts claims against the architect, reasoning that the plans drawn by the architect are intended to serve as a basis for reliance by the contractor who forms a bid on the basis of them and is then hired to carry them out. The Restatement views the architect's plans as analogous to the audit report that an accountant supplies to a client for distribution to potential investors—which is a standard case of liability for negligent misrepresentation. The court in this case, while acknowledging that there is some analogy between the architect's plans and an accountant's audit report, concluded that the audit report is not an invitation to all investors to rely, but only those to whom it is more specifically directed, and that the architect's plans are no more an invitation to all potential bidders to rely.

Quicknotes

ECONOMIC LOSS RULE In products liability cases, economic losses can include repair and replacement costs, as well as lost profits and the commercial value lost.

NEGLIGENT MISREPRESENTATION A misrepresentation that is made pursuant to a business relationship, in violation of an obligation owed, upon which the plaintiff relies to his detriment.

▬▬▬

---

532 Madison Avenue Gourmet Foods, Inc. v. Finlandia Center, Inc.

Businesses within city closures (P) v. Building owner, ground lessee
and managing agent (D)

N.Y. Ct. App., 96 N.Y.2d 280, 750 N.E.2d 1097 (N.Y. 2001).

NATURE OF CASE: Appeal of one dismissed and one allowed action for economic loss based on negligence and public nuisance.

FACT SUMMARY: Many business entities, including 532 Madison Avenue Gourmet Foods, Inc. (532 Madison) (P), 5th Ave. Chocolatiere (P) and Goldberg Weprin & Ustin (Goldberg Weprin) (P), were harmed when two separate buildings partially collapsed at separate times, and they sued to recover for their losses.

🏛 RULE OF LAW
(1) A landowner has no duty in negligence to protect an entire urban neighborhood against purely economic loss.
(2) When businesses are forced to close their establishments because of the collapse of nearby structures and incur damages as a result, if the businesses do not incur special damages beyond those suffered by the public, they do not have a valid cause of action for public nuisance.

FACTS: A construction project on a 39-story office tower known as 540 Madison Avenue aggravated existing structural defects on the property causing a section of its south wall to partially collapse. As a result, bricks and mortar fell onto Madison Avenue, which is a heavily occupied prime commercial location. New York City officials (the City) closed 15 blocks of Madison Avenue for about two weeks. As a result of the accident, 532 Madison Avenue Gourmet Foods, Inc. (532 Madison) (P) had to close its 24-hour delicatessen for five weeks and it subsequently sued Finlandia Center, Inc. (D), collectively the building owner, ground lessee and managing agent, for damages. In a companion case, 5th Ave. Chocolatiere (5th Ave. Chocolatiere) (P), collectively a group of business entities, also sued alleging that shoppers were unable to gain access to their stores. In another case, three actions involving the collapse of a 48-story construction elevator tower on West 43rd Street, near Times Square, were consolidated. In that case, the City prohibited all traffic in a wide area of midtown Manhattan. Goldberg Weprin (P), collectively a law firm, a public relations firm and a clothing manufacturer, sought damages for economic loss based on gross negligence, strict liability and public and private nuisance. Both complaints were dismissed at trial. The appellate division affirmed the dismissal of Goldberg Weprin, but reinstated the public nuisance and negligence claims in 532 Madison and 5th

Ave. Chocolatiere for economic loss. Goldberg Weprin (P) and Finlandia (D) appealed.

ISSUE:
(1) What is a landlord's duty in negligence when the sole injury is lost income?
(2) Do 532 Madison (P), 5th Ave. Chocolatiere (P) and Goldberg Weprin (P) have a valid claim for public nuisance based on the collapses forcing closure of their establishments, and thereby causing special damages beyond those suffered by the public?

HOLDING AND DECISION: (Kaye, C.J.)
(1) None. We have never held that a landowner owes a duty to protect an entire urban neighborhood against purely economic loss.
(2) No. 532 Madison (P), 5th Ave. Chocolatiere (P) and Goldberg Weprin (P) claims for public nuisance based on the collapses forcing closure of their establishments and thereby causing special damages beyond those suffered by the public are invalid. A public nuisance occurs when conduct substantially interferes with common rights of the public. Such a nuisance is a violation against the State, and is remedied by the proper governmental authority. A private person only has a public nuisance action when that person suffers a special injury beyond that suffered by the community at large. A nuisance is the invasion of interests in land. In the present case, the right to use the public space around Madison Ave. and Times Square was invaded by the building collapses and the City's decision to close off those areas and, therefore, a public nuisance occurred. However, there was no special loss sustained. The closures of the subject areas caused widespread economic loss to the businesses in the areas and therefore 532 Madison (P), 5th Ave. Chocolatiere (P) and Goldberg Weprin (P) claimed injuries are no different from the injuries suffered by the public at large. Reversed as to *532 Madison* (P) and *5th Ave. Chocolatiere* (P) and affirmed as to *Goldberg Weprin* (P).

▶ **ANALYSIS**

As in *Anonymous,* Y.B. Mich. 27 Hen 8, f. 27, pl. 10 (1536), the plaintiff's remedy in the present case is to be sought through a governmental authority, and not via a private action in the courts.

■━■

Continued on next page.

Quicknotes

NEGLIGENCE Conduct falling below the standard of care that a reasonable person would demonstrate under similar conditions.

PUBLIC NUISANCE An activity that unreasonably interferes with a right common to the overall public.

Emerson v. Magendantz

Injured patient (P) v. Physician (D)

R.I. Sup. Ct., 689 A.2d 409 (1997).

NATURE OF CASE: Certified questions regarding tort of negligent sterilization.

FACT SUMMARY: The Emersons (P) alleged that Magendantz's (D) negligence in performing a sterilization procedure had caused them damages.

🏛 RULE OF LAW
Recovery may be allowed for the negligent performance of a sterilization procedure.

FACTS: The Emersons (P) consulted Magendantz (D), a gynecological specialist, concerning sterilization procedures. Magendantz (D) performed a tubal ligation on Mrs. Emerson (P). Several months later she became pregnant and subsequently gave birth to a child with congenital problems. The Emersons (P) sued Magendantz (D) for negligently performing the sterilization procedure. The trial court certified two questions to the state supreme court: (1) Is there a cause of action under Rhode Island law when a physician negligently performs a sterilization procedure? (2) If so, what is the measure of damages?

ISSUE: May recovery be allowed for the negligent performance of a sterilization procedure?

HOLDING AND DECISION: (Weisberger, C.J.) Yes. Recovery may be allowed for the negligent performance of a sterilization procedure. Under the limited-recovery rule, the Emersons (P) may recover the medical expenses of the ineffective medical procedure, the medical and hospital costs of the pregnancy, the expense of subsequent sterilization procedure, loss of wages, and perhaps for emotional distress and loss of consortium, as well as medical expenses for prenatal care, delivery, and postnatal care. No recovery for emotional distress is allowable for emotional distress arising out of the birth of a healthy child. Remanded.

CONCURRENCE AND DISSENT: (Bourcier, J.) I agree with the majority's answer to the first certified question, but disagree with the answer to the second. Full recovery for all damages proximately resulting from the physician's negligence should be recoverable.

▶ ANALYSIS

The dissent claimed that the suit was really a medical malpractice claim. If the child is born with health problems, additional medical expense damages are recoverable. Some jurisdictions permit recovery of the cost of child rearing.

Quicknotes

DAMAGES Monetary compensation that may be awarded by the court to a party who has sustained injury or loss to his or her person, property or rights due to another party's unlawful act, omission or negligence.

NEGLIGENCE Conduct falling below the standard of care that a reasonable person would demonstrate under similar conditions.

PROXIMATE CAUSE The natural sequence of events without which an injury would not have been sustained.

WRONGFUL LIFE A medical malpractice action brought by the parents of a child born with severe birth defects against a doctor, claiming that but for the doctor's negligent treatment or advice they would not have given birth to the child.

CHAPTER 5

Factual Causation

Quick Reference Rules of Law

Stubbs v. City of Rochester

Typhoid fever victim (P) v. Municipality (D)

N.Y. Ct. App., 226 N.Y. 516, 124 N.E. 137 (1919).

NATURE OF CASE: Suit for damages.

FACT SUMMARY: Stubbs (P) contracted typhoid fever, allegedly as a result of drinking contaminated water supplied by the City of Rochester (D). The City (D) argued that Stubbs's (P) contagion could have been from some other origin.

🏛 RULE OF LAW
In a negligence action, the fact that the plaintiff's condition could have been caused by factors other than the defendant's negligence does not obligate the plaintiff to prove that none of those factors was actually the cause.

FACTS: Stubbs (P) resided in the City of Rochester (D) and was employed in a factory located within the City (D), but approximately three miles from his home. The City (D) supplied water and made water from the Hemlock system available for drinking purposes while water from the Holly system was utilized for firefighting. In September of 1910, Stubbs (P) contracted typhoid fever. Later, Stubbs (P) sued the City (D) for damages, alleging that the Hemlock and Holly systems had negligently been permitted to intermingle near the Brown Street Bridge. Stubbs (P) offered highly persuasive evidence that the incidence of typhoid fever near his place of employment had increased markedly during the latter part of 1910 and that contaminated water had been the cause of his own illness. The City (D), however, submitted evidence that typhoid fever may result from myriad causes, including contaminated water, fertilized foods, contact with infected individuals, shell fish, house flies and impure ice. The trial judge, concluding that Stubbs (P) had failed to prove that his typhoid fever had not resulted from one of these other sources, granted a nonsuit. An appellate court affirmed but Stubbs (P) again appealed, arguing that he did not have any burden of proving that his illness had not been caused by one of the factors cited by the City (D).

ISSUE: In order to establish that his condition resulted from the defendant's negligence, must a plaintiff prove conclusively that none of the other possible causes of his harm actually caused it?

HOLDING AND DECISION: (Hogan, J.) No. In a negligence action, the fact that the plaintiff's condition could have been caused by factors other than the defendant's negligence does not obligate the plaintiff to prove that none of those factors was actually the cause. It is undisputed that Stubbs (P) contracted typhoid fever, and that he worked within a block of the Brown Street Bridge.

Residents of the neighborhood near the bridge testified that their water had seemed contaminated during the summer of 1910, and the City's (D) health officer acknowledged that tests performed by a chemist had confirmed contamination. The health officer, himself a physician, stated that it was his opinion that Stubbs's (P) typhoid fever had resulted from contaminated water. Two other doctors testified to the same effect. Statistical evidence confirmed that typhoid fever was unusually prevalent in Rochester (D) during the latter part of 1910. In fact, it was stipulated that more than fifty witnesses were available to testify that they had drunk water in the area near the bridge and had later contracted typhoid fever, and the statistics clearly showed that a disproportionate share of the City's (D) typhoid cases were reported in the region near the bridge. It would be totally unreasonable to require Stubbs (P) to prove that none of the other possible causes of typhoid fever was the cause of his own infection especially since evidence was presented that some of the causes of the disease are unknown. Stubbs (P) rode the streetcar to and from work during the period that his infection apparently began its incubation period. If the City's (D) theory were accepted, Stubbs (P) could not recover without first finding everyone who rode on his streetcar during the period and proving that none of them infected him with typhoid fever. Such a burden of proof obviously is absurdly onerous. Stubbs (P) has offered persuasive evidence that he contracted his typhoid fever because of the City's (D) negligent operation of the water supply system. The courts below erred in holding that Stubbs (P) was obliged to discount all other possible causes of his illness. It follows that Stubbs (P) is entitled to a reversal and to a new trial.

▶ ANALYSIS

Causation is an element of every tort action. At a minimum, the plaintiff must satisfy the trier of facts that some act or omission of the defendant was the cause in fact of the damages suffered by the plaintiff. Normally, the plaintiff has no obligation to discount all other potential factors to which his damages might be attributable, although his failure to prove an especially likely cause was not the one that actually caused his injuries may severely diminish the persuasiveness of his case. Obviously, the nature of some occurrences is such that their potential causes are infinite in number. Thus, it would clearly be unreasonable to require the plaintiff in all cases to establish conclusively

Continued on next page.

that none of the causes, other than the one he has alleged, could have resulted in his condition.

Quicknotes

CAUSATION The aggregate effect of preceding events that bring about a tortious result; the causal connection between the actions of a tortfeasor and the injury that follows.

NEGLIGENCE Conduct falling below the standard of care that a reasonable person would demonstrate under similar conditions.

Zuchowicz v. United States

Decedent's estate (P) v. Federal government (D)

140 F.3d 381 (2d Cir. 1998).

NATURE OF CASE: Appeal from damage award for plaintiff in negligence action.

FACT SUMMARY: Mrs. Zuchowicz (P) brought suit against the Government (D), alleging the Government's (D) negligence in prescribing an overdose of Danocrine, thereby causing her to develop primary pulmonary hypertension.

RULE OF LAW

Where a negligent act increases the chances that a particular type of accident would occur, and such an accident does in fact occur, a court may conclude that the negligent conduct was the cause of the injury.

FACTS: Mrs. Zuchowicz (P) filed a prescription for Danocrine at the Naval Hospital. The prescription incorrectly instructed her to take 1600 milligrams of Danocrine per day. Defendants stipulated its doctors and/or pharmacists were negligent and violated the prevailing standard of care by prescribing this dosage. Mrs. Zuchowicz (P) took 1600 milligrams per day for one month, and 800 milligrams per day thereafter. She experienced abnormal weight gain, bloating, edema, hot flashes, night sweats, a racing heart, chest pains, dizziness, headaches, acne and fatigue. She was examined by an obstetrician/gynecologist who told her to stop taking the drug. Shortly thereafter, she was diagnosed with primary pulmonary hypertension (PPH). She was on the waiting list for a lung transplant when she became pregnant. She gave birth to a son and died one month later. Mrs. Zuchowicz's (P) expert witness testified that he was confident that the prescribed overdose caused her illness. The district court awarded plaintiff's husband, as representative of Mrs. Zuchowicz's (P) estate, $1,034,236.02 in damages. The Government (D) appealed.

ISSUE: Where a negligent act increases the chances that a particular type of accident would occur, and such an accident does in fact occur, may a court conclude that the negligent conduct was the cause of the injury?

HOLDING AND DECISION: (Calabresi, J.) Yes. Where a negligent act increases the chances that a particular type of accident would occur, and such an accident does in fact occur, a court may conclude that the negligent conduct was the cause of the injury. On the basis of the expert testimony alone, the court could have held that the prescribed overdose more likely than not caused Mrs. Zuchowicz's (P) illness. In order for the causation element to be satisfied, the trier of fact must be able to determine, by a preponderance of the evidence, that the defendant's

negligence was responsible for the injury. Here the trier of fact must be able to conclude that the overdose was, more likely than not, the cause of Mrs. Zuchowicz's (P) illness and ultimate death. Courts have held that where a negligent act was deemed wrongful because the act increased the chances that a particular type of accident would occur, and such an accident did in fact happen, this was sufficient to support a finding by the trier of fact that the negligent conduct caused the injury. Then the burden shifts to the negligent party to show evidence rebutting such but for cause and showing that the wrongful conduct was not a substantial factor. Here Mrs. Zuchowicz (P) met her burden of demonstrating that the excessive dosage was a substantial factor in causing her illness. Affirmed.

ANALYSIS

Cause-in-fact is also an issue in slip-and-fall cases. In such cases courts have noted that the mere fact that such injury could have occurred in the absence of negligence is insufficient to break the chain of causation, where the defendant's conduct greatly increases the chances of injury and is of the type that would normally lead to the happening of such an injury. *Reynolds v. Texas & Pacific Ry.*, 37 La. Ann. 694, 698 (1995).

Quicknotes

CAUSE IN FACT The event without which an injury would not have been incurred.

NEGLIGENCE Conduct falling below the standard of care that a reasonable person would demonstrate under similar conditions.

PREPONDERANCE OF THE EVIDENCE A standard of proof requiring the trier of fact to determine whether the fact sought to be established is more probable than not.

Matsuyama v. Birnbaum

Estate (P) v. Doctor (D)

Mass. Sup. Jud. Ct., 890 N.E.2d 819 (2008).

NATURE OF CASE: Appeal of district court judgment following a jury trial.

FACT SUMMARY: Dr. Birnbaum (D) failed to order tests to rule out the possibility of gastric cancer for Matsuyama, a patient with symptoms that might have indicated gastric cancer. When Birnbaum (D) finally did diagnose Matsuyama's cancer, it was too late and Matsuyama died. Matsuyama's estate (P) sued Birnbaum (D) for negligence. The trial court ruled in favor of the estate (P), and Birnbaum (D) appealed.

🏛 RULE OF LAW
Where a physician's negligence reduces or eliminates the patient's prospects for achieving a more favorable medical outcome, the physician is liable for damages, regardless of how low those prospects are.

FACTS: Dr. Birnbaum (D) was the primary-care physician of the decedent, Matsuyama, from July 1995 until his death in 1999. Matsuyama complained about gastric distress first in 1988, and reiterated his complaint when he began seeing Birnbaum (D). Birnbaum noted Matsuyama's complaints and recommended that he take over-the-counter medicines to relieve the symptoms of heartburn and acid reflux. When Matsuyama developed moles on his body and over his eye, Birnbaum (D) concluded they were benign. When Matsuyama told Birnbaum (D) he had visited an urgent care facility for severe stomach pain, Birnbaum (D) ordered a test for bacteria, H. pylori, which is connected to several diseases, including gastric cancer. The test was positive, but Birnbaum (D) still did not order tests to confirm his working diagnosis of gastritis, a non-malignant irritation, or to rule out the possibility of gastric cancer. Birnbaum (D) did not finally diagnose Matsuyama's cancer until 1999, when it was too late. A few months after the gastric cancer was diagnosed, Matsuyama died. Matsuyama's estate (P) sued Birnbaum (D) for negligence. A jury found that Birnbaum (D) was negligent, and that it was a substantial contributing factor to Matsuyama's death, and awarded the estate (P) $160,000 for pain and suffering and $328,125 for loss of chance damages. In computing the loss of chance damages, the jury first found that $875,000 would be the full wrongful death damages, that Matsuyama was suffering from stage 2 cancer at the time of Birnbaum's (D) initial negligence and had a 37.5 percent chance of survival at that time, and that final loss of chance damages to be awarded were $328,125 ($875,000 multiplied by .375). Birnbaum (D) appealed.

ISSUE: Where a physician's negligence reduces or eliminates the patient's prospects for achieving a more favorable medical outcome, is the physician liable for damages, regardless of how low those prospects are?

HOLDING AND DECISION: (Marshall, C.J.) Yes. Where a physician's negligence reduces or eliminates the patient's prospects for achieving a more favorable medical outcome, the physician is liable for damages, regardless of how low those prospects are. The loss of chance doctrine is based on a person's prospects for surviving a serious medical condition, and considers those prospects something of value, even if, prior to the physician's negligence, the possibility of recovery is less than even. If a physician's negligence reduces or eliminates the patient's prospects for a more favorable outcome, the physician has harmed the patient and is liable. The loss of chance doctrine was developed to answer for the inadequacies of the all or nothing rule of tort recovery, which states that a plaintiff may recover damages only by showing that the defendant's negligence more likely than not caused the ultimate outcome of death or injury. Under the all or nothing rule, if a patient had a 51 percent chance of survival, and the negligent misdiagnosis or treatment caused that chance to drop to zero, the plaintiff would be awarded full wrongful death damages, because the negligence more likely than not caused the death. But if the patient had a 49 percent chance of survival, and the negligent misdiagnosis caused that chance to drop to zero, the plaintiff receives nothing, because the plaintiff cannot show that the negligence more likely than not caused the death—it was already more likely than not that she would not survive. If the patient's chance of survival before the physician's negligence is less than even—that is, 50-50—it is impossible for her to show that the physician's negligence was the cause of her death, so she can recover nothing. The all or nothing rule therefore released from doctors from liability any time there was less than a 50 percent chance of survival, regardless of how extreme the negligence.

Birnbaum's (D) arguments against the loss of chance doctrine are not persuasive. The argument that it lowers the threshold of proof of causation by diluting the preponderance of the evidence standard is rejected, because in a loss of chance case, as in any negligence case, a plaintiff still must establish by a preponderance of the evidence that the defendant caused the injury or death. The loss of chance doctrine does not change the prevailing rule about causation. Loss of chance goes to injury, not causation; the probability of survival is part of the patient's condition,

Continued on next page.

and when a physician's negligence diminishes the chance of survival, the patient has suffered real injury. Something of value has been lost. So loss of chance is not a theory of causation, but a theory of injury. Birnbaum's (D) argument that the loss of chance doctrine relies too heavily on speculation is likewise rejected, because survival rates are based on data that is accepted by the medical community. Whatever complexities and problems attach to the loss of chance doctrine apply also to ordinary negligence cases in the area of medical malpractice. Medical science has progressed to the point that physicians can gauge a patient's chances of survival to a reasonable degree of medical certainty, and use such statistics as a tool of medicine. Finally, Birnbaum's (D) argument that the ramifications of adoption of loss of chance are immense across all areas of tort is rejected, because this ruling limits the doctrine to medical malpractice actions. And anyway, whatever difficulties exist in recognizing loss of chance as an item of damages in a medical malpractice action, they are outweighed by the strong reasons to adopt the doctrine. So loss of chance is a separate, compensable item of damages in a medical malpractice action.

As to how the loss of the likelihood of a more favorable outcome is to be valued for damages sake, there are two questions. The first question is what is being valued, and the second is how to calculate the monetary value for the lost chance. What is being valued is lost chances for a more favorable outcome, and that is measured by Matsuyama's likelihood of surviving for a number of years based on the medical standard applicable to him. With respect to loss of chance damages, they are measured as the percentage probability by which Birnbaum's (D) tortious conduct diminished the likelihood of achieving some more favorable outcome. The fact finder must (1) calculate the total amount of damages allowed for the injury or death, (2) calculate the patient's chance of survival immediately before the medical malpractice, (3) calculate the chance of survival that the patient had as a result of the medical malpractice, (4) subtract the amount derived in step (3) from step (2), and (5) multiply the amount determined in step (1) by the percentage calculated in step (4) to figure out the proportional damages award for loss of chance. So if the full wrongful death damages are $600,000 and the patient had a 45 percent chance of survival before the malpractice, and the physician's negligence reduced the chance of survival to 15 percent, the patient's chance of survival are reduced to 30 percent due to the negligence, and the patient's loss of chance damages would be $600,000 multiplied by 30 percent, for a total of $180,000. Affirmed.

▶ ANALYSIS

This is a landmark case in medical malpractice, and the key to its importance is this: The Massachusetts high court found that in spite of the fact that the jury found that Matsuyama had less than a 50 percent chance of survival. The court held that the 50 percent all or nothing rule was unsatisfactory, noting what might seem to be common sense: a blanket release from liability for doctors and hospitals any time there was less than a 50 percent chance of survival, regardless of how obvious the medical malpractice was, is absurd. The trend among states is to adopt this rule.

━━━

Quicknotes

NEGLIGENCE Conduct falling below the standard of care that a reasonable person would demonstrate under similar conditions.

━━━

Summers v. Tice

Shooting victim (P) v. Hunters (D)

Cal. Sup. Ct., 33 Cal. 2d 80, 199 P.2d 1 (1948).

NATURE OF CASE: Damages for personal injury.

FACT SUMMARY: Summers (P) sued two defendants for personal injury caused when both defendants shot in his direction.

🏛 RULE OF LAW

When two or more persons by their acts are possibly the sole cause of a harm, and the plaintiff has introduced evidence that one of the two persons is culpable (responsible), then the defendant has the burden of proving that the other person was the sole cause of the harm.

FACTS: Summers (P) and the two defendants were members of the same hunting party. Both defendants fired at the same time at a quail in the direction of Summers (P). Summers (P) was struck in the eye by a shot from one of the two guns. There was no evidence from which to determine which gun had caused the injury. The trial court held both defendants liable. They appealed on grounds they were not joint tortfeasors, they were not acting in concert, and there was insufficient evidence to show which defendant was guilty of the negligence which caused the injuries.

ISSUE: When two persons by their acts are possibly the sole cause of a harm, and the plaintiff has introduced evidence that one of the two persons is culpable, do the defendants have the burden of proving which of them was the sole cause of the harm?

HOLDING AND DECISION: (Carter, J.) Yes. When two or more persons by their acts are possibly the sole cause of a harm, and the plaintiff has introduced evidence that one of the two persons is culpable, then each defendant has the burden of proving that the other person was the sole cause of the harm. The reason behind the rule that each joint tortfeasor is responsible for the whole damage is the practical unfairness of denying the injured person redress simply because he cannot prove how much damage each did, when it is certain that between the defendants they did all the damage. The rule applies whenever the harm has plural causes, and not merely when the causes acted in conscious concert. Here it is clear that the two defendants were the sole cause of the plaintiff's injuries. Plaintiff has introduced evidence that one of the two defendants is culpable. The defendants now have the burden of proving which one of them was the sole cause of the harm. Affirmed.

▶ ANALYSIS

At common law, two situations in which two or more defendants acted tortiously toward the plaintiff gave rise to what is now referred to as joint and several liability: (1) where the defendants acted in concert to cause the harm, and (2) where the defendants acted independently but caused indivisible harm. Liability in the case of concerted action is a form of vicarious liability, in which all the defendants will be responsible for the harm actually caused by only one of the defendants.

Quicknotes

JOINT AND SEVERAL LIABILITY Liability amongst tortfeasors allowing the injured party to bring suit against any of the defendants, individually or collectively, and to recover from each up to the total amount of damages awarded.

JOINT TORTFEASORS Two or more parties that either act in concert, or whose individual acts combine to cause a single injury, rendering them jointly and severally liable for damages incurred.

NEGLIGENCE Conduct falling below the standard of care that a reasonable person would demonstrate under similar conditions.

VICARIOUS LIABILITY The imputed liability of one party for the unlawful acts of another.

Hymowitz v. Eli Lilly & Co.

Daughter of DES user (P) v. DES manufacturer (D)

N.Y. Ct. App., 73 N.Y.2d 487, 539 N.E.2d 1069 (1989).

NATURE OF CASE: Review of denial of summary judgment in product liability/personal injury action.

FACT SUMMARY: Hymowitz (P) contended that liability among manufacturers of the drug diethylstilbestrol (DES) should be apportioned per market share.

🏛 RULE OF LAW
Liability among manufacturers of the drug DES shall be apportioned per national market share.

FACTS: Starting in 1941, the drug diethylstilbestrol (DES) was prescribed for the treatment of various maladies. By 1971, it had become clear that use of the drug by pregnant women had a tendency to cause certain otherwise rare cancers in their female offspring. During the thirty years the drug was produced, about 300 manufacturers contributed to the national supply, and seldom were records kept as to which manufacturer supplied which patient. Hymowitz (P) brought an action against various drug companies, contending that she had cancer due to her mother's ingestion of DES. The defendants moved for summary judgment, contending that Hymowitz (P) could not prove who distributed the specific units of DES her mother had ingested. The trial court denied the motion, and the appellate division affirmed. The state high court accepted review.

ISSUE: Shall liability among manufacturers of the drug DES be apportioned per national market share?

HOLDING AND DECISION: (Wachtler, C.J.) Yes. Liability among manufacturers of the drug DES shall be apportioned per national market share. Traditionally, for a defendant to be liable for a plaintiff's harm, that plaintiff had to show that a particular defendant's conduct had resulted in that harm. However, given the unique problems of proof presented in litigation over DES-induced injury, these traditional notions must give way. It would be inconsistent with the expectations of a modern society to deny plaintiffs who have suffered certain harm compensation because of the insidious nature of an injury that remains long dormant, thus allowing the evidentiary trail to become so cold as to be unfollowable. The most appropriate method to fairly compensate the plaintiffs in this type of case is to apportion liability among the national market share of each manufacturer during the time that DES was being used by a plaintiff's mother. National market share will provide a rough approximation of the likelihood that any particular defendant was involved with any particular plaintiff. Affirmed.

CONCURRENCE AND DISSENT: (Mollen, J.) If a defendant can prove its product did not reach a particular plaintiff's mother, that defendant should be exculpated from liability.

▶ ANALYSIS

The approach used by the court here was first formulated in *Sindell v. Abbott Laboratories*, 26 Cal. 3d 588 (1980). This "market share" liability can be seen as approaching the imposition of the status of insurer of a defective product upon a manufacturer. Market share liability represents something of a radical departure from traditional requirements of tort liability, and not all jurisdictions have elected to adopt it.

Quicknotes

JOINT AND SEVERAL LIABILITY Liability amongst tortfeasors allowing the injured party to bring suit against any of the defendants, individually or collectively, and to recover from each up to the total amount of damages awarded.

MARKET SHARE LIABILITY The apportionment of liability between each participant in an industry equal to the participant's market share.

Proximate Cause (Scope of Liability)

Quick Reference Rules of Law

Benn v. Thomas

Injured customer (P) v. Store (D)

Iowa Sup. Ct., 512 N.W.2d 537 (1994).

NATURE OF CASE: Review of reversal of judgment for negligence.

FACT SUMMARY: Benn (P) alleged that the trial court erred in denying a jury instruction on the eggshell plaintiff rule.

RULE OF LAW

A tortfeasor whose act, superimposed upon a prior latent condition, results in an injury may be liable in damages for the full disability.

FACTS: Benn (P) died several days after Thomas (D) rear-ended the van in which he was riding. At trial, Benn's (P) medical expert testified that Benn (P) had a history of coronary disease and that the accident was the straw that broke the camel's back, and had caused his death. The trial court refused to give a jury instruction on the eggshell plaintiff rule that requires the defendant to take the plaintiff as he finds him. The jury determined that the accident was not the cause of Benn's (P) death. The court of appeals reversed and remanded because the charge to the jury failed to convey the applicable law. The state Supreme Court granted review.

ISSUE: May a tortfeasor whose act, superimposed upon a prior latent condition, results in an injury be liable in damages for the full disability?

HOLDING AND DECISION: (McGiverin, C.J.) Yes. A tortfeasor whose act, superimposed upon a prior latent condition, results in an injury may be liable in damages for the full disability. Once it was established that Thomas (D) caused some injury to Benn (P), the eggshell plaintiff rule imposed liability for the full extent of those injuries, not merely those that were foreseeable to Thomas (D). The record in this case warranted an instruction on the eggshell plaintiff rule. Court of appeals affirmed, district court reversed, and remanded.

▶ ANALYSIS

The court found that depriving the plaintiff estate of the requested instruction failed to convey to the jury a central principal of tort liability. Thomas (D) claimed that the proposed instruction concerned damages only. The court found that the eggshell plaintiff rule was also a rule of proximate cause.

injury or condition, regardless of whether the magnitude of the injury was foreseeable.

NEGLIGENCE Conduct falling below the standard of care that a reasonable person would demonstrate under similar conditions.

PROXIMATE CAUSE The natural sequence of events without which an injury would not have been sustained.

Quicknotes

EGGSHELL PLAINTIFF RULE Doctrine, that the defendant is liable in tort for the aggravation of a plaintiff's existing

In re an Arbitration Between Polemis and Another and Furness, Withy & Co., Ltd.

Shipowner (Polemis) v. Ship charterer (Furness)

Ct. App., 3 K.B. 560, All E.R. 40 (1921).

NATURE OF CASE: Arbitration for damages for injury due to negligence.

FACT SUMMARY: The ship Polemis, while being unloaded, was destroyed by fire when Furness' servant negligently dropped a plank setting off a spark in the hold, which exploded vapor seeping from the cargo of petrol and benzine.

🏛 **RULE OF LAW**
The fact that the kind of damage which an act might probably cause was not the damage anticipated is immaterial so long as the resulting damage is directly traceable to the negligent act, and not due to an independent cause having no connection with the negligent act.

FACTS: Furness chartered the ship, Polemis, from its owners. It carried a cargo of petrol and benzine. While unloading in Casablanca, a heavy plank fell into the hold setting off a spark, which ignited petrol vapor. The resulting explosion completely destroyed the Polemis. Arbitrators found that while a spark resulting from the dropping of the plank would not be reasonably foreseen, the dropping of the plank was due to negligence of Furness's servants. Also found was that some damage could be reasonably anticipated from the dropping of the plank. Damages were stated at £ 96 1s. 11d.

ISSUE: Were the damages too remote as to be recoverable?

HOLDING: (Lord Bankes, J.) No. The arbitors are affirmed. It is immaterial that the spark could not be reasonably anticipated; the act of dropping the plank itself was negligent. If the act would or might probably cause damage, the fact that the damage it in fact causes is not the exact kind of damage one would expect is immaterial, so long as the damage is in fact directly traceable to the negligent act, and not due to the operation of independent causes having no connection with the negligent act, except that they could not avoid its results. Appeal must be dismissed.

HOLDING: (Lord Scrutton, J.) When damage is directly traceable to a negligent act, and no independent cause separates the damage from the negligent act, the unexpectedness of the specific kind of damage is irrelevant. In this case, the fact that some foreseeable damage would result from knocking down the planks makes the act negligent. That the resulting spark was unexpected is irrelevant

because the negligent act directly caused the damage. Appeal dismissed.

▶ **ANALYSIS**

This case follows the rule set out in *Christianson v. Chicago, St. P., M.G.O. Ry. Co.*, 69 N.W. 640 (1896), a minority rule in the United States. The rule is rather mechanical. Basically, if X can be foreseen to result in Y, but instead results in Z, the wrongdoer is still liable for Z even though it may be totally out of proportion to X. Z is proximate to X and, hence, there is liability. Prosser, among others, has called this decision "absurd." Basically, the criticism is that damages are usually just too high, with the rule being "artificial." This case remained a controversy for forty years until it was overruled in 1961.

■▬■

Quicknotes

FORESEEABILITY A reasonable expectation that an act or omission would result in injury.

■▬■

Overseas Tankship (U.K.) Ltd. v. Mort's Dock & Engineering Co., Ltd. (The Wagon Mound)

Wharf owner (P) v. Workman's employer (D)

Privy Council, A.C. 388 (1961).

NATURE OF CASE: Action for damages for injury due to negligence.

FACT SUMMARY: A wharf operated by Mort's Dock & Engineering Co., Ltd. (P) was seriously damaged by fire when oil negligently discharged from a ship, the Wagon Mound [owned by Overseas Tankship (U.K.) Ltd. (Overseas) (D)], spread across the water and later caught fire when molten metal dropped by workmen of Overseas (D) ignited cotton waste floating on the surface.

> 🏛 **RULE OF LAW**
> Even though injury may result from a negligent act, liability for that injury is limited to the risk reasonably to be foreseen.

FACTS: Mort's Dock & Engineering Co., Ltd. (Mort's) (P) operated a wharf in Port of Sydney, Australia. The ship, Wagon Mound, owned by Overseas Tankship (U.K.) Ltd. (Overseas) (D) and moored about 600 feet away, carelessly discharged a large quantity of furnace oil that spread across the surface of the water and washed against Mort's (P) wharf. Damage was so minor that no claim was made. Cotton waste floating on the surface was ignited by molten metal dropped by workmen of Overseas (D). This set the oil afire, seriously damaging Mort's (P) wharf. The trial court found that Overseas (D) did not know, and could not reasonably know that the oil with a flash point of 170° F could be set afire when spread on water. Mort's (P) was awarded judgment and Overseas (D) appealed to the Privy Council (the appeals court for all Commonwealth nations except England).

ISSUE: Should a defendant be liable for all damage directly resulting from his negligent act?

HOLDING AND DECISION: (Viscount Simonds) No. It is not "consonant with current ideas of justice and morality that for an act of negligence, however slight or venial, which results in some trivial foreseeable damage the actor should be liable for all consequences however unforeseeable and however grave, so long as they can be said to be 'direct.'" One should be responsible only for the probable consequences of his act, not the improbable. This keeps the rule from being too harsh while requiring all persons to observe a minimum standard of behavior. There should be some limitation on the consequences of a negligent act for which the wrongdoer will be held responsible. It seems unreasonable to substitute the reasonable foreseeability test with a direct causation test that leads to nothing but "insolvable problems of causa-

tion." The appeal should be allowed, and the respondent's action dismissed.

▶ **ANALYSIS**

This case overruled *In re Polemis*, Ct. of Appeals, 3 K.B. 560 (1921). One is responsible for the reasonably foreseeable or probable consequences of his negligent acts. The old rule of responsibility for all damage, foreseeable or not as long as some damage was reasonably foreseeable, was found unjust and harsh. This rule does not apply to the "eggshell skull" doctrine as that deals with the inherent weakness of plaintiff, while foreseeable consequences deals with the extent of damage done.

Quicknotes

CAUSATION The aggregate effect of preceding events that bring about a tortious result; the causal connection between the actions of a tortfeasor and the injury that follows.

FORESEEABILITY A reasonable expectation that an act or omission would result in injury.

NEGLIGENCE Conduct falling below the standard of care that a reasonable person would demonstrate under similar conditions.

Doe v. Manheimer

Raped pedestrian (P) v. Landowner (D)

Conn. Sup. Ct., 212 Conn. 748, 563 A.2d 699 (1989).

NATURE OF CASE: Appeal from a trial court's setting aside of plaintiff's judgment and award in a negligence suit against a landowner.

FACT SUMMARY: When Doe (P) was raped by an unknown assailant, she brought suit for her injuries against Manheimer (D), the landowner on whose property the rape occurred, arguing that overgrown vegetation on the property prevented persons on the sidewalk from seeing and assisting her.

🏛 RULE OF LAW

A landowner is not liable in tort for damages arising from the rape of a pedestrian committed on the landowner's property behind brush and trees that shield the area from view.

FACTS: Doe (P), while working as a meter reader, was raped on property owned by Manheimer (D). The assailant forced her from a sidewalk and onto Manheimer's (D) property where he committed the rape. The area of the property where Doe (P) was raped was bounded by overgrown sumac bushes and tall grass which shielded the area from view from the sidewalk and street. Doe (P), whose injuries were extensive, sued Manheimer (D) for her injuries sustained in the rape, arguing that he had failed to remove the overgrown vegetation although he should have known that, because the neighborhood was a high crime area, third persons might use the overgrowth to conceal the perpetration of crimes against pedestrians. Manheimer (D) presented no evidence but moved for a directed verdict. The jury found for Doe (P) and awarded her $540,000. Subsequently, the trial court set aside the verdict, stating that as a matter of law the jury could not find that Manheimer's (D) maintenance of overgrowth was a substantial factor in producing Doe's (P) injuries, hence Doe (P) had failed to establish proximate cause. Doe (P) appealed.

ISSUE: Is a landowner liable in tort for damages arising from the rape of a pedestrian committed on the landowner's property behind brush and trees that shield the area from view?

HOLDING AND DECISION: (Glass, J.) No. A landowner is not liable in tort for damages arising from the rape of a pedestrian committed on the landowner's property behind brush and trees that shield the area from view. Even if liability could extend beyond injury caused by physical contact with dangerous conditions on a defendant's property, here the relationship between the opportunity of shielding and the plaintiff's harm was accidental. There could have been any number of nonnatural conditions on Manheimer's (D) property that would have shielded the assault. Not every conceivable item that could have shielded the occurrence of a violent crime should be deemed a basis for negligence because of the potential for crime endemic in an urban neighborhood. This court is not prepared to extend the scope of the foreseeable risk presented by obnoxious overgrowth or accumulated debris beyond injury produced by physical contact with such conditions. The harm suffered by Doe (P) in this case was not of the same general type that allegedly made Manheimer (D) negligent. That negligent conduct is a "cause in fact" of an injury, obviously, does not mean that it is also a "substantial factor" for the purposes of a proximate cause inquiry. Affirmed.

⬛ ANALYSIS

In the *Manheimer* decision, the court noted that there was no evidence tending to demonstrate that the landowner had had any past experience that might reasonably have led him to perceive and act on the atypical association between "natural shields" such as overgrown vegetation and violent criminal activity. Nor was there any evidence presented that any of the individuals who frequented the adjoining vacant lot threatened or assaulted any passersby or local residents.

■━■

Quicknotes

FORESEEABILITY A reasonable expectation that an act or omission would occur.

NEGLIGENT FAILURE TO PROTECT The breach of duty by a person with a special relationship or other fiduciary duty owed to the plaintiff to intercede and prevent a threatened injury.

PROXIMATE CAUSE The natural sequence of events without which an injury would not have been sustained.

SUBSTANTIAL FACTOR TEXT In determining whether one of several joint acts was the proximate cause of an injury for purposes of tort liability, the inquiry is whether the act or omission was a substantial factor in causing the damage and whether the damage was the direct or probable result of the act or omission.

■━■

Palsgraf v. Long Island Railroad Co.

Injured (P) v. Railroad (D)

N.Y. Ct. App., 248 N.Y. 339, 162 N.E. 99 (1928).

NATURE OF CASE: Action for damages for personal injury due to negligence.

FACT SUMMARY: Mrs. Palsgraf (P) was injured on Long Island Railroad's (LIRR) (D) train platform when LIRR's (D) servant helped a passenger aboard a moving train, jostling his package, causing it to fall to the tracks. The package, containing fireworks, exploded creating a shock which tipped a scale onto Mrs. Palsgraf (P).

RULE OF LAW
When a negligent act results in injury to another, but the risk of harm to the injured party was not a reasonably foreseeable consequence of the negligent act, no duty of care exists as to the injured party, and, thus, the negligent party is not held liable for damages.

FACTS: Mrs. Palsgraf (P) purchased a ticket to Rockaway Beach from Long Island Railroad Co. (LIRR) (D) and was waiting on the train platform. While standing there, two men ran to catch a train that was pulling out from the platform. The first man jumped aboard, but the second man, who appeared as if he might fall, was helped aboard by the guard who had kept the door open so they could jump aboard. A guard on the platform also helped him by pushing him onto the train. The man was carrying a package wrapped in newspaper. In the process, the man dropped his innocent-looking package, which fell to the tracks. The package contained fireworks and exploded. The shock of the explosion was apparently of great enough strength to tip over some scales at the other end of the platform. The scale fell onto Mrs. Palsgraf (P) and injured her. She was awarded damages and LIRR (D) appealed.

ISSUE: When a negligent act results in injury to another, but the risk of harm to the injured party was not a reasonably foreseeable consequence of the negligent act, does a duty of care exist as to the injured party that will hold the negligent party liable for damages?

HOLDING AND DECISION: (Cardozo, C.J.) No. If there was no foreseeable hazard as the result of an outwardly-seeming innocent act with reference to the injured party, the act does not become a tort simply because it happened to be a wrong. To be a tort, the act must result in an injury to a foreseeable victim. Negligence is not enough upon which to base liability—there must be a duty to the injured party which could have been averted or avoided by observance of the duty. There can be no duty owed to an injured party when the wrong was committed towards someone else. The range of the duty is limited by the range of danger. The risk reasonably to be perceived defines the duty to be obeyed. In this case, there was nothing to suggest that the parcel from its appearance contained fireworks. Had the guard purposefully thrown down the package, he would have had no warning of a threat of harm to Mrs. Palsgraf (P). Just because the act was inadvertent does not impose liability. In the abstract, negligence itself is not a tort. To be a tort it must result in the commission of a wrong. A wrong imports the violation of a right. If the wrong was not willful it must be shown by the plaintiff that the act as to him had such great possibilities of danger, so many and so apparent, as to entitle him to protection against it though the harm was unintended. Had there been liability for the negligence toward Mrs. Palsgraf (P), she would recover for all injury "however novel or extraordinary." Reversed.

DISSENT: (Andrews, J.) The concept that "there is no negligence unless there is in the particular case a legal duty to take care, and that this duty must be one owed to the plaintiff himself and not to others" is too narrow. Negligence in itself is a wrong. The rule of *In re Polemis*, 3 K.B. 560 (1921), is the correct statement of the law. A person who does a negligent act should be liable for its proximate results. Mrs. Palsgraf's (P) claim is for a breach of duty to herself and there cannot only be a duty when the harm is expected. Her right is not lesser to the right of the man with the parcel.

ANALYSIS
Cardozo states that negligence is a matter of relationship between the parties. That relationship must be based upon the foreseeability of harm to the person who is, in fact, injured. Just because defendant's act was negligent, it is not necessarily wrong to the injured party. The act must be negligent and wrong to the injured party to enable him to sue in his own right. If there is no duty to the injured party, there can be no violation of a right, so even if an act was negligent it could not have violated a wrong to the injured party. The dissent, on the other hand, states that each person owes a duty of due care to society at large. Each person must refrain from any act which unreasonably threatens the safety of others. Accordingly, any party injured by a negligent act would suffer a wrong as the duty owed to each member of society at large would have been violated. A right of action must then arise despite the unforeseeability of the injury. The Restatement has accepted the view of this case that without any duty there can be

Continued on next page.

no negligence, hence, never any liability to the unforesee-able injured party. Note that the determination on any question of duty is a question of law and never one for the jury. Cardozo, on the question of duty, went even farther by suggesting that the defendant could owe a duty to one particular interest of the injured party, but not to a different interest of the same party. That is to say that there could be a duty to the injured party's prop-erty interest but not to his person. So if defendant negligently sets afire plaintiff's unoccupied building, and plaintiff is injured extinguishing the blaze, damages only to the building are recoverable, or vice versa depending upon the original duty. This theory advanced in the dictum of Palsgraf was approved by the Restatement § 281, but it has been widely opposed by most other courts. In fact, there is much authority against it and even Prosser has called this aspect of Cardozo's view "artificial." "There are of course interests which, as a matter of public policy, should not be protected against certain types of wrongful conduct, but it does not follow from this that protection should always be limited to the interest which is threatened in advance."

Quicknotes

DUTY OF CARE A principle of negligence requiring an individual to act in such a manner as to avoid injury to a person to whom he or she owes an obligatory duty.

FORESEEABILITY A reasonable expectation that an act or omission would result in injury.

NEGLIGENCE Conduct falling below the standard of care that a reasonable person would demonstrate under simi-lar conditions.

Defenses

Quick Reference Rules of Law

Fritts v. McKinne

Patient (P) v. Physician (D)

Okla. Civ. App., 934 P.2d 371 (1996).

NATURE OF CASE: Appeal from judgment for Plaintiff.

FACT SUMMARY: Fritts (P) alleged that the trial court erred in admitting evidence regarding the decedent's history of drug abuse and in allowing the jury to consider comparative negligence.

RULE OF LAW
The negligence of a party, which necessitated medical treatment, is irrelevant to the issue of possible subsequent medical malpractice.

FACTS: Mr. Fritts received serious injuries in a one-vehicle accident. He died following surgery. Mrs. Fritts (P) sued Dr. McKinne (D) for negligence. McKinne (D) asserted a comparative negligence defense based on the contention that Mr. Fritts had been driving drunk at the time of the accident. The trial court denied Mrs. Fritts's (P) motion to exclude the evidence of decedent's prior drug and alcohol use. The jury returned a verdict in favor of McKinne (D). Fritts (P) appealed, claiming that the trial court erred in admitting the evidence of substance abuse and in allowing the jury to consider comparative negligence.

ISSUE: Is the negligence of a party, which necessitated medical treatment, irrelevant to the issue of possible subsequent medical malpractice?

HOLDING AND DECISION: (Stubblefield, J.) Yes. The negligence of a party, which necessitated medical treatment, is irrelevant to the issue of possible subsequent medical malpractice. The interjection of Fritts's possible negligence in the accident was a matter unrelated to proper medical procedures and it constituted a substantial error that was highly prejudicial. The submission of the issue of comparative negligence was error. Reversed and remanded.

ANALYSIS

The jury was led on a journey to irrelevant and highly prejudicial matters here. The relevant issues were obscured by the allegations of comparative negligence. The history of substance abuse would only be relevant in considering damages based on probable life expectancy.

Quicknotes

COMPARATIVE NEGLIGENCE Doctrine whereby the court in assessing the appropriate measure of damages compares the relative fault of the parties and reduces the amount of damages to be collected by the plaintiff in proportion to his degree of fault.

JURY INSTRUCTION A communication made by the court to a jury regarding the applicable law involved in a proceeding.

PREJUDICE A preference of the court toward one party prior to litigation.

RELEVANCE The admissibility of evidence based on whether it has any tendency to prove or disprove a matter at issue to the case.

Hanks v. Powder Ridge Restaurant Corp.

Injured snow tuber (P) v. Resort (D)

Conn. Sup. Ct., 885 A.2d 734 (2005).

NATURE OF CASE: Appeal of summary judgment.

FACT SUMMARY: [Plaintiff not stated in casebook excerpt.] The plaintiff and four children went snowboarding at Powder Ridge (D). Before doing so, they signed an exculpatory agreement, which essentially waived any rights they had to hold the resort liable for its own negligence. Plaintiff got hurt and sued for negligence, and the trail court granted summary judgment for Powder Ridge (D).

RULE OF LAW
A clear and well-drafted exculpatory clause signed by patrons at a snow resort violates public policy.

FACTS: [Plaintiff not stated in casebook excerpt.] Powder Ridge Restaurant Corp. (D) operates a winter resort for skiing, snowboarding, and snowtubing. The plaintiff and his three children, along with another child, went to Powder Ridge (D) to snowtube. None of them had snowtubed at Powder Ridge (D), but the area for snowtubing was open to the general public regardless of prior experience, except that children under six years old or forty-four inches tall could not participate. To snowtube, Powder Ridge (D) required patrons to sign an exculpatory contract that waives and releases the resort (D) from any liability for injuries, including negligence. The plaintiff read and signed it on behalf of himself and the four children. While snowtubing, the plaintiff's right foot got caught between his snowtube and the bank of the run, resulting in serious injuries and multiple surgeries. The plaintiff filed a lawsuit against Powder Ridge (D) for negligence, and Powder Ridge (D) moved for summary judgment because the waiver barred the negligence claim as a matter of law. The trial court granted Powder Ridge (D) summary judgment, holding that the plaintiff, by signing the agreement, released Powder Ridge (D) from liability for negligence. On appeal, the plaintiff claimed that a person of ordinary intelligence reasonably would not have believed that by signing the agreement, he was releasing Powder Ridge (D) from liability for personal injuries caused by negligence, and that the agreement violates public policy, because a recreational operator cannot release itself from liability for its own negligence where it services the public.

ISSUE: Does a clear and well-drafted exculpatory clause signed by patrons at a snow resort violate public policy?

HOLDING AND DECISION: (Sullivan, C.J.) Yes. A clear and well-drafted exculpatory clause signed by patrons at a snow resort violates public policy. First, prece-

dent for this case exists in *Hyson v. White Water Mountain Resorts of Connecticut, Inc.*, 829 A.2d 827 (Conn. 2003), in which the plaintiff was injured while snowtubing at the same resort and sued. In that case, the plaintiff signed an exculpatory agreement as well. The issue in that case was whether the exculpatory agreement released the defendant from liability for its negligent conduct and barred the negligence action as a matter of law, and the court decided that it did not. The holding was based on the theory that the law disfavors exceptions from negligence when the public has a right to expect a safe operation. But the agreement in Hyson did not specifically refer to possible negligence by the defendant, and a person of ordinary intelligence reasonably could believe that by signing the release, he or she was releasing the defendant only from liability for damages caused by the inherent dangers in snowtubing. So the conclusion in that case was that the exculpatory agreement did not expressly release the defendants from liability for future negligence and did not bar the plaintiff's claims. The agreement in this case does expressly release Powder Ridge (D) from liability for personal injuries incurred as a result of its own negligence, in contrast to the agreement in Hyson. Part of the agreement states, "I fully assume all risks associated with snowtubing, even if due to the negligence" of Powder Ridge (D). The agreement expressly and unambiguously purports to release Powder Ridge (D) from prospective liability for negligence. But the question of whether exculpatory agreements such as the one in this case violate public policy was not considered in Hyson. While people are free to contract for whatever terms they wish, contracts that violate public policy are unenforceable. Exculpatory provisions undermine the policy considerations governing the tort system, which is to compensate innocent parties, shifting the loss to responsible parties or distributing it among appropriate entities. The standard most often relied upon for determining whether exculpatory agreements violate public policy was set forth in *Tunkl v. Regents of the University of California*, 383 P.2d 441 (Cal. 1963), in which the court said that exculpatory agreements violate public policy if they affect the public interest adversely, based on six factors: (1) the agreement concerns a business that is generally thought of as publicly regulated; (2) the party seeking exculpation is engaged in performing a service of great importance to the public; (3) the party holds itself out as willing to perform this service for any member of the public who seeks it; (4) the party invoking exculpation has a superior bargaining position against the public seeking the service; (5) in

Continued on next page.

exercising the superior bargaining power, the party confronts the public with a standardized adhesion contract of exculpation; and (6), as a result of the transaction, the person or property of the purchaser is placed under the control of the seller, and is subject to the risk of carelessness by the seller. But the ultimate determination of what constitutes the public interest must be made considering the totality of the circumstances of a case in the context of current societal expectations. So the *Tunkl* factors are a guide, but not the final word, in this analysis. Powder Ridge (D) is in the business of providing snowtubing services to the general public, regardless of experience, with minimal restrictions. Because there is virtually unrestricted access, a reasonable person would presume that Powder Ridge (D) was offering an activity the whole family could enjoy safely. Societal expectations that family oriented recreational activities will be reasonably safe is even more important where patrons are under the care and control of the operator as a result of an economic transaction, because as a result of that transaction, the plaintiff was under the care and control of Powder Ridge (D) and was subject to its carelessness. So the plaintiff voluntarily relinquished control to Powder Ridge (D) with the reasonable expectation of an exciting but reasonably safe experience. Additionally, the plaintiff lacked the knowledge, experience, and authority to discern whether the runs were maintained in a reasonably safe condition. It is illogical to permit snowtubers and the general public to bear the costs of risks that they lack ability and right to control. The agreement also was an adhesion contract offered on a take-it-or-leave-it basis. If they didn't sign it, they could not snowtube, so their bargaining power was less than Powder Ridge's (D). Powder Ridge (D) argues that they did not have superior bargaining power because snowtubing is not an essential public service. But while snowtubing is a voluntary activity, there can be disparity in bargaining power in the context of voluntary activities. Recreational activities are pursued by the majority of the population and are an important and healthy part of everyday life. Public policy promotes participation in such activities. The agreement here is contrary to public policy and is unenforceable. While most states uphold adhesion contracts releasing recreational operators from liability for personal injuries caused by their own negligent conduct, this court disagrees. Reversed and remanded.

DISSENT: (Norcott, J.) Parties are free to contract for whatever terms on which they may agree, and this freedom includes the right to contract for the assumption of the risk that may arise as a consequence of signing the contract. While contracts that violate public policy are unenforceable, under *Tunkl*, this contract does not violate public policy and is therefore enforceable. With respect to the first factor, the business is not of a type generally thought of as suitable for regulation, which favors upholding the release, since there are not statutes or regulations affecting snowtubing. As to the second factor, snowtubing is not an

important public service. The fourth factor also weighs against the plaintiff, since the plaintiff's only incentive for snowtubing was recreation, not an important personal interest like banking; he would have suffered no harm if he had not snowtubed. So the conclusion that Powder Ridge (D) enjoyed a significant bargaining advantage is wrong. The sixth *Tunkl* factor also weighs against a determination that the release implicates the public interest, because the plaintiff did not place his person or property under Powder Ridge's (D) control. This isn't a case where the patient was unconscious on the operating table. The third and fifth *Tunkl* factors support the plaintiff's position. Powder Ridge (D) offers its services to the general public, and the contract was an adhesion contract. The majority of the *Tunkl* factors and the approach taken by the vast majority of states support upholding the release in this case. People participating in recreational activities can decide to forego the activity if they don't want to release the activity from liability. The average person is capable of reading a release agreement and deciding not to snowtube because of the risks that he or she is asked to assume. The trial court properly granted summary judgment.

▶ **ANALYSIS**

It is understandable that the court was divided on this issue, because neither the majority opinion nor the dissent is completely persuasive. With respect to the majority decision, the argument that voluntary recreational activities cannot be abandoned in lieu of signing an exculpatory adhesion contract is specious, at best. But the dissent's application of *Tunkl* factors to this case is also not completely persuasive, since *Tunkl* involved a release of patients entering a hospital.

■—■—■

Quicknotes

ADHESION CONTRACT A contract that is not negotiated and is usually prepared by the dominant party on a "take it or leave it" basis.

EXCULPATORY CLAUSE A clause in a contract relieving one party from liability for certain unlawful conduct.

PUBLIC POLICY Policy administered by the state with respect to the health, safety and morals of its people in accordance with common notions of fairness and decency.

■—■—■

Murphy v. Steeplechase Amusement Co.

Amusement seeker (P) v. Amusement park (D)

N.Y. Ct. App., 250 N.Y. 479, 166 N.E. 173 (1929).

NATURE OF CASE: Action to recover damages for personal injuries.

FACT SUMMARY: Murphy (P) was injured when he fell while riding an amusement ride, "The Flopper," which was a moving belt that ran up an inclined plane and caused people to fall on padded walls and flooring.

🏛 RULE OF LAW
One who takes part in a sport accepts the dangers that inhere in it so far as they are obvious and necessary and they are not so serious as to justify the belief that precautions of some kind must have been taken to avert them.

FACTS: While visiting the amusement park at Coney Island, New York (run by Steeplechase Amusement Co. (Steeplechase) (D)), Murphy (P), his wife, and their friends decided to ride "The Flopper" after watching others do so. "The Flopper" consists of a moving belt, running up an inclined plane, on which passengers sit or stand. There are four-foot high padded walls on either side of the groove in which the belt runs and padded flooring beyond those walls at the same angle as the belt (which is driven by a motor that runs on electrical current). The whole purpose of the ride was the laughter and merriment occasioned by the numerous spills the passengers took. In fact, Mrs. Murphy, who preceded her husband in boarding the ride, testified that she took a chance when she was asked if she thought a fall might be expected. When Murphy (P) fell on the ride, however, he blamed the fractured knee cap he suffered on a sudden start and stop of the belt. In a suit to recover for his injuries, Murphy (P) specifically charged that (1) the belt was dangerous to life and limb, (2) it was not properly equipped to prevent injuries to persons using it, (3) it was operated at a fast and dangerous rate of speed, and (4) there was no proper railing, guard, or other device to prevent a fall. At trial, Murphy (P) gave uncorroborated testimony (which was also contradicted by photographs and witnesses for Steeplechase (D)) that he fell on wood and not canvas padding. At the same trial, the president of Steeplechase (D) said such an accident had never occurred before, but a nurse in the emergency hospital serving the amusement park said there had been other injuries (she did not know how many), none of which involved broken bones or serious injuries. On this evidence, a verdict in favor of Murphy (P) was entered. Following an affirmation of that verdict on appeal, Steeplechase (D) brought the matter before this court on appeal.

ISSUE: Does one assume the risks that are inherent in a sport?

HOLDING AND DECISION: (Cardozo, C.J.) Yes. When one engages in a sport, he accepts the dangers that inhere in it insofar as they are obvious and necessary. The whole design of the ride in question was to illicit amusement and merriment from the spills taken by the riders. Murphy (P) observed this before he got on the ride. His injuries are no more than what common experience tells us could well happen at any time as the consequence of a sudden fall. As to the allegation that an abnormal and extraordinary spasm in the machine's operation caused the fall, such a bare allegation is insufficient to provide the basis for a verdict absent some evidence firmer than a mere descriptive epithet (Murphy's (P) saying that he felt a jerk). All in all, the best advice is for the timorous to stay at home. Otherwise they must accept the risks inherent in the actions and adventures they undertake. Reversed.

▶ ANALYSIS

The legal maxim "volenti non fit injuria" (no wrong is done to one who is willing), cited by the court, is the basis for the assumption of risk doctrine. Precisely what one has "willingly" chosen to risk is usually determined subjectively. However, there are certain risks all adults are held to appreciate.

Quicknotes

ASSUMPTION OF RISK DOCTRINE An affirmative defense to a negligence suit by the defendant contending that the plaintiff knowingly and voluntarily subjected himself to the hazardous condition wholly absolving the defendant of liability for injuries incurred.

SUBJECTIVE A belief that is personal to an individual.

Davenport v. Cotton Hope Plantation Horizontal Property Regime

Injured lessee (P) v. Owner (D)

S.C. Sup. Ct., 333 S.C. 71, 508 S.E.2d 565 (1998).

NATURE OF CASE: Review of reversal of directed verdict for defendant in negligence claim.

FACT SUMMARY: Davenport (P) alleged that Cotton Hope's (D) negligence caused him to trip and injure himself in a stairway, but Cotton Hope (D) claimed that Davenport (P) had assumed the risk for the accident when he decided to use that stairway.

🏛 RULE OF LAW
A plaintiff is not barred from recovery by the doctrine of assumption of risk, unless the degree of fault arising therefrom is greater than the negligence of the defendant.

FACTS: Davenport (P) knew that the floodlight in a stairway near his apartment was not working and had reported it to management. When Davenport (P) fell and injured himself in the stairway, he sued Cotton Hope Plantation Horizontal Property Regime (Cotton Hope) (D), the landlord. Cotton Hope (D) argued that Davenport (P) had assumed the risk by knowingly using that stairway and that, even if comparative negligence applied, Davenport (P) was more negligent as a matter of law. The trial court directed a verdict against Davenport (P) and the court of appeals reversed. The South Carolina Supreme Court granted review to decide whether assumption of risk survived as a complete bar to recovery under South Carolina's comparative negligence system.

ISSUE: Is a plaintiff barred from recovery by the doctrine of assumption of risk if the degree of fault arising therefrom is not greater than the negligence of the defendant?

HOLDING AND DECISION: (Toal, J.) No. A plaintiff is not barred from recovery by the doctrine of assumption of risk unless the degree of fault arising therefrom is greater than the negligence of the defendant. In this case, it could be reasonably concluded that Davenport's (P) negligence in proceeding down that stairway did not exceed Cotton Hope's (D) negligence. The case was properly remanded for a new trial. Assumption of risk is abolished as an absolute bar to recovery. Reversed and remanded.

▶ ANALYSIS

The court discussed various approaches taken by other states on this issue. Express assumption of risk can still be an absolute defense to negligence claims. That is be-

cause express assumption of risk is a contract theory, not a tort theory.

■■■

Quicknotes

ASSUMPTION OF RISK DOCTRINE An affirmative defense to a negligence suit by the defendant contending that the plaintiff knowingly and voluntarily subjected himself to the hazardous condition wholly absolving the defendant of liability for injuries incurred.

COMPARATIVE NEGLIGENCE Doctrine whereby the court in assessing the appropriate measure of damages compares the relative fault of the parties and reduces the amount of damages to be collected by the plaintiff in proportion to his degree of fault.

CONTRIBUTORY NEGLIGENCE Behavior on the part of an injured plaintiff falling below the standard of ordinary care that contributes to the defendant's negligence, resulting in the plaintiff's injury.

DIRECTED VERDICT A verdict ordered by the court in a jury trial.

■■■

Riegel v. Medtronic, Inc.

Injured patient (P) v. Medical device manufacturer (D)

552 U.S. 312 (2008).

NATURE OF CASE: Appeal from appeals court affirmation of a district court grant of summary judgment.

FACT SUMMARY: A catheter used in an angioplasty burst, causing the patient, Charles Riegel (P) extreme medical complications. He sued the manufacturer, Medtronic, Inc. (D) for negligence. The district court granted summary judgment to Medtronic (D) and the appeals court affirmed.

RULE OF LAW
Section 360k(a) of the Medical Device Amendments to the Food, Drug, and Cosmetic Act preempts state-law claims seeking damages for injuries caused by medical devices that received premarket approval from the Food and Drug Administration.

FACTS: Charles Riegel's (P) surgeon used an Evergreen Balloon Catheter to dilate his coronary artery during his angioplasty. The catheter burst, causing extreme complications. Riegel (P) sued the manufacturer, Medtronic, Inc. (D), for negligence in the design, manufacture, and labeling of the device. Medtronic (D) argued that Riegel (P) could not bring these state-law negligence claims because Section 360k(a) of the Medical Device Amendments (MDA) to the Food, Drug, and Cosmetic Act preempted them. The Food and Drug Administration (FDA) has for a long time required FDA approval for the introduction of new drugs into the market, but until the MDA was passed, states regulated the introduction of new medical devices into the market. Now, under the MDA, premarket approval (PMA) is a rigorous process that includes review of reports on all studies and investigations of the device's safety and effectiveness, a full statement of its components, and an example of the proposed labeling, among other things. The FDA may consult outside experts before approving the application. The FDA spends an average of 1200 hours reviewing each application, and grants approval when there is reasonable assurance of the device's safety and effectiveness. In addition to setting forth a federal regulatory process for ensuring the safety of medical devices, the MDA provides that no state may set requirements that differ from or add to the federal ones. The district court dismissed Riegel's (P) claims as preempted by the MDA on grounds that they were based on New York law. The U.S. Court of Appeals for the Second Circuit agreed that the suits based on medical devices like the catheter used in this case are preempted by the MDA. The catheter had been through the PMA process, and federal regulators ensured that it met federal requirements. To allow state common-law suits for PMA-approved devices would be to add a state requirement to the regulatory process despite the MDA's preemption clause.

ISSUE: Does Section 360k(a) of the Medical Device Amendments to the Food, Drug, and Cosmetic Act preempt state-law claims seeking damages for injuries caused by medical devices that received premarket approval from the Food and Drug Administration?

HOLDING AND DECISION: (Scalia, J.) Yes. Section 360k(a) of the Medical Device Amendments to the Food, Drug, and Cosmetic Act preempts state-law claims seeking damages for injuries caused by medical devices that received premarket approval from the Food and Drug Administration. The catheter in this case received premarket approval from the FDA in 1994, and in *Medtronic, Inc. v. Lohr*, 518 U.S. 470 (1996), this Court held that state requirements are preempted when the FDA has established specific counterpart regulations or there are other specific requirements applicable to a particular device. The MDA preempted state common-law claims for defective devices such as this one after they have undergone PMA through the FDA, because the FDA's determination about the safety of a device cannot be second-guessed. Riegel's (P) negligence and strict liability claims relating to the safety and effectiveness of the catheter were based on New York's requirements and were therefore "different from, or in addition to" the federal requirements. Affirmed.

DISSENT: (Ginsburg, J.) The MDA's preemption clause cannot spare medical device manufacturers from personal injury claims alleging flaws in a design or label once the application for the design or label has gained premarket approval from the FDA. Congress did not intend the MDA to curtail state common-law suits so severely. There is a presumption against preemption, because Congress does not lightly preempt state-law causes of action, and federal laws containing preemption clauses do not automatically escape the presumption against preemption. The purpose of the MDA is to provide for the safety and effectiveness of medical devices, and Congress meant only to preempt state premarket regulation of medical devices, not the suppression of common-law tort claims. Riegel's (P) suit is not preempted.

▶ ANALYSIS

This case stands for the proposition that the FDA's PMA of a device indicates sound design and labeling, and that the

Continued on next page.

design cannot be questioned in state-based lawsuits. Following this decision, lawyers expected personal injury lawsuits to abandon issues related to possible design defects questions and focus on whether patients were harmed because the manufacturing company did not make or handle the product according to the safety processes laid out in the documents approved by the FDA, which is a focus on manufacturing defects. Another question raised by this case and yet to be determined is whether personal injury lawsuits are barred in cases where manufacturers deceived the regulators by providing false data or withholding data on safety and effectiveness to get their marketing approval.

━━■■■━━

Quicknotes

FEDERAL FOOD, DRUG, AND COSMETIC ACT Consumer-protection statute authorizing promulgation of rules governing food and drugs.

PREEMPTION Doctrine holding that matters of national interest take precedence over matters of local interest; the federal law takes precedence over state law.

━━■■■━━

Strict Liability

Quick Reference Rules of Law

Fletcher v. Rylands

Mine operator (P) v. Reservoir owner (D)

Ex. Ch., L.R. 1 Ex. 265 (1866).

NATURE OF CASE: Action in strict liability for damages to property.

FACT SUMMARY: Water from Rylands's (D) reservoir escaped down through mine shafts below his property and flooded Fletcher's adjoining mine.

🏛 RULE OF LAW
A person who brings something onto his land that is potentially harmful if it escapes is strictly liable for all the natural consequences of such escape.

FACTS: Rylands (D) had a reservoir built on his property. His engineers found old mine shafts beneath the reservoir, but thought that they would support the reservoir, because they were filled up with dirt. Unknown to both Rylands (D) and the engineers, the filled mine shafts were connected to open shafts on Fletcher's (P) adjoining property. When the reservoir was filled, the water burst through the filled shafts underneath the reservoir and then flooded Fletcher's (P) mine.

ISSUE: Is a person who brings something onto his land that is potentially harmful if it escapes, strictly liable for the natural consequences of such escape?

HOLDING AND DECISION: (Blackburn, J.) Yes. A person who brings something dangerous onto his land has an absolute duty to prevent its escape. He is therefore strictly liable for the damage resulting from its escape, even though he may have taken all reasonable precautions to keep it safely on his land. Rylands (D) dammed up huge quantities of water on his land. The stored water was harmless while contained in the reservoir, but was capable of doing great damage to Fletcher's (P) property if the reservoir did not hold. Therefore, although Rylands (D) was free from blame for the flooding, he should be held strictly liable for the damage to Fletcher's (P) mines. Judgment for the plaintiff.

▶ ANALYSIS

This is the leading case from which developed the doctrine that persons engaged in abnormally dangerous activities are absolutely liable for resulting damage, regardless of fault. The House of Lords reviewed the decision of the Exchequer Chamber in this case and limited the holding so that it applied to "nonnatural" or exceptional uses of the land only. In the United States, courts initially rejected *Rylands v. Fletcher*. Today, however, a majority of courts apply the doctrine to unusual or abnormal uses of land. Examples of activities upon which strict liability has been imposed are storage of water in large quantities, storage and use of explosives and highly volatile substances, blasting, pile driving, crop dusting, fumigation with cyanide gas, and drilling of oil wells in densely populated communities.

■=■

Quicknotes

STRICT LIABILITY Liability for all injuries proximately caused by a party's conducting of certain inherently dangerous activities without regard to negligence or fault.

■=■

Rylands v. Fletcher

Reservoir owner (D) v. Mine operator (P)

H.L., All E.R. 1, L.R. 3 H.L. 330 (1868).

NATURE OF CASE: Appeal from an award of damages for injury to land.

FACT SUMMARY: Rylands (D) built a reservoir on his land, but the water escaped through an abandoned mine shaft and flooded an adjoining mine owned by Fletcher (P).

RULE OF LAW

A person using his land for a dangerous, non-natural use is strictly liable for damage to another's property resulting from such nonnatural use.

FACTS: Rylands (D) built a water reservoir on his land. The water escaped through an abandoned coal mine shaft and flooded an adjoining coal mine owned by Fletcher (P). Fletcher (P) sued for damages to his land caused by the water.

ISSUE: Is a person who uses his land for a dangerous, nonnatural use, strictly liable for damage to another's property resulting from such nonnatural use?

HOLDING AND DECISION: (Lord Cairns, Ch.) Yes. A person using his land for a dangerous, nonnatural use is strictly liable for damage to another's property resulting from such nonnatural use. If water had naturally accumulated upon the land and, by the laws of nature had run off on to adjoining land, there would be no liability. But if water, not being a natural condition of the land, is introduced upon it, any water that escapes does so at the landowner's peril; for which any damage to adjoining land he is strictly liable. These were the principles stated by Justice Blackburn in the court below. Judgment of the Court of Exchequer Chamber affirmed.

CONCURRENCE: (Lord Cranworth, Ch.) No matter how cautious a person is, he will be liable if he brings upon his land something that causes damage to his neighbor's land. The determinative factor is not whether the defendant has acted with due care but rather if his actions caused the damage. Rylands (D) brought onto his land water and stored it into a reservoir that ended up harming Fletcher (P) and, therefore, Rylands (D) is liable.

▶ *ANALYSIS*

This is the leading case from which was developed the doctrine of strict liability for abnormally dangerous activities or conditions. In determining whether a certain activity is a nonnatural use, the court looks to the place where the activity occurs, the customs of the community, and the natural fitness or adaptation of the premises for the pur-

pose. The restatement, while accepting the principle of the case, has limited it to ultrahazardous activities.

Quicknotes

DUE CARE The degree of care that can be expected from a reasonably prudent person under similar circumstances; synonymous with ordinary care.

STRICT LIABILITY Liability for all injuries proximately caused by a party's conducting of certain inherently dangerous activities without regard to negligence or fault.

Sullivan v. Dunham

Decedent (P) v. Dynamite blasting landowner (D)

N.Y. Ct. App., 161 N.Y. 290, 55 N.E. 923 (1900).

NATURE OF CASE: Appeal from an affirmation of a trial court decision in an action to recover damages for death of the decedent.

FACT SUMMARY: Sullivan's (P) decedent was walking along a public highway when she was killed by a fragment of wood hurled into the air by a dynamite blast designed to fell a 60-foot tree on Dunham's (D) land.

🏛 RULE OF LAW
One is strictly liable for injury to person or property that is occasioned by trespass resulting from his blasting activities.

FACTS: Dunham (D) hired two men to dynamite a 60-foot tree on his land, but the blast hurtled a fragment of wood 412 feet onto a highway—where Sullivan's (D) decedent was killed when it struck her. As a result, Sullivan (P) sued Dunham (D) and the two blasters under a New York statute allowing a decedent's personal representative to maintain an action to recover damages for a wrongful act, neglect, or default which caused decedent's death if decedent himself could have maintained the same action. At trial, the judge charged that proof of negligence was not necessary to establish liability, and the subsequent recovery by Sullivan (P) was affirmed by the appellate division. From that affirmation, Dunham (D) appealed.

ISSUE: Must negligence be proven before one can be held liable for injury to person or property resulting from a trespass by debris from his blasting activities?

HOLDING AND DECISION: (Vann, J.) No. Where injuries are occasioned by trespass to person or property due to any activities, like blasting, in which the landowner is engaged, liability therefore is not predicated upon proof of negligence (unlike cases where the injury is not direct but is consequential). Although one has a right to use his land as he sees fit, it has long been held that that right must yield when it deprives another of the beneficial use of his property altogether—injury of such nature being prohibited without regard to negligence. The safety of a person from such trespass is certainly as important and entitled to a similar degree of protection. Previous cases have allowed recovery for personal injury due to intentional explosion; even some have denied recovery where the explosion was accidental. They have also protected people from injury even if they did not own the land where they were injured. Thus, it seems well within our settled principles to protect a person who is where he has a right to be—such as standing on a public highway. The safety of travelers thereupon is certainly paramount to improvement of one piece of property. For these reasons, the judgment is affirmed.

▶ ANALYSIS

This case reflects the now-defunct approach that concussion damage and debris damage gave rise to different standards of liability (negligence being a prerequisite to recovery for the former). The underlying rationale was that debris damage could support a trespass action, where intent and fault were irrelevant, whereas the indirect and consequential harm typified by concussion damage was sufficient solely for an action on the case, where the concept of fault being relevant was developed earlier. It was not until the 1969 case of *Spano v. Perini Corp.,* 25 N.Y.2d 11, 250 N.E.2d 31, that New York did away with this archaic distinction and focused on the problem of who should bear the cost of blasting damages.

━━━

Quicknotes

ABNORMALLY DANGEROUS ACTIVITY An activity, as set forth in Restatement (Second) of Torts § 520, giving rise to strict liability on the part of the actor for damages caused thereby.

STRICT LIABILITY Liability for all injuries proximately caused by a party's conducting of certain inherently dangerous activities without regard to negligence or fault.

TRESPASS Unlawful interference with, or damage to, the real or personal property of another.

Indiana Harbor Belt Railroad Co. v. American Cyanamid Co.

Railroad (P) v. Chemical manufacturer (D)

916 F.2d 1174 (7th Cir. 1990).

NATURE OF CASE: Appeal of damages awarded for injury to property.

FACT SUMMARY: American Cyanamid Co. (D), manufacturer of a dangerous chemical, was held strictly liable when a quantity of it spilled during transportation.

🏛 RULE OF LAW
Strict liability will not be imposed against the manufacturer of a toxic chemical for accidents occurring during transportation.

FACTS: American Cyanamid Co. (D), a chemical manufacturer, engaged a railroad car to transport 20,000 gallons of liquid acrylonitrile, a toxic substance, to a processing plant in New Jersey. While the car was sitting in a Chicago railroad yard owned by Indiana Harbor Belt R.R. (P), about 5,000 gallons spilled, which necessitated an evacuation of nearby homes and nearly $1 million in cleanup. Indiana Harbor Belt R.R. (P) filed suit against American Cyanamid (D) to recover the cost of cleanup, contending that the transportation of toxic chemicals was an ultrahazardous activity for which the manufacturer should be strictly liable. A district court, sitting in diversity, agreed and so instructed the jury. A verdict for damages was rendered, and American Cyanamid (D) appealed.

ISSUE: Will strict liability be imposed against the manufacturer of a toxic chemical for accidents occurring during transportation?

HOLDING AND DECISION: (Posner, J.) No. Strict liability will not be imposed against the manufacturer of a toxic chemical for accidents occurring during transportation. The Restatement (Second) of Torts, at § 520, lists six factors to be considered in determining whether an activity is ultrahazardous: (1) great probability of harm; (2) potentially serious level of harm; (3) the activity is not a matter of common usage; (4) harm cannot be prevented by utmost care; (5) the activity is inappropriate for the location; and (6) the social value of the activity is not sufficient to offset the risks. The basic purpose behind the ultrahazardous activity doctrine is to encourage the use of alternative methods when possible. In this case, no alternative exists to transport chemicals other than truck transport, which is not inherently safer. It would not be feasible to reroute the shipment of all hazardous materials around Chicago. Moreover, the negligence regime is perfectly adequate for deterring railway spills. Finally, the ultrahazardous activity doctrine concentrates on the activity, not the subject of the activity. American Cyanamid (D) is not considered to be engaged in an abnormally danger-

ous activity just because a product it manufactures becomes dangerous when handled. It is the transportation, not the manufacture of the chemical, which is under scrutiny. For these reasons, strict liability is inappropriate in this context. Reversed and remanded.

▶ ANALYSIS

The classic case of ultrahazardous activity is dynamite blasting in an urban area. It entails a great risk of harm, and a less dangerous (albeit more expensive) method building demolition exists—the wrecking ball. The ultrahazardous activity rule will make the demolisher strictly liable if he chooses the more dangerous method.

■==■

Quicknotes

ABNORMALLY DANGEROUS ACTIVITY An activity, set forth in Restatement (Second) of Torts § 520, as giving rise to strict liability on the part of the actor for damages caused thereby.

STRICT LIABILITY Liability for all injuries proximately caused by a party's conducting of certain inherently dangerous activities without regard to negligence or fault.

■==■

CHAPTER 9

Liability for Defective Products

Quick Reference Rules of Law

MacPherson v. Buick Motor Co.

Car owner (P) v. Automobile manufacturer (D)

N.Y. Ct. App., 217 N.Y. 382, 111 N.E. 1050 (1916).

NATURE OF CASE: Appeal from judgment for plaintiff.

FACT SUMMARY: MacPherson (P) was injured when his car collapsed due to a defective wheel.

RULE OF LAW

Where a product which, if negligently made, will be dangerous to life or property and it is foreseeable that third parties will use or come in contact with it, a cause of action exists in favor of the injured third party.

FACTS: MacPherson (P) purchased a used Buick from a dealer. The wheel had been negligently manufactured by a third party. Buick Motor Co. (Buick) (D) could have discovered the defect by a simple inspection. The wheel collapsed and MacPherson (P) was severely injured. Buick (D) argued that it should not be liable for the negligence of others. Buick (D) further argued that since no privity of contract existed between it and MacPherson (P) it owed him no duty of care. Finally, Buick (D) argued that an automobile was not considered a dangerous item, hence, no third-party recovery should be allowed. MacPherson (P) argued that strict liability should be extended to any product which, if negligently made, would be likely to cause serious injury or death if it were likely that third parties would use or come into contact with the product. The court found that Buick (D) was negligent in failing to inspect the wheel; that a defect in a car was likely to cause serious injury or death; that it was also both foreseeable and likely that a third party would purchase the automobile. Judgment was granted for MacPherson (P).

ISSUE: Should a third person, injured by a manufacturer's negligence, be permitted to recover where the negligence is likely to render the product dangerous to human life?

HOLDING AND DECISION: (Cardozo, J.) Yes. This is a negligence action. Buick (D) knew or had reason to know that if its automobile was negligently manufactured it was likely to cause serious injury. Its failure to inspect the wheel for obvious defects was negligence. It was foreseeable that the car would be sold to other parties who could be injured by the negligence. Where a manufacturer voluntarily places his product in the stream of commerce, and he knows that if it were negligently manufactured there was a serious risk of bodily injury or death, he will be liable to the purchaser of the vehicle. He will also be liable to other parties who could foreseeably be injured by the product. No privity is required, since this is a tort action.

While we have previously denied recovery except in cases involving dangerous products, this coverage should be extended to all products which, if negligently manufactured, are likely to cause the risk of serious bodily injury or death. Affirmed.

DISSENT: (Bartlett, C.J.) Earlier decisions can all be explained by the "inherently dangerous" analysis; hence this Court should not venture beyond that formulation.

ANALYSIS

Plaintiff purchased a sealed bottle of ginger beer at a cafe. After drinking from it, a decomposed snail floated to the top. She was allowed to recover from the manufacturer/bottler for emotional distress and shock, *M'Alister v. Stevenson*, A.C. 562 (1932). Before liability of the manufacturer can be found, it must be established that the defect was caused solely by its negligence and could not have resulted from the negligence of others or the plaintiff's contributory negligence in misusing the product.

Quicknotes

CONTRIBUTORY NEGLIGENCE Behavior on the part of an injured plaintiff falling below the standard of ordinary care that contributes to the defendant's negligence, resulting in the plaintiff's injury.

DUTY OF CARE A principle of negligence requiring an individual to act in such a manner as to avoid injury to a person to whom he or she owes an obligatory duty.

NEGLIGENCE Conduct falling below the standard of care that a reasonable person would demonstrate under similar conditions.

PRIVITY OF CONTRACT A relationship between the parties to a contract that is required in order to bring an action for breach.

STRICT LIABILITY Liability for all injuries proximately caused by a party's conducting of certain inherently dangerous activities without regard to negligence or fault.

Escola v. Coca Cola Bottling Co. of Fresno

Exploding bottle victim (P) v. Soft drink manufacturer (D)

Cal. Sup. Ct., 24 Cal. 2d 453, 150 P.2d 436 (1944).

NATURE OF CASE: Negligence action.

FACT SUMMARY: A Coca Cola bottle exploded in Escola's (P) hand.

🏛 RULE OF LAW
Res ipsa loquitur may be applied if plaintiff can show that the condition of the product did not change after it left defendant's hands, the plaintiff exercised due care, and the accident would not have occurred without negligence.

FACTS: A Coca Cola bottle exploded in Escola's (P) hand. Escola (P) sued for negligence. The case went to the jury with a res ipsa loquitur instruction even though Escola (P) had produced no testimony concerning negligence and an expert had testified that Coca Cola (D) subjected its bottles to nearly infallible testing. Coca Cola (D) appealed a verdict against it alleging that there was no proof of negligence. Escola (P) alleged that where an accident would not have happened except for negligence and the instrumentality was not damaged after leaving a defendant's control, res ipsa loquitur instructions may be given.

ISSUE: May res ipsa loquitur instructions be given if a plaintiff can establish that the condition of the product did not change after it left defendant's hands, the plaintiff exercised due care, and the accident would not have occurred without negligence?

HOLDING AND DECISION: (Gibson, C.J.) Yes. Although here the evidence is unclear whether the explosion was caused by an excessive charge or a defect in the glass, there is a sufficient showing that neither cause would ordinarily have been present if due care had been used. Further, Coca Cola Bottling Company (D) had exclusive control over both the charging and inspection of the bottles. Thus, all the requirements necessary to entitle Escola (P) to rely on the doctrine of res ipsa loquitur to supply an inference of negligence are present. The rule is well settled that when a defendant produces evidence to rebut the inference of negligence which arises upon application of the doctrine of res ipsa loquitur, it ordinarily is a question of fact for the jury to determine whether the inference has been dispelled. Escola's (P) award is affirmed.

CONCURRENCE: (Traynor, J.) A manufacturer's negligence should no longer be singled out as the basis of a plaintiff's right to recover in cases such as the instant one. It should now be recognized that a manufacturer incurs an absolute liability when an article they have placed in the market, knowing that it is to be used without inspection, proves to have a defect that causes injury to human beings.

▶ ANALYSIS

This case is considered to be the classic example of a court's adjusting the duty of a defendant while applying the doctrine of res ipsa loquitur. Notice that the doctrine does not prove conclusively that the defendant is liable. It merely creates an inference of negligence in most jurisdictions which, if not overcome by the defendant, at least allows the case to go to the jury. Many jurisdictions would hold Coca Cola (D) guilty under a strict liability theory, i.e., liability without a showing of negligence based on public policy considerations.

Quicknotes

EXCLUSIVE CONTROL RULE Necessary element of res ipsa loquitur doctrine that the defendant have total control of the instrument that inflicted the injury.

NEGLIGENCE Conduct falling below the standard of care that a reasonable person would demonstrate under similar conditions.

PREPONDERANCE OF THE EVIDENCE A standard of proof requiring the trier of fact to determine whether the fact sought to be established is more probable than not.

RES IPSA LOQUITUR A rule of law giving rise to an inference of negligence where the instrument inflicting the injury is in the exclusive control of the defendant and where such harm could not ordinarily result in the absence of negligence.

STANDARD OF CARE A uniform degree of behavior against which a person's conduct can be measured when determining liability in negligence cases.

Soule v. General Motors Corporation

Driver (P) v. Automobile manufacturer (D)

Cal. Sup. Ct., 8 Cal. 4th 548, 882 P.2d 298 (1994).

NATURE OF CASE: Appeal from award of damages in action alleging design defect.

FACT SUMMARY: Soule (P) sued General Motors Corp. (GM) (D), alleging a design defect after suffering severe ankle injuries in a collision involving her Camaro and another vehicle.

🏛 RULE OF LAW
In establishing liability for a design defect in a complex product, the standard is the "excessive preventable danger" test, i.e., that the risk of danger in the design outweighs the benefits of the design.

FACTS: Soule (P) was driving her Camaro on a drizzly afternoon without her seatbelt. An oncoming Datsun skidded into Soule's (P) path and the cars collided at estimated combined speeds of 30 to 70 miles per hour. The collision bent the frame of the Camaro in the area of the driver's side front wheel and tore a bracket loose. As a result, the wheel collapsed into the underside of the "toe pan" and crumpled it, causing fractures in both of Soule's (P) ankles. Soule (P) sued General Motors Corp. (GM) (D), alleging defective design in the placement of the bracket and the configuration of the frame. Numerous expert witnesses appeared at trial for both Soule (P) and GM (D) and testimony was given on topics including design engineering, orthopedics, and biomechanics. GM (D) argued that the force of the accident and the fact that Soule (P) was not wearing a seatbelt were the causes of her ankle injuries. The court gave the jury a conventional "ordinary consumer expectations" instruction. The jury found that the Camaro contained a design defect that was the legal cause of Soule's (P) injuries and awarded her $1.65 million. The court of appeals affirmed. GM (D) appealed.

ISSUE: Is an "ordinary consumer expectations" instruction appropriate in a design defect case involving a complex product?

HOLDING AND DECISION: (Baxter, J.) No. In establishing liability for a design defect in a complex product, the standard is the "excessive preventable danger" test, i.e., that the risk of danger in the design outweighs the benefits of the design. The instruction given to the jury was incorrect in this case; however, the error was harmless. The jury should have been given an instruction that the design is defective if it embodies "excessive preventable danger." Under this test, the danger inherent in the design is weighed against its benefits, and factors such as practicality, cost, and risk are all considered. Although this instruction was not given, all of the expert testimony given at trial was precisely on these issues. The consumer expectations theory was never presented or argued by witnesses for either Soule (P) or GM (D). Therefore, even though the wrong instruction was given, there is no indication that it affected the jury's decision, and therefore there is no basis for reversing their verdict. Affirmed.

▶ ANALYSIS

The "ordinary consumer expectations" instruction is appropriately given when a product causes injury in a way that does not meet the consumer's most minimum assumptions about the product's proper usage. The court points out that the test might be appropriate in a case involving a complex product such as a car, but not if design defect is at issue. For example, one would not expect a car to roll over when making a right hand turn at 5 miles per hour, but if this occurred the "ordinary consumer expectations" instruction would likely be given.

■━■

Quicknotes

DESIGN DEFECT A defect in a product manufactured according to the intended design, but present because the design of the product itself presents a risk of harm to consumers.

PRODUCT LIABILITY The legal liability of manufacturers and sellers for damages and injuries suffered by buyers, users, and even bystanders because of defects in goods purchased.

■━■

Camacho v. Honda Motor Co., Ltd.

Motorcycle rider (P) v. Motorcycle manufacturer (D)

Colo. Sup. Ct., 741 P.2d 1240 (1987).

NATURE OF CASE: Review of summary judgment dismissing products liability action.

FACT SUMMARY: Camacho's (P) product liability action was dismissed on the grounds that the danger posed by the motorcycle he was riding would have been within the contemplation of the ordinary user.

⚖ RULE OF LAW
Whether the danger presented by a product would have been within a user's contemplation is not relevant in a products liability action.

FACTS: Camacho (P) suffered severe leg injuries in a motorcycle accident. He filed a products liability suit against Honda Motor Co., Ltd. (D), alleging that certain leg guards should have been installed. The trial court granted summary judgment dismissing the action, concluding that, as a matter of law, the danger posed by the motorcycle was within the contemplation of the ordinary consumer. The court of appeals affirmed, and the Colorado Supreme Court accepted review.

ISSUE: Is whether the danger presented by a product would have been within a user's contemplation relevant in a products liability action?

HOLDING AND DECISION: (Kirshbaum, J.) No. Whether the danger presented by a product would have been within a user's contemplation is not relevant in products liability action. In a products liability action, the focus is on the product itself, not the consumer or the manufacturer. Looking to a user's expectations improperly shifts the focus to the user. The proper test for whether a product is defective is whether the product is unreasonably dangerous when used in an intended manner. Whether this is so in any case requires an analysis of numerous factors, such as the usefulness of the product and a cost-benefit analysis of making the product safer. This is a fact-intensive inquiry, normally one for the jury. The basis for the summary judgment here was therefore improper. Reversed and remanded.

DISSENT: (Vollack, J.) When a common consumer product is involved, the consumer expectation test is appropriate.

▶ ANALYSIS

"Unreasonably dangerous" is the standard test for defective design. It is embodied in § 402A of the Restatement. The main rejection of this standard can be found in the case *Cronin v. J.B.E. Olson Corp.*, 8 Cal. 3d 121 (1972), wherein the California Supreme Court held that a defect did not have to make a product unreasonably dangerous for strict liability to apply. *Cronin* has not, for the most part, been followed by other states.

■━■

Quicknotes

DESIGN DEFECT A defect in a product manufactured according to the intended design, but present because the design of the product itself presents a risk of harm to consumers.

PRODUCT LIABILITY The legal liability of manufacturers and sellers for damages and injuries suffered by buyers, users and even bystanders because of defects in goods purchased.

STRICT LIABILITY Liability for all injuries proximately caused by a party's conducting of certain inherently dangerous activities without regard to negligence or fault.

■━■

Hood v. Ryobi America Corp.

Injured consumer (P) v. Manufacturer (D)

181 F.3d 608 (4th Cir. 1999).

NATURE OF CASE: Appeal from summary judgment for defendant.

FACT SUMMARY: Hood (P) alleged that Ryobi America Corp. (D) failed to adequately warn of dangers of using an allegedly defectively designed saw.

🏛 RULE OF LAW
A manufacturer may be liable for placing a product on the market that bears inadequate instructions and warnings or that is defective in design.

FACTS: Hood (P) purchased a saw manufactured by Ryobi America Corp. (Ryobi) (D) to use for home repairs. The saw itself warned that the saw blade guards, which were attached to the saw, should never be removed. The owner's manual also contained similar warnings. Disregarding the warnings, Hood (P) removed the saw blade guards and was later seriously injured when the spinning saw blade flew off the saw. Hood claimed that Ryobi's (D) warnings were not adequate because they were not specific enough, and that the saw had been defectively designed. Hood (P) sued under negligence, strict liability, and breach of warranty. The district court granted Ryobi's (D) motion for summary judgment and Hood (P) appealed.

ISSUE: May a manufacturer be liable for placing a product on the market that bears inadequate instructions and warnings or that is defective in design?

HOLDING AND DECISION: (Wilkinson, C.J.) Yes. A manufacturer may be liable for placing a product on the market that bears inadequate instructions and warnings or that is defective in design. A warning need only be one that is reasonable under the circumstances. Ryobi's (D) warnings were clear and unequivocal. Ryobi (D) placed three labels on the saw itself and at least four warnings in the owner's manual. The warnings were adequate as a matter of law. Affirmed.

▶ ANALYSIS

The court declined to hold the manufacturer liable because of the affirmative misuse by Hood (P). The additional warnings Hood (P) had claimed were necessary were found by the court to be more confusing and unnecessary. Some courts rule on the issue of the adequacy of the warnings as a matter of law. Other courts leave this issue for the jury to decide.

Quicknotes

DUTY TO WARN An obligation owed by an owner or occupier of land to persons who come onto the premises, to inform them of defects or active operations, which may cause injury.

NEGLIGENCE Conduct falling below the standard of care that a reasonable person would demonstrate under similar conditions.

PRODUCT LIABILITY The legal liability of manufacturers and sellers for damages and injuries suffered by buyers, users and even bystanders because of defects in goods purchased.

STRICT LIABILITY Liability for all injuries proximately caused by a party's conducting of certain inherently dangerous activities without regard to negligence or fault.

State v. Karl

Drug manufacturer (D) v. Estate (P)

W. Va. Sup. Ct. App., 220 W. Va. 463, 647 S.E.2d 899 (2007).

NATURE OF CASE: Appeal of denial of summary judgment.

FACT SUMMARY: A woman died suddenly after three days of taking a drug prescribed by her doctor, and her estate filed a products liability/medical malpractice action against the doctor and drug manufacturer. The court refused to dismiss the claim against the manufacturer, and the manufacturer appealed.

🏛 RULE OF LAW
Under West Virginia products liability law, the learned intermediary doctrine does not absolve manufacturers of prescription drugs of the same duty to warn consumers about the risks of their products as other manufacturers.

FACTS: Propulsid was a drug manufactured and distributed by Janssen (D), a pharmaceutical company. Nancy J. Gellner (P) was prescribed Propulsid by her primary care physician, Daniel J. Wilson (D). She died suddenly on the third day of taking the drug, and her estate (P) filed a products liability/medical malpractice action against Janssen (D) and Wilson (D). Janssen (D) filed a motion for summary judgment, arguing that the learned intermediary doctrine absolved it of liability. The court denied the motion, and the company appealed.

ISSUE: Under West Virginia products liability law, does the learned intermediary doctrine absolve manufacturers of prescription drugs of the same duty to warn consumers about the risks of their products as other manufacturers?

HOLDING AND DECISION: (Davis, C.J.) No. Under West Virginia products liability law, the learned intermediary doctrine does not absolve manufacturers of prescription drugs of the same duty to warn consumers about the risks of their products as other manufacturers. West Virginia does not recognize the learned intermediary doctrine. The doctrine provides an exception to the general rule imposing a duty on pharmaceutical companies to warn consumers about the risks associated with the drugs they produce, on grounds that the manufacturer's duty to warn consumers about the dangers of its drugs extends only to the prescribing physician, who is the "learned intermediary" between the pharmaceutical company and the consumer, and the physician assumes responsibility for advising individual patients of the risks associated with the drug. While a majority of courts apply the doctrine, it is a slight majority, and the primary justifications advanced for the doctrine are outdated or unpersuasive. They are (1) the

difficulty manufacturers encounter in trying to provide warnings to ultimate users of the drugs; (2) patients' reliance on their treating physician's judgment; (3) the fact that it is physicians who exercise their judgment in selecting appropriate drugs; (4) the belief that physicians are in the best position to provide appropriate warnings to their patients; and (5) the concern that direct warnings to ultimate users would interfere with the doctor/patient relationship. The doctrine dates back to 1925 when these concerns might have been valid, but changes in the drug industry, including the enormous amount of money spent by pharmaceutical companies on advertising directly to consumers, as well as the development of the internet as a common method of dispensing and obtaining prescription information show the means and effectiveness of communication directly with patients. In addition, the relationship between doctor and patient has changed: Informed consent requires a patient-based decision rather than a paternalistic approach, and managed care has reduced the time allotted per patient, so that physicians have less time to inform patients of the risks and benefits of a drug. Interference with the doctor-patient relationship is less of a concern in current context. Furthermore, the Restatement (Third) of Torts, which recognizes the learned intermediary doctrine, includes a general exception to the doctrine in circumstances where the manufacturer knows or should know that a physician will not be in a position to provide an adequate warning. If drug manufacturers are able to provide warnings to consumers under the exceptions provided in the Restatement, they should be able to provide them in general. Finally, it is not unreasonable to require the manufacturers to provide warnings to the ultimate users of their product; it is the companies that benefit financially from sale of their products, and it is the consumer bearing the ultimate risk. Physicians have certain duties and responsibilities regarding their role in providing prescription medications, and manufacturers should also carry some weight. Writ denied.

DISSENT: (Albright, J.) It is unwise to completely abandon the learned intermediary doctrine, because some cases warrant it. The doctrine is most needed where the drugs at issue are not the subject of a massive advertising campaign, and where the physician did in fact assume the role of a "learned intermediary" in advising and recommending that the patient use a particular drug.

CONCURRENCE: (Maynard, J.) The argument of the dissent leads to an unfair result, because consumers

Continued on next page.

are bombarded with advertisements for drugs, and consumers are well educated about the effects of these drugs, and there's no reason why they should be exempt from the general duty to warn that the state places on other manufacturers, putting only the doctors on the hook.

▶ ANALYSIS

The effect of this defense is to shift the focus and ultimate responsibility for any failure to warn about the medication's risks from the manufacturer to the prescribing physician. Courts have typically reasoned that requiring the manufacturer to warn only the prescribing physician is a reasonable way in which to handle prescription medication warnings, in light of the fact that medications are complex and varied in effect, and that the prescribing physician is in a unique position to consider the unique situation of individual patients, and then exercise an individualized medical judgment. In addition, the physician has an independent duty to warn the patient of the risks associated with treatment already. But note that the mere fact that a prescribing physician was warned of the proper use and the risks of a prescription medication does not necessarily shift liability from the manufacturer to the prescribing physician. A warning from the manufacturer to the prescribing physician discharges the manufacturer's duty to warn only if the warning given is "adequate and not misleading." This is a hotly litigated subject.

■■■■

Vassallo v. Baxter Healthcare Corporation

Breast implant recipient (P) v. Manufacturer (D)

Mass Sup. Jud. Ct., 428 Mass. 1, 696 N.E.2d 909 (1998).

NATURE OF CASE: Products liability action.

FACT SUMMARY: Vassallo (P) brought suit seeking recovery of damages for injuries sustained as a result of the rupturing of her silicone breast implants, on the basis that the implants were negligently designed and that the manufacturer negligently failed to provide adequate warnings in breach of the implied warranty of merchantability.

🏛 RULE OF LAW
A defendant is not liable under the implied warranty of merchantability for failure to warn or to provide instructions about risks that were not reasonably foreseeable at the time of sale, or could not have been reasonably discovered through reasonable testing, prior to the marketing of the product.

FACTS: Vassallo (P) underwent breast implant surgery. The implants were manufactured by a company subsequently bought by Baxter Healthcare Corporation (Baxter) (D). When the implants caused Vassallo (P) injuries, she sued Baxter (D), arguing that the implants had been negligently designed, that they were accompanied by negligent product warnings, and that they breached the implied warranty of merchantability. The jury found for Vassallo (P) on the negligence counts, and the intermediate appellate court affirmed. Baxter (D) appealed to the state's supreme court.

ISSUE: Is a defendant liable under the implied warranty of merchantability for failure to warn or to provide instructions about risks that were not reasonably foreseeable at the time of sale, or could not have been reasonably discovered through reasonable testing, prior to the marketing of the product?

HOLDING AND DECISION: (Greaney, J.) No. A defendant is not liable under the implied warranty of merchantability for failure to warn or to provide instructions about risks that were not reasonably foreseeable at the time of sale, or could not have been reasonably discovered through reasonable testing, prior to the marketing of the product. This holding is a revision of this court's law and is in recognition of the clear judicial trend regarding the duty to warn in products liability cases and the principles set forth in the Restatement (Third) of Torts and the Products Liability Restatement. The majority of jurisdictions support this proposition. The rationale behind the principle is that unforeseeable risks arising from foreseeable product use by definition cannot be warned against. A seller is, however, charged with knowledge of what reasonable testing would reveal. A manufacturer will be held to the standard of knowledge of an expert in the appropriate field and will remain subject to a continuing duty to warn (at least purchasers) of risks discovered following the sale of the product at issue. Affirmed.

▌ ANALYSIS

The majority of jurisdictions follow the Restatement of Torts (Second) § 402A comment j rule requiring a warning if the seller has knowledge, or if "by the application of reasonable, developed human skill and foresight should have knowledge, of the danger." Restatement of Torts (Third): Products Liability § 2(c) comment m ratifies this rule and clarifies that the manufacturer has a duty to perform testing prior to marketing a product to discover risks. Furthermore, a seller of the product is also charged with knowledge of the risks as discovered by the reasonable testing.

Quicknotes

STRICT LIABILITY Liability for all injuries proximately caused by a party's conducting of certain inherently dangerous activities without regard to negligence or fault.

WARRANTY OF MERCHANTABILITY An implied promise made by a merchant in a contract for the sale of goods that such goods are suitable for the purpose for which they are purchased.

General Motors Corporation v. Sanchez

Manufacturer (D) v. Decedent's estate (P)

Texas Sup. Ct., 997 S.W.2d 584 (1999).

NATURE OF CASE: Review of damages award for product defect and negligence.

FACT SUMMARY: The estate of Sanchez (P) alleged that General Motors Corp. (GM) (D) was negligent, the transmission on its pickup trucks was defectively designed, and it failed to provide adequate warnings, but GM (D) claimed that Sanchez (P) had been negligent as well.

🏛 **RULE OF LAW**
A consumer has no duty to discover or guard against a product defect, but a consumer's conduct other than the mere failure to discover or guard against a product defect is subject to comparative responsibility.

FACTS: Sanchez (P) was crushed and bled to death when he left his pickup truck running while opening a corral gate and the pickup rolled backward. Sanchez's estate (P) alleged that General Motors Corp. (GM) (D) had defectively designed the transmission on the pickup truck, was negligent, and had failed to provide adequate warnings. The jury found that GM (D) was negligent and awarded actual and punitive damages of $8.5 million. GM (D) claimed that the court had ignored the jury finding that Sanchez (P) was fifty percent responsible for the accident, and that the court should have applied the comparative responsibility statute, and appealed.

ISSUE: Does a consumer have no duty to discover or guard against a product defect, but is a consumer's conduct other than the mere failure to discover or guard against a product defect subject to comparative responsibility?

HOLDING AND DECISION: (Gonzales, J.) Yes. A consumer has no duty to discover or guard against a product defect, but a consumer's conduct other than the mere failure to discover or guard against a product defect is subject to comparative responsibility. Under comparative responsibility a court reduces a claimant's damages recovery by the percentage of responsibility attributed to him by the trier of fact. Sanchez's conduct prior to the accident amounted to conduct other than a failure to discover or guard against a product defect. Sanchez had a responsibility to operate his truck in a safe manner; his actions must be considered under the duty to use ordinary care. There was sufficient evidence to support the jury's verdict that Sanchez (D) breached the duty to use ordinary care and was fifty percent responsible for the accident. The punitive damages award was reversed and remanded for reduction by fifty percent of the actual damages award.

▶ **ANALYSIS**

The Texas statute was revised in 1987. Comparative negligence was replaced by comparative responsibility. The court found that a reasonably prudent driver should know enough to take safety precautions to prevent a runaway car.

■━■

Quicknotes

ACTUAL DAMAGES Measure of damages necessary to compensate victim for actual injuries suffered.

COMPARATIVE NEGLIGENCE Doctrine whereby the court in assessing the appropriate measure of damages compares the relative fault of the parties and reduces the amount of damages to be collected by the plaintiff in proportion to his degree of fault.

DUTY OF CARE A principle of negligence requiring an individual to act in such a manner as to avoid injury to a person to whom he or she owes an obligatory duty.

FAILURE TO WARN The failure of an owner or occupier of land to inform persons present on the property of defects or active operations that may cause injury.

PRODUCT LIABILITY The legal liability of manufacturers and sellers for damages and injuries suffered by buyers, users and even bystanders because of defects in goods purchased.

PUNITIVE DAMAGES Damages exceeding the actual injury suffered for the purposes of punishment, deterrence and comfort to plaintiff.

Jones v. Ryobi, Ltd.

Printing press employee (P) v. Printing press manufacturer (D)

37 F.3d 423 (8th Cir. 1994).

NATURE OF CASE: Appeal from defense motion granted for judgment as a matter of law in negligence and product liability action.

FACT SUMMARY: Jones (P), employed as the operator of a printing press, brought suit against Ryobi, Ltd. (D), its manufacturer, for strict product liability after she injured her hand while operating the modified press.

🏛 RULE OF LAW
If a product has been modified by a third party in a way that makes it unsafe, the seller of the product is relieved of liability even if the modification is foreseeable.

FACTS: Jones (P) was employed at Business Cards Tomorrow (BCT) as the operator of a small printing press. The press operated by passing blank sheets of paper through several moving parts during the course of which an image is imprinted. Jones (P) was required to ensure that the wheels that ejected the freshly printed paper did not streak the image. When BCT purchased the press, it was equipped with a plastic guard that prevented the operator from reaching into the moving parts and a switch that automatically shut off the press if the guard was opened while the press was on. BCT, as was common in the printing industry, had modified the press to save time by removing the guard and disabling the shut-off switch. One day, while Jones (P) was adjusting the eject-wheels, she was startled by a loud noise. She jumped and her hand was crushed in the moving parts. Jones (P) sued Ryobi, Ltd. (D), the manufacturer of the press, and A.B. Dick Corp. (D), the distributor, alleging strict product liability for defective design. Ryobi (D) and A.B. Dick (D) moved for judgment as a matter of law (JAML). The district court granted the motions and Jones (P) appealed.

ISSUE: If a product has been modified by a third party in a way that makes it unsafe, is the seller of the product relieved of liability even if the modification is foreseeable?

HOLDING AND DECISION: (Fagg, J.) Yes. If a product has been modified by a third party in a way that makes it unsafe, the seller of the product is relieved of liability even if the modification is foreseeable. In this case, Jones (P) would have to prove that she was injured as a direct result of a defect that existed when the press was sold to BCT to recover on a theory of strict product liability. Because the press was substantially modified by a third party not related to the manufacturer or distributor, Ryobi (D) or A.B. Dick (D), they cannot be held liable. The fact that BCT encouraged Jones (P) to use the press with the safety features dismantled does not mean that the press was sold with an unreasonably dangerous defect. Jones (P) failed to show that the press was dangerous when used in the condition in which it was sold, as strict product liability law requires. Affirmed.

DISSENT: (Heaney, J.) The district court should not have granted the JAML as there was sufficient conflicting evidence to send the case to a jury. The evidence does not show that the press was safe in the condition in which it was originally sold. Testimony at trial indicated that the safety shut off switch was not "fail-safe." Furthermore, the fact that so many companies removed the safety guards is evidence that the press was incapable of operating efficiently according to industry standards.

▶ ANALYSIS

Contrary to the holding in this case, many courts have found that if a modification is foreseeable, and the manufacturer knows its products are being modified, the manufacturer cannot escape liability. Instead, the manufacturer has a duty to consider such modifications when designing the product. At the very least, the dissent was probably correct in stating that there was sufficient evidence on the safety of the press in its original condition to present to a jury.

━■━

Quicknotes

DEFECTIVE DESIGN A defect in a product manufactured according to the intended design, which in itself causes a risk of harm to users.

NEGLIGENCE Conduct falling below the standard of care that a reasonable person would demonstrate under similar conditions.

PRODUCT LIABILITY The legal liability of manufacturers and sellers for damages and injuries suffered by buyers, users and even bystanders because of defects in goods purchased.

STRICT LIABILITY Liability for all injuries proximately caused by a party's conducting of certain inherently dangerous activities without regard to negligence or fault.

━■━

Liriano v. Hobart Corp.

Injured user (P) v. Manufacturer (D)

N.Y. Ct. App., 92 N.Y.2d 232, 700 N.E.2d 303 (1998).

NATURE OF CASE: Certified question in products liability suit.

FACT SUMMARY: Liriano (P) was injured when he used a saw manufactured by Hobart Corp. (D) and later alleged that Hobart (D) had failed to adequately warn of dangers associated with the saw's use.

RULE OF LAW
A manufacturer may be liable for failure to warn in cases where the substantial modification defense would preclude liability on a design defect theory.

FACTS: Liriano (P) lost his right hand and forearm when using a meat grinder at a supermarket where he was employed. The supermarket had removed the safety guard from the meat grinder and there was no warning on the grinder about the danger of using it without a guard. Liriano (P) sued the manufacturer, Hobart Corp. (D), under both negligence and strict products liability for defective product design and failure to warn. The jury found Hobart (D) 5 percent liable and the supermarket 95 percent liable. Hobart (D) appealed, claiming that the failure-to-warn claims were barred because a manufacturer was not liable for injuries caused by substantial alterations to the product by a third party that rendered the product defective or unsafe.

ISSUE: May a manufacturer be liable for failure to warn in cases where the substantial modification defense would preclude liability on a design defect theory?

HOLDING AND DECISION: (Ciparick, J.) Yes. A manufacturer may be liable for failure to warn in cases where the substantial modification defense would preclude liability on a design defect theory. Just as a manufacturer may be liable for failing to warn against the foreseeable misuse of its product, it may also be liable for failure to warn of foreseeable alteration of its product. It is for the jury to decide whether a danger was open and obvious based on the facts of the case.

ANALYSIS

The plaintiff in this case was seventeen years old and had recently arrived in the United States. There is an exception to the duty to warn for bulk suppliers. If one company supplies a product in bulk to a large enterprise where it will be used by many workers, no direct warnings are necessary.

Quicknotes

COMPARATIVE NEGLIGENCE Doctrine whereby the court in assessing the appropriate measure of damages compares the relative fault of the parties and reduces the amount of damages to be collected by the plaintiff in proportion to his degree of fault.

DEFECTIVE DESIGN A product that is manufactured in accordance with a particular design; however, such design is inherently flawed so that it presents an unreasonable risk of injury.

DEFECTIVE PRODUCTS Products that contain a weakness or flaw in manufacture that is responsible for damages or injuries.

FAILURE TO WARN The failure of an owner or occupier of land to inform persons present on the property of defects or active operations that may cause injury.

Royer v. Catholic Medical Center

Patient (P) v. Hospital (D)

N.H. Sup. Ct., 741 A.2d 74 (1999).

NATURE OF CASE: Appeal from dismissal of products liability case.

FACT SUMMARY: Royer (P) alleged that Catholic Medical Center (CMC) (D) was liable because the prosthesis the doctors at CMC (D) had implanted in his knee was defective.

RULE OF LAW

Where a health care provider supplies a prosthetic device to be implanted into a patient, the health care provider is not engaged in the business of selling prostheses for purposes of strict products liability.

FACTS: Royer (P) had his knee replaced at CMC (D). The prosthesis was defective and a second operation was necessary to replace it. Royer (P) sued CMC (D) in strict liability for allegedly selling a defectively designed prosthesis that was in an unreasonably dangerous condition. CMC (D) claimed that it was not a seller of goods for purposes of strict products liability. The trial court granted CMC's (D) motion to dismiss the complaint. Royer (P) appealed.

ISSUE: Where a health care provider supplies a prosthetic device to be implanted into a patient, is the health care provider engaged in the business of selling prostheses for purposes of strict products liability?

HOLDING AND DECISION: (Brock, C.J.) No. Where a health care provider supplies a prosthetic device to be implanted into a patient, the health care provider is not engaged in the business of selling prostheses for purposes of strict products liability. Health care providers primarily render services; the provision of a prosthetic device is merely incidental to that service. Affirmed.

ANALYSIS

The majority of jurisdictions have similar decisions. Patients do not enter hospitals for the purpose of buying prosthetics. Prosthetics are supplied along with many other medical services that hospitals provide.

Quicknotes

DEFECTIVE DESIGN A product that is manufactured in accordance with a particular design; however, such design is inherently flawed so that it presents an unreasonable risk of injury.

NEGLIGENCE Conduct falling below the standard of care that a reasonable person would demonstrate under similar conditions.

PRODUCT LIABILITY The legal liability of manufacturers and sellers for damages and injuries suffered by buyers, users and even bystanders because of defects in goods purchased.

STRICT LIABILITY Liability for all injuries proximately caused by a party's conducting of certain inherently dangerous activities without regard to negligence or fault.

East River Steamship Corp. v. Transamerica Delaval Inc.

Tanker company (P) v. Turbine manufacturer (D)

476 U.S. 858, (1986).

NATURE OF CASE: Appeal from summary judgment denying damages for economic loss.

FACT SUMMARY: In East River Steamship Corp.'s (East River) (P) action against Transamerica Delaval Inc. (Delaval) (D), East River (P) contended that Delaval (D) was liable for damages for the malfunction of a high-pressure turbine aboard a supertanker which injured only the turbine itself and caused purely economic loss.

RULE OF LAW

A manufacturer in a commercial relationship has no duty under either negligence or a strict products liability theory to prevent a product from injuring itself.

FACTS: Transamerica Delaval Inc. (Delaval) (D) made turbines for supertankers chartered by East River Steamship Corp. (East River) (P). When one of East River's (P) tankers made its maiden voyage, the high-pressure turbine malfunctioned, but the ship was able to get to port. Inspection showed that an essential ring had disintegrated, causing additional damage to other parts of the turbine. East River's (P) complaint against Delaval (D) set forth tort damage claims for the cost of repairing the ship and for income lost while the ship was out of service. The district court granted Delaval (D) summary judgment, and the court of appeals affirmed. East River (P) appealed.

ISSUE: Does a manufacturer in a commercial relationship have a duty under either a negligence or strict products liability theory to prevent a product from injuring itself?

HOLDING AND DECISION: (Blackmun, J.) No. A manufacturer in a commercial relationship has no duty under either a negligence or strict products liability theory to prevent a product from injuring itself. Even when the harm to the product itself occurs through an abrupt, accident-like event, the resulting loss due to repair costs, decreased value, and lost profits is essentially the failure of the purchaser to receive the benefit of its bargain— traditionally the core concern of contract law. The increased cost to the public that would result from holding a manufacturer liable in tort for injury to the product itself is not justified. Damage to the product itself is most naturally understood as a warranty claim. Here, contract law, and the law of warranty in particular, is well suited to compensate the parties because the parties may set the terms of their own agreements. There is no great disparity in the bargaining power between East River (P) and

Delaval (D), and, thus, there is no reason to intrude into the parties' allocation of risks. Even assuming Delaval (D) was negligent, it owed no duty under a products liability theory based on negligence to avoid causing purely economic loss. Thus, whether stated in negligence or strict liability, no products liability claim lies when the only injury claimed is economic loss. Affirmed.

ANALYSIS

As can be seen from the above case, courts tend to use a comparative approach to defenses in tort cases. A different outcome may occur when a case is brought under the Uniform Commercial Code. The Code nowhere contemplates shared responsibility. Rather, it speaks in terms of proximate cause, suggesting that once a buyer discovers a defect or should reasonably have discovered it, there can no longer be reasonable reliance on the warranty, and thus no recovery.

◼▬◼

Quicknotes

NEGLIGENCE Conduct falling below the standard of care that a reasonable person would demonstrate under similar conditions.

PRODUCT LIABILITY The legal liability of manufacturers and sellers for damages and injuries suffered by buyers, users and even bystanders because of defects in goods purchased.

STRICT LIABILITY Liability for all injuries proximately caused by a party's conducting of certain inherently dangerous activities without regard to negligence or fault.

◼▬◼

Quick Reference Rules of Law

Boomer v. Atlantic Cement Co.

Property owner (P) v. Cement plant (D)

N.Y. Ct. App., 26 N.Y.2d 219, 257 N.E.2d 870 (1970).

NATURE OF CASE: Appeal from denial of plaintiff's injunction.

FACT SUMMARY: Dirt, smoke, and vibrations issuing from a cement factory interfered with the use and enjoyment of neighboring property.

🏛 **RULE OF LAW**
In an action to abate a nuisance, a court may award permanent damages in lieu of an injunction where there is a marked disparity in economic consequences between the effect of an injunction and the effect of the nuisance.

FACTS: Neighboring landowners were damaged by dirt, smoke, and vibrations emanating from a factory owned by Atlantic Cement Co. (D). The total permanent damage caused by the factory to these landowners was stipulated to be $185,000. The owners of Atlantic Cement Co. (D) had invested more than 45 million dollars in the factory, which employed over 300 people. It was agreed at trial that if the court were to issue an injunction, the factory would have to close down.

ISSUE: In an action to abate a nuisance, may a court award damages in lieu of an injunction if there is a marked disparity in economic consequences between the effect of an injunction and the effect of the nuisance?

HOLDING AND DECISION: (Bergan, J.) Yes. Where the effect of an injunction would be grossly disproportionate to the consequences of allowing the nuisance to continue, damages may be awarded in lieu of an injunction. In this case, an award of damages seems to be fair, because the landowners can be fully compensated for their injuries, while an injunction would close down the factory completely. The only other alternative would be to grant the injunction but to postpone its effect to a future date, to give Atlantic Cement Co. (D) an opportunity to eliminate the nuisance. This alternative, however, is unworkable, because the cement company is unlikely to be able to develop suitable techniques in a short enough time. Such technical research and development is beyond the resources of Atlantic Cement Co. (D). However, the risk of having to pay permanent damages not only to these landowners, but to others as well, will spur Atlantic Cement Co. (D) to use its best efforts to minimize the nuisance as quickly as technical advances in the industry permit. Therefore, the circumstances here justify the denial of an injunction if Atlantic Cement Co. (D) pays permanent damages to Boomer (P) and the other property owners. Reversed and remanded to grant injunction unless and until permanent damages paid.

DISSENT: (Jasen, J.) The injunction should issue, because to award damages is to license a continuation of a wrong. The court, in effect, is telling defendants that they may continue to pollute the air if they pay a fee. Moreover, once the damages are paid, a polluter has no incentive to alleviate the disastrous consequences of his enterprise.

▶ **ANALYSIS**

The arguments advanced by the majority and by the dissenting justices are typical examples of the considerations involved in "balancing the equities" in granting or denying an injunction. The majority opinion correctly considered the public interest in allowing the cement company to continue its operations; but as the minority opinion recognizes, there was no weighing of the public interest in clean air in this case. The outcome in cases of this type usually depends upon the economic importance of the industry to the community in terms of number of people employed and the dependence of the community on the existence of the particular plant.

━■━■

Quicknotes

INJUNCTION A court order requiring a person to do or prohibiting that person from doing a specific act.

NUISANCE An unlawful use of property that interferes with the lawful use of another's property.

━■━■

State of Rhode Island v. Lead Industries Association, Inc.

State (P) v. Paint manufacturers (D)

R.I. Sup. Ct., 951 A.2d 428 (2008).

NATURE OF CASE: Appeal of denial of motion to dismiss.

FACT SUMMARY: The attorney general of the state of Rhode Island filed a public nuisance action against former lead paint manufacturers. The trial court denied the manufacturers' motion to dismiss.

🏛 RULE OF LAW
A public nuisance action cannot proceed against manufacturers of a product where there is no unreasonable interference with a right common to the general public, and the manufacturers have no control over the product complained about at the time it caused harm.

FACTS: The Rhode Island Attorney General (P) filed a public nuisance action against former paint manufacturers (D) whose products contained lead. The manufacturers (D) moved to dismiss the action, and the trial court denied the motion.

ISSUE: Can a public nuisance action proceed against manufacturers of a product where there is no unreasonable interference with a right common to the general public, and the manufacturers have no control over the product complained about at the time it caused harm?

HOLDING AND DECISION: (Williams, C.J.) No. A public nuisance action cannot proceed against manufacturers of a product where there is no unreasonable interference with a right common to the general public, and the manufacturers have no control over the product complained about at the time it caused harm. A public nuisance is an unreasonable interference with a right common to the general public. There are three elements to a public nuisance lawsuit: (1) an unreasonable interference; (2) with a right common to the general public; (3) by a person or people with control over the instrumentality alleged to have created the nuisance when the damage occurred. With respect to the first element, the interference must deprive all members of the community of a right to some resource to which they otherwise are entitled. The term "public right" implies those indivisible resources shared by the public at large, such as air, water, or public rights of way. The right of an individual child to not be poisoned by lead paint is a nonpublic right. But even if the state (P) adequately alleged an interference with a public right, the state (P) also fails to satisfy the third element by alleging any facts that support a conclusion that the manufacturers (D) were in control of the lead pigment at the time it harmed Rhode Island children. Control at the time

the damage occurs is critical in public nuisance cases because the principal remedy for the harm caused is abatement. This is not to say that Rhode Islanders have no remedy against the manufacturers (D). An injunction requiring abatement or private causes of action can be brought, based on product liability. Whereas public nuisance focuses on the abatement of annoying or bothersome activities, products liability law is designed specifically to hold manufacturers liable for harmful products that the manufacturers have distributed. Reversed.

▶ ANALYSIS

The court held that the "control" requirement was related to the ability to prevent harm and the defendant's conduct in failing to do so, and "public right" was defined as an "indivisible resource" such as air, land or water, giving it a defined and limited scope. These limitations on common-law public nuisance make public nuisance inapplicable to "stream of commerce" cases, which must be governed by product liability law. Because the state tried to broaden the concept of public nuisance to include products in the stream of commerce, the court considered it a completely new cause of action, one that would dramatically expand public nuisance concepts in a way that is inconsistent with the incremental growth of the common law and the role of the legislature to determine matters of broad public policy.

Quicknotes

PUBLIC NUISANCE An activity that unreasonably interferes with a right common to the overall public.

Damages and Insurance

Quick Reference Rules of Law

Seffert v. Los Angeles Transit Lines

Bus rider (P) v. Bus company (D)

Cal. Sup. Ct., 56 Cal. 2d 498, 364 P.2d 337 (1961).

NATURE OF CASE: Appeal from award of damages to plaintiff.

FACT SUMMARY: The doors of a Los Angeles Transit Lines (D) bus closed on Seffert (P) as she was attempting to board. The bus then dragged Seffert (P) for some distance before she was thrown onto the pavement.

RULE OF LAW
An appellate court should not reduce the amount of a jury verdict unless it is so large as to suggest that the jurors were motivated by passion, prejudice, or corruption.

FACTS: Seffert (P) was boarding a Los Angeles Transit Lines (Transit Lines) (D) bus when the doors suddenly closed, catching her right hand and left foot. The bus then dragged Seffert (P) for some distance until she was thrown to the pavement. As a result of the incident, Seffert (P) sustained severe injuries. She underwent nine operations, several of them extremely uncomfortable ones, and was advised that the need to amputate her left foot would continue to be a possibility. Skin grafts were performed, but Seffert's (P) left heel remained severely disfigured and was marred by an open ulcer that drained continuously. Doctors were forced to sever certain nerves and tie off various blood vessels, and placed Seffert (P) in an awkward cast for a month so that skin from her thigh could be grafted to her foot. Despite eight months in hospitals and treatment centers, Seffert (P) remained permanently crippled and faced the prospect of continuous suffering and medical care for the rest of her life. At the time of the accident she had been a 42-year-old file clerk, supporting herself on a salary of $375 per month. Although she eventually returned to work, Seffert (P) claimed past and future medical bills and lost earnings totalling $53,903.75. Her counsel argued that, in addition to these pecuniary losses, Seffert (P) should be able to recover $100 in pain and suffering for each of the 660 days between the accident and the trial as well as an additional $2,000 in pain and suffering for each of the 34 years which Seffert (P) could be expected to live. Although the Transit Lines (D) disputed both its liability and Seffert's (P) computation of damages, the jury awarded Seffert (P) $187,903.75, the precise amount which she had sought. The judge denied Transit Lines' (D) motion for a new trial but the company (D) appealed, citing various legal errors but arguing chiefly that the damages awarded by the jury were excessive.

ISSUE: Should a damage award be reduced by an appellate court merely because it seems unusually large?

HOLDING AND DECISION: (Peters, J.) No. An appellate court should not reduce the amount of a jury verdict unless it is so large as to suggest that the jurors were motivated by passion, prejudice, or corruption. In this case, the jury heard the witnesses and had the opportunity to observe Seffert's (P) condition. The amount awarded by the jury was upheld by the trial judge, who was also able to see Seffert (P). Although the verdict in this case is larger than has been awarded in others, each case clearly must be evaluated on its own merits. Considering Seffert's (P) pain and anguish, her embarrassment, humiliation, and other emotional suffering, the fact that she remains crippled and will be disfigured for life, the fear of future amputation, and the certainty of life-long medical care, it cannot be said that Seffert's (P) recovery is shocking, excessive, or likely to be the result of passion, prejudice, or corruption. Although it was arguably improper for Seffert's (P) counsel to have resorted to a mathematical formula in arguing the amount of damages owed for pain and suffering, counsel for the Transit Lines (D) offered no objection to this practice and in fact presented a similar argument himself. Affirmed.

DISSENT: (Traynor, J.) The $134,000 awarded for pain and suffering is so excessive as to create the suspicion that the jury was motivated by passion or prejudice. Evidently, the jury accepted Seffert's (P) own assessment of her damages without exercising any restraint or common sense of its own. It is unusual for an amount exceeding the victim's pecuniary losses to be awarded for pain and suffering. In fact, the award in this case is greater than any award ever sustained in this state in a case of this type. It is necessary for an appellate court to take due regard for the effect which cases decided today will have on future litigation. Obviously, the excessive award in this case was the result of the mathematical formula approach adopted by Seffert's (P) counsel in his address to the jury. Several states have ruled that arguments of this type are improper. Although the mathematical approach provides some standard for jurors to seize upon, it is unlikely to be an accurate one. Unfortunately, such pure conjecture may impress the jury unduly, providing as it does a method by which an award may be readily calculated. The argument employed by Seffert's (P) counsel was misleading and improper, and should not be tolerated merely because the Transit Lines' (D) attorney used a similar argument and failed to object to that of his adversary. Therefore, the case should be remanded for a new trial on the issue of damages.

Continued on next page.

▶ *ANALYSIS*

Justice Traynor, in reaching the conclusion that the $187,903.75 awarded to Seffert (P) was excessive, alluded to the need to protect the interests of future litigants. No doubt Traynor was anticipating the advent of the astronomically high judgments that were awarded in the later 1960s and 1970s. Some have argued vociferously that these multimillion dollar judgments are unwarranted and unreasonable. However, they can be justified by citing mounting costs of medical care, the costs and attorney fees involved in protracted personal injuries litigation, and the notion that no amount of money can ever really compensate a person for physical agony, mental anguish, and the consequences of permanent disfigurement.

Quicknotes

DAMAGES Monetary compensation that may be awarded by the court to a party who has sustained injury or loss to his or her person, property or rights due to another party's unlawful act, omission or negligence.

McDougald v. Garber

Comatose patient (P) v. Physician (D)

N.Y. Ct. App., 73 N.Y.2d 246, 536 N.E.2d 372 (1989).

NATURE OF CASE: Review of award of damages for medical malpractice.

FACT SUMMARY: The trial court, over Garber's (D) objections in a malpractice action, held that an ability to experience suffering was not a condition precedent to obtaining pain and suffering damages, and that loss of the pleasures of life was a separate category of recovery.

🏛 RULE OF LAW
An ability to experience suffering is a condition precedent to pain and suffering damages, and loss of the pleasures of life is not a separate category of recovery.

FACTS: McDougald (P) was rendered permanently comatose due to medical malpractice. At trial, damages were requested on her behalf consisting of actual expenses, pain and suffering, and loss of enjoyment of life. The trial court rejected the contention of Garber (D) that ability to experience suffering was a condition precedent to recovering pain and suffering damages, and that loss of enjoyment of life was not a separate category of damages from pain and suffering. A jury returned a verdict of $4.5 million, which the court remitted to $2 million. The state court of appeals granted review, Garber (D) arguing that to award such damages to a comatose patient who lacked the ability to experience suffering was reversible error.

ISSUE: Is an ability to experience suffering a condition precedent to being awarded pain and suffering damages, and is loss of the pleasures of life not a separate category of recovery?

HOLDING AND DECISION: (Wachtler, C.J.) Yes. An ability to experience suffering is a condition precedent to pain and suffering damages, and loss of the pleasures of life is not a separate category of recovery. Money can never truly ameliorate suffering, but the law indulges in the fiction that it can, simply because no better source of compensation can be provided by the law. However, this rationale becomes imperative when a victim cannot be aware of either his suffering or compensation therefor. Simply put, such damages cannot compensate, and compensation is the purpose of the tort system. Consequently, for a person to be entitled to pain and suffering damages, he must be aware of his condition. As to the issue of loss of enjoyment of life, the bottom line is that such a loss can be placed within the concept of suffering. To contend the contrary places an unduly restrictive definition upon "suffering." This court is not convinced that allowing a separate category of recovery in this area will result in greater accuracy of awards; in fact, it could lead to confusion and duplicative awards. Therefore, loss of enjoyment of life will not be recognized as a separate category of damages from pain and suffering. New trial ordered on nonpecuniary damages.

DISSENT: (Titone, J.) Loss of enjoyment of life is analytically distinguishable from pain and suffering. Further, no ability to comprehend such loss should be required for such damages to be awarded.

▌ANALYSIS

Pain and suffering, called "general" damages, have been the source of much debate in the legal community. Some commentators have called for their abolition, stating that, at the societal level, they are nothing more than a device for wealth distribution and have nothing to do with compensation. Most accept the need for such damages, however, for reasons cited in the present case. The difficulty with the majority view is that a wrongdoer pays less compensation when his actions turn the victim into a "vegetable" than had the victim retained consciousness.

■═■

Quicknotes

CONDITION PRECEDENT The happening of an uncertain occurrence, which is necessary before a particular right or interest may be obtained or an action performed.

MEDICAL MALPRACTICE Conduct on the part of a doctor falling below that demonstrated by other doctors of ordinary skill and competency under the circumstances, resulting in damages.

■═■

Mathias v. Accor Economy Lodging, Inc.

Bedbug-bitten individual (P) v. Motel operator (D)

347 F.3d 672 (7th Cir. 2003).

NATURE OF CASE: Appeal from punitive damages award.

FACT SUMMARY: Accor Economy Lodging, Inc. (Accor) (D) was aware its Motel was infested with bedbugs, but it continued to rent rooms to guests. Guests bitten by bedbugs sought compensatory as well as punitive damages for Accor's (D) conduct.

🏛 RULE OF LAW
(1) Punitive damages are permitted where a defendant's conduct has been willful and wanton.
(2) Punitive damages should be proportional to the wrongfulness of defendant's actions.

FACTS: Accor Economy Lodging, Inc. (Accor) (D) owned and operated a "Motel 6" chain and a "Red Roof Inn" (the Motel). In 1998, the Motel's exterminator informed the manager of a bedbug infestation in several rooms. The exterminator offered to spray each room for $500 total, but the Motel refused. In 1999, the exterminator was again hired to spray just one affected room instead of the entire building. By 2000, the manager noticed an increase in room refunds and reports of ticks and bugs in rooms. One guest was moved three times with bugs in each room. The Motel conceded to its exterminator it had a major problem but would not close the motel for a thorough spray. It flagged rooms "Do not rent until treated" but the rooms were often rented anyway. The Motel desk clerks were told to inform inquiring guests the bugs were "ticks." Plaintiffs, guests who had been bitten by bedbugs, brought suit, claiming that Accor (D) was guilty of wanton and willful conduct that would support compensatory and punitive damages. Accor (D) asserted that, if anything, it had merely been negligent, so that punitive damages were inappropriate. The jury awarded compensatory damages of about $5,000 and each plaintiff received $186,000 in punitive damages. Accor (D) appealed, arguing that the punitive damages award was unwarranted and excessive. The court of appeals granted review.

ISSUE:
(1) Are punitive damages permitted where a defendant's conduct has been willful and wanton?
(2) Should punitive damages be proportional to the wrongfulness of defendant's actions?

HOLDING AND DECISION: (Posner, J.)
(1) Yes. Punitive damages are permitted where a defendant's conduct has been willful and wanton. It was amply shown that Accor (D) recklessly and unjustifiably failed to avoid a known risk. Its failure either to warn guests or to take effective measures to eliminate the bedbugs amounted to fraud and probably to battery as well. This amounted to "willful and wanton" conduct, so that an award of punitive damages was permitted.

(2) Yes. Punitive damages should be proportional to the wrongfulness of defendant's actions. [Federal constitutional cases suggest "guideposts" for punitive damages awards. Those guideposts require the trial judges to consider a given award in light of the reasons the punitive damages were awarded.] The term "punitive damages" implies punishment, and general penal principles are applicable: generally, the punishment should fit the crime; the defendant should have reasonable notice of the sanction for unlawful acts, and sanctions should be based on the wrong done. However, what follows from these general principles is that there should be reasonably clear standards for determining punitive damages for particular wrongs. Punitive damages may provide civil redress for minor criminal infractions. For example, a civil fine for the tort of battery might be a more appropriate deterrent for the minor criminal assault of deliberately spitting in someone's face, especially where compensatory damages might be slight. Accor (D) may have profited from its continued refusal to address the infestation and calling the bedbugs "ticks." Punitive damages here limit the defendant's ability to avoid prosecution by hiding the misconduct through the payment of nominal compensatory damages. The jury cannot award punitive damages based solely on defendant's ability to pay because that would be discriminatory. The net worth of Accor (D) is relevant to the extent it could mount a heavy defense and increase plaintiffs' expenses. The award cannot be considered excessive although it is arbitrary. With no guidelines attaching specific amounts to certain behaviors, it is bound to be arbitrary. The judicial function is to police a range, not a point. Although the parties failed to present evidence concerning the regulatory or criminal penalties to which Accor (D) exposed itself through its conduct, the court takes judicial notice that the deliberate exposure of hotel guests to the health risks created by insect infestations exposes the hotel's owner to sanctions under state and municipal law that in the aggregate are comparable in severity to the punitive damages awarded. Affirmed.

Continued on next page.

▶ ANALYSIS

Juries can, and do, consider a defendant's net worth when awarding punitive damages. If the intent is to deter similar conduct, the net worth becomes relevant when deciding the deterrence amount. Some corporations or wealthy individuals might not be deterred from misconduct if the punitive damages were only a negligible percentage of the tortfeasor's worth. The punitive damages must, however, be related to the extent of the misconduct. Juries across jurisdictions could award massive amounts in one case or nothing in the next case for the same conduct if guidelines requiring a consideration of the wrongfulness were not in place.

Quicknotes

PUNITIVE DAMAGES Damages exceeding the actual injury suffered for the purposes of punishment of the defendant, deterrence of the wrongful behavior or comfort to the plaintiff.

WANTON AND RECKLESS Unlawful intentional or reckless conduct without regard to the consequences.

State Farm Mutual Automobile Insurance Co. v. Campbell

Insurer (D) v. Insured (P)

538 U.S. 408 (2003).

NATURE OF CASE: Certiorari review of damages awarded in a bad faith, fraud, and intentional infliction of emotional distress action.

FACT SUMMARY: Campbell (P) sued State Farm Mutual Automobile Insurance Co. (State Farm) (D), his automobile insurer, for bad faith, fraud, and intentional infliction of emotional distress action when State Farm (D) refused to settle a claim brought against Campbell (P) by Ospital's estate and by Slusher.

RULE OF LAW

In determining the validity of a punitive damage award, consideration is given to the degree of reprehensibility of the defendant's misconduct, the disparity between the actual or potential harm suffered by the plaintiff and the punitive damages award, and the difference between the punitive damages awarded by the jury and the civil penalties authorized or imposed in comparable cases.

FACTS: Campbell (P) caused a collision that killed Ospital and left Slusher permanently disabled. Ospital's estate and Slusher sued Campbell (P) for wrongful death and in tort. Campbell's (P) insurance company, State Farm Mutual Automobile Insurance Co. (State Farm) (D) refused to settle with Ospital and Slusher even though Ospital and Slusher agreed to settle for the policy limit of $25,000 each. State Farm (D) assured Campbell (P) State Farm (D) would represent Campbell's (P) interests, Campbell's (P) assets were safe and that Campbell (P) did not need to procure separate counsel. A jury found Campbell (P) to be at fault and awarded $185,849 to Ospital and Slusher. Initially, State Farm (D) refused to cover the $135,849 in excess liability and refused to post a bond so Campbell (P) could appeal. State Farm (D) told Campbell (P) that he may as well put a for sale sign on his house. Campbell (P) obtained his own attorney, filed his appeal and, in the meantime, agreed to let Slusher and Ospital's attorney represent him (P) in a case against State Farm (D) for bad faith, fraud, and intentional infliction of emotional distress. In exchange, Slusher and Ospital agreed not to seek satisfaction from Campbell (P), but would play a central role in the bad faith action, including receiving 90 percent of any verdict against State Farm (D). The appeals court denied Campbell's (P) appeal in the wrongful death and tort actions and State Farm (D) paid the entire judgment, including the amounts in excess of the policy limits. Despite State Farm's (D) payment, Campbell (P) filed suit against State Farm (D) alleging bad faith, fraud, and intentional infliction of emotional distress. The trial court found

in favor of Campbell (P) and awarded him $2.6 million in compensatory damages and $145 million in punitive damages. The award was subsequently reduced to $1 million and $25 million, respectively. The appeals court affirmed the $1 million and reinstated the $145 million in punitive damages. The U.S. Supreme Court granted certiorari.

ISSUE: Is an award of $145 million in punitive damages, where full compensatory damages are $1 million, excessive and in violation of the Due Process Clause?

HOLDING AND DECISION: (Kennedy, J.) Yes. An award of $145 million in punitive damages, where full compensatory damages are $1 million, is excessive and in violation of the Due Process Clause because the reprehensibility of State Farm's (D) misconduct could have been punished in a more modest way and still have satisfied state objectives. The disparity between the actual or potential harm suffered by Campbell (P) and the punitive damages awarded was significant, and the difference between the punitive damages awarded by the jury and the civil penalties authorized or imposed in comparable cases was great. Although states have discretion over the amount of punitive damages allowed, there are constitutional limitations on these awards. The imposition of grossly excessive or arbitrary punishments on a tortfeasor is prohibited because of fundamental notions of fairness. Moreover, because defendants subjected to punitive damages in civil cases do not have the same protections applicable in criminal proceedings, such awards pose an acute danger of arbitrary deprivation of property. In the present case, it was erroneous for the $145 million to be reinstated. Although State Farm's (D) handling of the claims against Campbell (P) was reprehensible, in that they would probably get a judgment over the policy limits, but still went to trial and then told Campbell (D) to sell his house, a more modest punishment for these actions could have satisfied the state's legitimate objectives. Instead, this case was used to expose State Farm's (D) perceived nationwide deficiencies, and a state does not have a legitimate concern in imposing punitive damages to punish a defendant for unlawful acts committed outside the state's jurisdiction. A state cannot punish a defendant for conduct that may have been lawful where it occurred. Lawful out-of-state conduct may be probative when it demonstrates the deliberateness and culpability of the defendant's action in the state where it is tortuous, but that conduct must have a nexus to the specific harm suffered by the plaintiff. Moreover, the courts

Continued on next page.

erred in awarding punitive damages to punish and deter conduct that bore no relation to Campbell's (P) harm. Due process does not permit courts to adjudicate the merits of other parties' hypothetical claims against a defendant. Furthermore, the disparity between the actual or potential harm suffered by Campbell (P) and the punitive damages award is much too large to be valid. Few awards exceeding a single-digit ratio between punitive and compensatory damages will satisfy due process. Usually an award of no more than four times the amount of compensatory damages is the maximum. The ratio in the present case is 145 to 1. The measure of punishment in this case was neither reasonable nor proportionate to the amount of harm to Campbell (P) and to the general damages recovered. The harm Campbell (P) suffered was minor economic damage and not physical, and the excess verdict was paid before the complaint was filed. Lastly, the disparity between the punitive damages award and the civil penalties authorized or imposed in comparable cases is great. The civil sanction is a $10,000 fine for an act of fraud. Reversed and remanded.

DISSENT: (Scalia, J.) The Due Process Clause provides no substantive protections against excessive or unreasonable awards of punitive damages.

DISSENT: (Ginsburg, J.) Punitive damage issues are traditionally within the states' domain until legislators initiate systemwide change.

▶ **ANALYSIS**

In subsequent cases citing this case, the Court has limited punitive damages, as a matter of due process, to a maximum 1:1 ratio on a classwide basis—regardless of the size of any individual class member's claim. See for example *Exxon Shipping Co., et al. v. Baker, et al.*, 554 U.S. 471 (2008), where, following a jury trial, the district court entered judgment for respondents in the amount of $507.5 million in compensatory damages and $5 billion in punitive damages arising from the 1989 Exxon Valdez oil spill. The Ninth Circuit later remitted the punitive damages award to $2.5 billion and the petitioners appealed. The Supreme Court held that a 1:1 ratio represented the "upper limit" as a matter of federal maritime law, and vacated the punitive damages award. The Court arrived at this conclusion after thoroughly surveying and considering the law in several states, academic studies that have documented the frequency and amounts of punitive damages verdicts, and its own decision in State Farm.

■══■

Quicknotes

BAD FAITH Conduct that is intentionally misleading or deceptive.

DUE PROCESS CLAUSE Clauses, found in the Fifth and Fourteenth Amendments to the United States Constitu-

tion, providing that no person shall be deprived of "life, liberty, or property, without due process of law."

FRAUD A false representation of facts with the intent that another will rely on the misrepresentation to his detriment.

INTENTIONAL INFLICTION OF EMOTIONAL DISTRESS Intentional and extreme behavior on the part of the wrongdoer with the intent to cause the victim to suffer from severe emotional distress, or behavior performed with reckless indifference, resulting in the victim's suffering from severe emotional distress.

PUNITIVE DAMAGES Damages exceeding the actual injury suffered for the purposes of punishment, deterrence and comfort to plaintiff.

■══■

Kenney v. Liston

Intoxicated motorist (D) v. Injured motorist (P)

W. Va. Sup. Ct., 760 S.E.2d 434 (2014).

NATURE OF CASE: Appeal from award of compensatory damages in action based on injuries sustained in a motor vehicle accident.

FACT SUMMARY: Kenney (D), who admitted he severely injured Liston (P) in a car crash as a result of driving while intoxicated, contended that the amount of compensatory damages for the medical bills incurred by Liston (P) should be the amount actually paid by him or his insurance company as a result of discounts and write-offs pre-negotiated with healthcare providers, and that the collateral sources rule should not apply to the difference between the amounts billed and the amounts paid.

RULE OF LAW

Where an injured individual's health care provider agrees to reduce, discount, or write off a portion of the individual's medical bill, the collateral source rule permits the person to recover the entire reasonable value of the medical services necessarily required by the injury, so that the tortfeasor who caused the injuries is not entitled to receive the benefit of the reduced, discounted, or written-off amount.

FACTS: Kenney (D) severely injured Liston (P) in a car crash as a result of driving while intoxicated. Liston (P) brought suit for damages. Because Kenney (D) admitted his culpability, the only issue at trial was the determination of damages. Liston (P) had incurred medical bills in excess of $70,000. Kenney (D) pointed out that only a portion of each bill had been paid by Liston (P) or his insurance company, since the medical providers and the insurance company had pre-negotiated discounts, reductions, or downward adjustments for the medical services, and the unpaid portions of the medical bills were "written off" by the providers. Accordingly, Kenney (D) asserted that Liston's (P) damages should be limited to the amounts actually paid by Liston (P) and amounts paid on his behalf by any collateral source, such as his health insurance carrier. Kenney (D) also contended that since the full bills were neither paid nor actually incurred by Liston (P) or his health insurance carrier, Liston (P) should not be allowed to introduce evidence of those written-off amounts at trial. The trial court rejected Kenney's (D) argument, concluding that the discounts or write-offs were a collateral source to Liston (P). The trial court reasoned that under the collateral source rule, Liston (P) was entitled to recover damages for the value of any reasonable and necessary medical services he received, whether such services were rendered gratuitously or paid for by another. The jury awarded

Liston (P) over $70,000 for his medical expenses. Kenney (D) appealed, and the state's highest court granted review.

ISSUE: Where an injured individual's health care provider agrees to reduce, discount, or write off a portion of the individual's medical bill, does the collateral source rule permit the person to recover the entire reasonable value of the medical services necessarily required by the injury, so that the tortfeasor who caused the injuries is not entitled to receive the benefit of the reduced, discounted, or written-off amount?

HOLDING AND DECISION: (Ketchum, J.) Yes. Where an injured individual's health care provider agrees to reduce, discount, or write off a portion of the individual's medical bill, the collateral source rule permits the person to recover the entire reasonable value of the medical services necessarily required by the injury, so that the tortfeasor who caused the injuries is not entitled to receive the benefit of the reduced, discounted, or written-off amount. First, by statute, medical bills are prima facie evidence that the amounts billed were necessary and reasonable. Second, the collateral source rule excludes payments from other sources to plaintiffs from being used to reduce damage awards imposed upon culpable defendants. The collateral source rule protects payments made to or benefits conferred upon an injured party from sources other than the tortfeasor by denying the tortfeasor any corresponding offset or credit against the injured party's damages, and it precludes the offsetting of payments made by health and accident insurance companies or other collateral sources, such as employers or family members, as against the damages claimed by the injured party. The collateral source rule operates as both a rule of evidence and a rule of damages. As a rule of evidence, it precludes the introduction of evidence that some of the plaintiff's damages were paid by a collateral source, since it is believed that a jury would not be able to disregard such evidence when awarding damages. As a rule of damages, it prevents the defendant from offsetting the judgment against any receipt of collateral sources by the plaintiff. The rationale for this rule is that the tortfeasor should not benefit from the contracts or relationships that may exist between the plaintiff and third parties. Thus, only amounts received from the tortfeasor, the tortfeasor's agent, or a joint tortfeasor reduce the tortfeasor defendant's liability. Here, the amounts written off by Liston's (P) medical providers come within the collateral source rule, because those amounts can be considered both a benefit of Liston's (P)

Continued on next page.

bargain with his health insurance carrier, and a gratuitous benefit arising from his bargain with his medical providers. Additionally, a creditor's write-down of debt is often considered to be the equivalent of payment. Regardless of how, or even whether, Liston's (P) obligation to his medical providers was later discharged, he became liable for the bills when the services were received; he is therefore entitled to recover the value of the services. The collateral source rule is pronouncement of public policy that favors the victim of wrongdoing over the wrongdoer: because the law must sanction one windfall and deny the other, it favors the victim of the wrong rather than the wrongdoer. It is also part of the tort system's goal of requiring tortfeasors to make right their wrongful acts. Here, Liston (P) would have been liable for the full amount billed by his medical providers absent his insurance coverage. Whether he took benefits from his health insurer in the form of medical expense payments or in the form of discounts and write-offs because of agreements between his health insurer and his health care providers is irrelevant. Those amounts written off are as much of a benefit for which he paid consideration as are the actual cash payments made by his health insurer to the health care providers. This is the very purpose of the collateral source rule: to prevent a defendant from reaping the benefits of a plaintiff's preparation and protection. Affirmed.

DISSENT: (Loughery, J.) The majority ignores that Liston (P) was never liable for what were inflated bills because at the time he incurred his medical charges, the medical provider and the insurer had already agreed on a different price for the medical services rendered. Additionally, the "write off" or discount did not primarily benefit Liston (P), and to the extent that it did, it was not intended as compensation for his injuries. Given the realities and complexities of health care pricing structures, it is absurd to conclude that the amount billed for a certain medical procedure reflects the "reasonable value" of that service. There is authoritative evidence that insurers generally pay about 40 cents per dollar of billed charges, and that hospitals accept such amounts in full satisfaction of the billed charges. Therefore, the collateral source rule should not permit plaintiffs to receive compensation for medical expenses that were never paid by anyone. Limiting the amounts that can be recovered as damages for medical expenses to those amounts actually paid, as opposed to fictitious amounts generated by medical providers to ensure they can still make a profit after giving a substantial discount, does not thwart the rationale behind the collateral source rule. If tortfeasors are automatically required to compensate plaintiffs for their medical expenses at the highest possible price, regardless of the actual amounts paid, those costs will inevitably be passed on to the public through higher insurance premiums.

ANALYSIS

Many courts do not take the approach taken by the majority in this case. Instead, those courts do not apply the collateral source rule in cases similar to the one at bar, and they permit the defendant to present evidence about discounts and write-offs of amounts billed for medical services so as to limit the plaintiff's recovery to amounts actually paid by the health insurer. These courts reason that insurers and medical providers negotiate rates in pursuit of their own business interests, that the benefits of the bargains made accrue directly to the negotiating parties, and that the parties do not agree on discounted payments as compensation for a plaintiff's injuries. They also do not see the discounted price as a payment, and they also emphasize that the value of damages a plaintiff has avoided has never been the measure of tort recovery.

Quicknotes

COLLATERAL SOURCE RULE The doctrine that compensation given to an injured party from a third party should not be considered in assessing the damages to be paid by the party who inflicted the injury.

Frost v. Porter Leasing Corp.

Injured motorists (P) v. Tortfeasor (D)

Mass. Sup. Jud. Ct., 386 Mass. 425, 436 N.E.2d 387 (1982).

NATURE OF CASE: Certified question regarding subrogation.

FACT SUMMARY: The Frosts (P) were involved in an auto accident and sued the other driver (D); the insurer who had paid for their medical expenses claimed a right of subrogation as to damages the Frosts (P) would receive.

> ## RULE OF LAW
> An insurer has no right, in the absence of a subrogation clause, to share in the insured's recovery against the tortfeasor.

FACTS: The Frosts (P) were in a motor vehicle accident and sued the other driver (D). When a settlement was reached, the insurance company that had paid the Frosts' (P) medical expenses claimed a right of subrogation in the proceeds of the settlement. The Frosts (P) claimed that the insurance policy had no provision for subrogation, and that courts had not recognized implied rights of subrogation in the area of personal insurance. The court certified the question to the Massachusetts Supreme Judicial Court.

ISSUE: Does an insurer have a right, in the absence of a subrogation clause, to share in the insured's recovery against the tortfeasor?

HOLDING AND DECISION: (Hennessey, C.J.) No. An insurer has no right, in the absence of a subrogation clause, to share in the insured's recovery against the tortfeasor. The principles that support subrogation under policies for property insurance would not be served by extending subrogation rights to cases involving personal injury insurance. Subrogation cannot be implied as to medical expense benefits. Question answered in the negative.

CONCURRENCE: (Wilkins, J.) In fairness to an insured a policy should disclose the possibility of subrogation claims.

▶ ANALYSIS

The medical insurance in this case had been bargained for by the insured's union. In some jurisdictions, it is possible for the insurer to proceed against the tortfeasor directly. Courts generally do not recognize subrogation rights in the area of personal insurance, which includes medical expense benefits, life insurance, and accident insurance.

Quicknotes

COMPENSATORY DAMAGES Measure of damages necessary to compensate victim for actual injuries suffered.

MEDICAL MALPRACTICE Conduct on the part of a doctor falling below that demonstrated by other doctors of ordinary skill and competency under the circumstances, resulting in damages.

PERSONAL INJURY Harm to an individual's person or body.

SUBROGATION The substitution of one party for another in assuming the first party's rights or obligations.

Pavia v. State Farm Mutual Automobile Insurance Co.

Insured (P) v. Insurer (D)

N.Y. Ct. App., 82 N.Y.2d 445, 626 N.E.2d 24 (1993).

NATURE OF CASE: Appeal from award of damages for bad faith in personal injury action.

FACT SUMMARY: Pavia (P), injured while a passenger in a car accident, and Rosato (P), the driver of the car, filed suit against State Farm Automobile Insurance Co. (D), alleging bad faith for failing to accept a settlement offer.

🏛 RULE OF LAW
To establish a prima facie case of bad faith, a plaintiff must establish that an insurer's conduct in failing to accept a settlement offer constituted a "gross disregard" of the insured's interests or a deliberate or reckless failure to give equal weight to the interests of the insured and its own interests.

FACTS: Rosato (P), driving his mother's car, turned a corner at an excessive speed and encountered a double-parked car. In an effort to avoid the parked car, Rosato (P) collided with another car, and Pavia (P), a passenger in Rosato's (P) car, was seriously injured. Pavia (P) initially filed a personal injury suit against Rosato (P), who was insured by State Farm Mutual Automobile Insurance Co. (State Farm) (D) for $100,000. Pavia's (P) attorney wrote a letter to State Farm (D) demanding the full amount of the policy in settlement of the personal injury claim and requiring acceptance of the offer within 30 days. State Farm (D), continuing to investigate the accident although it had received unfavorable liability forecasts, did not respond to Pavia's (P) offer within the deadline. When State Farm (P) later offered Pavia the $100,000, it was rejected as "too late." At trial the jury returned a verdict for Pavia (P) for $6,322,000, which was later reduced to $3,880,000. Rosato (P) subsequently assigned all causes of action against State Farm (D) to Pavia (P) in exchange for a promise by Pavia (P) that he would not pursue the excess portion of the judgment against Rosato (P). Next, Pavia (P) and Rosato (P) brought this action, alleging that State Farm (D) had acted in bad faith when it failed to accept Pavia's (P) settlement offer despite the very unfavorable liability reports it had received. A jury trial found for Pavia (P) and Rosato (P) and awarded an excess judgment of $4,688,030. On appeal, State Farm (D) argued that there was insufficient evidence to support a finding of bad faith as a matter of law, but the appellate division affirmed the award.

ISSUE: To establish a prima facie case of bad faith, must a plaintiff establish that an insurer's conduct in failing to accept a settlement offer constituted a "gross disregard" of the insured's interests or a deliberated or reckless failure to give equal weight to the interests of the insured and its own interests?

HOLDING AND DECISION: (Titone, J.) Yes. To establish a prima facie case of bad faith, a plaintiff must establish that an insurer's conduct in failing to accept a settlement offer constituted a "gross disregard" of the insured's interests or a deliberate or reckless failure to give equal weight to the interests of the insured and its own interests. All of the facts and circumstances relating to whether the insurer's investigatory efforts prevented it from making an informed evaluation of the risks of refusing settlement must be considered. These factors include the plaintiff's likelihood of success on the liability claim, the potential magnitude of damage exposure in refusing the settlement, and any other evidence that tends to indicate bad faith. Application of these standards in this case does not lead to the conclusion that Pavia (P) and Rosato (P) have established a prima facie case of bad faith. When the demand for settlement was made, the case was still under investigation by State Farm (D). The only thing Pavia (P) and Rosato (P) have shown is that State Farm (D) did not accept a unilaterally imposed deadline. To allow recovery would encourage others to make arbitrary settlement deadline offers with the hope of manufacturing a bad faith claim. Although it is possible that State Farm (D) could have worked more expeditiously, their actions do not constitute a "gross disregard" for Pavia's (P) and Rosato's (P) rights. Reversed and dismissed.

▶ ANALYSIS

The court's rationale in attempting to strike a balance between the interests of the insurer and insured is a valid one. Although it is a goal of insurance companies to handle their claims in an expedient manner, it is also in the best interests of all parties involved that they thoroughly research the claims before doing so. Insurance fraud is a growing problem, and many states have set limits on damage awards in hopes of discouraging those looking for a quick cash settlement.

■■■

Quicknotes

BAD FAITH Conduct that is intentionally misleading or deceptive.

PRIMA FACIE An action in which the plaintiff introduces sufficient evidence to submit an issue to the judge or jury for determination.

■■■

Note: There are no principal cases in Chapter 12 of the casebook.

CHAPTER

13

Intentional Harm

Quick Reference Rules of Law

Garratt v. Dailey

Arthritic woman (P) v. Five-year-old boy (D)

Wash. Sup. Ct., 46 Wash. 2d 197, 279 P.2d 1091 (1955).

NATURE OF CASE: Action to recover damages for battery.

FACT SUMMARY: Brian Dailey (D) pulled a chair out from under Ruth Garratt (P) as she began to sit down in it.

RULE OF LAW

The intent necessary for the commission of a battery is present when the person acts, knowing with substantial certainty that the harmful contact will occur.

FACTS: Ruth Garratt (P) alleged that Brian Dailey (D), who was five years old, pulled a chair out from under her as she was sitting down, thereby causing her to fall and break her hip. Brian Dailey (D) alleged that he picked up the chair and sat down in it, and then noticed that Ruth Garratt (P) was about to sit down where the chair had been. However, upon a second appeal, it was found that Dailey (P) knew, when he moved the chair, that Ruth Garratt (P) was about to sit down in it.

ISSUE: Is intent to harm another necessary for the commission of a battery, when the defendant knows that his actions will result in an offensive contact?

HOLDING AND DECISION: (Hill, J.) No. While battery requires an intentional infliction of a harmful bodily contact, this does not mean that there must be an intent (or desire) to cause harm or even to cause the contact. When a minor has committed a tort with force, as here, the latter is liable to be proceeded against as any other person would be. As may have been the case herein, the mere absence of any intent of five-year-old Brian Dailey (D) to injure Garratt (P) or to play a prank on her would not absolve him from liability if in fact he had such knowledge. Without such knowledge, there would be nothing wrongful about the act in moving the chair, and, there being no wrongful act, there would be no liability. While a finding that he had no such knowledge can be inferred from the findings made, there should be no question but that the trial court had passed upon that issue. Hence, the case should be remanded for clarification of the findings to specifically cover the question of Dailey's (D) knowledge because intent could be inferred therefrom. If Dailey (D) did not have such knowledge, there was no wrongful act by him, and the basic premise of liability on the theory of a battery was not established. Remanded.

ANALYSIS

This court's decision regarding the nature of the intent needed for battery is representative of the nature of intent required for any intentional tort (such as assault, false imprisonment, trespass). Thus, the general view of intent is that where a reasonable person in the position of the defendant would believe that a certain result was substantially certain to follow his acts, the defendant will be considered to intend that result.

Quicknotes

BATTERY Unlawful contact with the body of another person.

INTENT The state of mind that exists when one's purpose is to commit a criminal act.

Picard v. Barry Pontiac-Buick, Inc.

Car owner (P) v. Car dealership (D)

R.I. Sup. Ct., 654 A.2d 690 (1995).

NATURE OF CASE: Appeal from action for damages for assault and battery.

FACT SUMMARY: Picard (P) charged that an employee of Barry Pontiac-Buick (D) who was inspecting the brakes on her car assaulted and battered her when she brought a camera to photograph the inspection.

🏛 RULE OF LAW
(1) An assault occurs when a physical act or verbal threat places an individual in reasonable apprehension of imminent bodily harm.
(2) An unpermitted or offensive contact with an object attached to or identified with another's body is sufficient to constitute a battery.

FACTS: Picard (P), unhappy with the service work performed on her car during a brake inspection, contacted a local TV "troubleshooter" news reporter. When she returned for a reinspection with a camera, the serviceman allegedly became angry and threatening. Picard (P) claimed that he lunged at her and spun her around, injuring her back. The serviceman claimed that he only placed his index finger on her camera and repeatedly said, "who gave you permission to take my picture?" The serviceman denied grabbing or threatening Picard (P) in any way. Picard (P) filed a suit for assault and battery against the service station, Barry Pontiac-Buick (D), and claimed permanent damage to her back as a consequence of the altercation. Picard (P) prevailed at trial and was awarded compensatory and punitive damages. Barry Pontiac-Buick (D) appealed on three grounds: first, Picard (P) did not prove that an assault or battery occurred; second, she failed to show that her injuries were caused by the alleged harm; and third, the damage awards were excessive and inappropriate.

ISSUE:
(1) Does a physical act or verbal threat that places an individual in reasonable apprehension of imminent bodily harm constitute a prima facie case of assault?
(2) Is an unpermitted or offensive contact with an object attached to or identified with another's body sufficient to constitute battery?

HOLDING AND DECISION: (Lederberg, J.)
(1) Yes. An assault occurs when a physical act or verbal threat places an individual in reasonable apprehension of imminent bodily harm. An assault occurs when either a physical or verbal threat puts an individual in reasonable fear of imminent bodily harm. It is Picard's (P) interpretation of the confrontation that is the mea-

sure of whether an assault occurred. The circumstances indicate that her apprehension was reasonable.
(2) Yes. An unpermitted or offensive contact with an object attached to or identified with another's body is sufficient to constitute a battery. Battery is defined as an act that was intended to cause, and in fact did cause, an offensive or unconsented touching of the body of another. This doctrine has been held to apply to the unpermitted touching of an object attached to a plaintiff's body such as a cane or clothing. The serviceman's intentional contact with the camera Picard (P) held in her hand was sufficient to constitute a battery. However, the medical evidence as to Picard's (P) back injuries was inadequate and the damage awards were excessive. The judgment of the superior court is affirmed as to the commission of assault and battery, but the award of damages is vacated and remanded.

▶ ANALYSIS

Assault and battery, which often occur during a single confrontation, are the most common of the intentional torts. Note that assault requires a threat of "imminent" bodily harm. Therefore a threat of future harm, such as "I will kill you next week," is not sufficient, although it might be frightening. Other acts that have been held to constitute battery, although the defendant never actually touched the plaintiff's body, include pulling out a chair from underneath an individual about to sit and throwing a baseball at someone.

Quicknotes

ASSAULT AND BATTERY Any unlawful touching of another person without justification or excuse.

INTENTIONAL TORT A legal wrong resulting in a breach of duty, which is intentionally or purposefully committed by the wrongdoer.

PRIMA FACIE An action, in which the plaintiff introduces sufficient evidence to submit an issue to the judge or jury for determination.

Wishnatsky v. Huey

Battery victim (P) v. Alleged batterer (D)

N.D. Ct. App., 584 N.W.2d 859 (1998).

NATURE OF CASE: Appeal from summary judgment for defendant.

FACT SUMMARY: Wishnatsky (P) alleged that Huey (D) had committed a battery when he closed the door in his face.

🏛 RULE OF LAW
A bodily contact is offensive if it offends a reasonable sense of personal dignity.

FACTS: Huey (D), an assistant attorney general, was in a private conference with another attorney at that attorney's office. Wishnatsky (P), who was working as a paralegal for the attorney, attempted to enter the office without knocking first. Huey (D) pushed the door closed, thereby pushing Wishnatsky (P) out into the hall. Wishnatsky (P) sued for battery, and the district court granted Huey's (D) motion for summary judgment. Wishnatsky (P) appealed.

ISSUE: Is a bodily contact offensive if it offends a reasonable sense of personal dignity?

HOLDING AND DECISION: (Per curiam) Yes. A bodily contact is offensive if it offends a reasonable sense of personal dignity. The evidence presented at trial indicated that Wishnatsky (P) was unduly sensitive as to his personal dignity. An ordinary person not unduly sensitive as to his personal dignity intruding upon a private conversation would not have been offended by Huey's (D) response to the intrusion. Affirmed.

▶ ANALYSIS

The court relied on the Restatement (Second) of Torts' definition of battery. The kind of contact that would be offensive to a reasonable sense of personal dignity must be a contact which was unwarranted by the social usages prevalent at the time and place at which it was inflicted. The unpermitted and intentional contact, and not any physical harm, is the essence of the grievance.

■==■

Quicknotes

BATTERY Unlawful contact with the body of another person.

HARMFUL OR OFFENSIVE CONTACT Contact that causes injury or annoyance to another individual.

INTENTIONAL TORT A legal wrong resulting in a breach of duty, which is intentionally or purposefully committed by the wrongdoer.

Lopez v. Winchell's Donut House

Employee (P) v. Employer (D)

Ill. App. Ct., 126 Ill. App. 3d 46, 466 N.E.2d 1309 (1984).

NATURE OF CASE: Appeal of summary judgment dismissing action for damages for false imprisonment.

FACT SUMMARY: Lopez (P), accused of theft by her employer, remained in a room during interrogation because she felt compelled to protect her reputation.

🏛 RULE OF LAW
One who submits to an interrogation out of a concern for protecting his reputation has not been falsely imprisoned.

FACTS: Lopez (P) was employed by Winchell's Donut House (Winchell's) (D). At one point, the franchise manager and an investigator called Lopez (P) into a room and accused her of pocketing proceeds. According to later deposition testimony, Lopez (P) remained in the room to answer to the charges. Lopez (P) was not threatened with force, restrained, or told that she would be terminated if she did leave. Lopez (P) later sued for false imprisonment. Based on the deposition testimony, Winchell's (D) moved for summary judgment, which was granted. Lopez (P) appealed.

ISSUE: Has one who submits to an interrogation out of a concern for protecting his reputation been falsely imprisoned?

HOLDING AND DECISION: (Lorenz, J.) No. One who submits to an interrogation out of a concern for protecting his reputation has not been falsely imprisoned. For false imprisonment to occur, a person must be restrained by physical force, threat, or coercion. Voluntary consent to detention and/or interrogation, even if reluctantly given, will not constitute false imprisonment. Here, Lopez (P) was not restrained, threatened, nor coerced. She voluntarily submitted to the interrogation. In light of this, the situation she experienced was not false imprisonment. Affirmed.

▶ ANALYSIS

In this instance, Lopez (P) apparently was not told that she would be fired if she left, although this may have been implicit in the situation (she was fired later). The question here would have been closer if such statements had been made. This would probably not amount to restraint or threat, but could constitute coercion.

━━

Quicknotes

DISPOSITION A transferring of property; conveyance.

FALSE IMPRISONMENT Intentional tort whereby the victim is unlawfully restrained.

Womack v. Eldridge

Worker (P) v. Agent of co-worker (D)

Va. Sup. Ct., 215 Va. 338, 210 S.E.2d 145 (1974).

NATURE OF CASE: Appeal of dismissal of action for damages for infliction of emotional distress.

FACT SUMMARY: Womack (P) sued Eldridge (D) for infliction of emotional distress, despite a lack of physical injury.

RULE OF LAW
One may recover damages for emotional distress absent physical injury.

FACTS: Womack (P) worked at a facility called Skateland, as did one Seifert. Seifert was the subject of an investigation relating to an alleged molestation. Eldridge (D) was hired by Seifert's attorney to obtain a photo of Womack (P), in hopes that he, not Seifert, would be identified as the perpetrator. Eldridge (D) visited Womack (P) and claimed to be a local reporter doing a story on Skateland. He consented to a photograph. The photo went to Seifert's attorney, and eventually to the prosecutor's office. The prosecutor, believing Womack (P) to be somehow involved, subpoenaed him to court several times. Womack (P) later sued Eldridge (D) for intentional infliction of emotional distress. The trial court directed a defense verdict on the grounds that Womack (P) had not suffered physical injury. Womack (P) appealed.

ISSUE: May one recover damages for emotional distress absent physical injury?

HOLDING AND DECISION: (I'Anson, C.J.) Yes. One may recover damages for emotional distress absent physical injury. Other jurisdictions disagree on this issue, but the clear trend is to allow such damages to be recoverable. The Restatement also allows the awarding of such damages if the defendant's actions were reasonably certain to cause distress. This position comports with logic. Consequently, this court adopts the rule that emotional distress without physical injury may be compensable if the defendant's conduct was intentional or reckless, the defendant intended to inflict distress or the nature of the conduct was likely to cause distress, and the conduct was outrageous and contrary to common standards of decency and morality. Here, it is questionable whether Eldridge's (D) behavior fell within this standard, so the issue should have gone to the jury. Reversed.

▶ ANALYSIS

The court here did not say whether an objective or subjective standard was being used with respect to what might be considered likely to cause distress. It would appear from reading between the lines that an objective standard can be inferred. Most jurisdictions use such a standard. To allow a subjective standard would introduce a good deal of uncertainty in this area.

Quicknotes

INTENTIONAL INFLICTION OF EMOTIONAL DISTRESS Intentional and extreme behavior on the part of the wrongdoer with the intent to cause the victim to suffer from severe emotional distress, or with reckless indifference, resulting in the victim's suffering from severe emotional distress.

OBJECTIVE STANDARD A standard that is not personal to an individual but is dependent on some external source.

SUBJECTIVE STANDARD A standard that is based on the personal belief of an individual.

Hustler Magazine, Inc. v. Falwell

Adult magazine (D) v. Televangelist (P)

485 U.S. 46 (1988).

NATURE OF CASE: Appeal from an award of damages for emotional distress.

FACT SUMMARY: Falwell (P) contended that he could recover for emotional distress caused by a Hustler Magazine, Inc. (D) cartoon, even though actual malice had not been shown.

RULE OF LAW
Public figures may not recover for infliction of emotional distress due to an allegedly defamatory act unless actual malice is shown.

FACTS: Hustler Magazine, Inc. (Hustler) (D), an adult magazine, printed an ad parody labeled as such, depicting Falwell (P), a televangelist, as having had sex with his mother and being drunk. Falwell (P) sued for defamation and intentional infliction of emotional distress. The district court directed a verdict for Hustler (D) on a privacy invasion count, and the jury found for Hustler (D) on the libel count. It awarded Falwell (P) $200,000 for infliction of emotional distress. The court of appeals affirmed, holding actual malice standards need not be shown to recover an emotional distress theory. The United States Supreme Court granted certiorari.

ISSUE: May public figures recover for infliction of emotional distress in a defamation context without showing actual malice?

HOLDING AND DECISION: (Rehnquist, C.J.) No. Public figures may not recover for infliction of emotional distress due to allegedly defamatory act unless actual malice is shown. The state common law tort of infliction of emotional distress illustrates a legitimate state interest in the protection of its residents; however, such protection cannot impair First Amendment rights. To allow a recovery for emotional distress in this context would allow First Amendment freedoms to be subverted. Because no actual malice was shown, no recovery could be had. Reversed.

CONCURRENCE: (White, J.) Penalizing publication of parody precludes the free exercise of freedom of press.

ANALYSIS

Actual malice, in the constitutional context of defamation, means the knowledge of the falsity of a statement or a reckless disregard for its truth. In the area of parody, this seems to be inapplicable. No assertion of fact exists to determine whether such was true. However, in the other areas of defamation, this case will have a widespread effect.

Quicknotes

ACTUAL MALICE The issuance of a publication with knowledge of its falsity or with reckless disregard as to its truth.

DEFAMATION An intentional false publication, communicated publicly in either oral or written form, subjecting a person to scorn, hatred or ridicule, or injuring him or her in relation to his or her occupation or business.

FIRST AMENDMENT Prohibits Congress from enacting any law respecting an establishment of religion, prohibiting the free exercise of religion, abridging freedom of speech or the press, the right of peaceful assembly and the right to petition for a redress of grievances.

INTENTIONAL INFLICTION OF EMOTIONAL DISTRESS Intentional and extreme behavior on the part of the wrongdoer with the intent to cause the victim to suffer from severe emotional distress, or with reckless indifference, resulting in the victim's suffering from severe emotional distress.

Martin v. Reynolds Metals Co.

Farm owner (P) v. Aluminum plant (D)

Or. Sup. Ct., 221 Or. 86, 342 P.2d 790 (1959).

NATURE OF CASE: Action to recover damages for trespass.

FACT SUMMARY: Although Martin (P) sued for trespass for the damage done to his farm land by the fluorides sent into the air and deposited on his land from Reynolds Metals Co.'s (Reynolds) (D) aluminum reduction plant, Reynolds (D) insisted that the proper action was one of nuisance.

🏛 RULE OF LAW

Trespass is defined as any intrusion that invades the possessor's protected interest in exclusive possession, whether that intrusion is by visible or invisible pieces of matter or by energy.

FACTS: Fluoride compounds not visible to the naked eye were put into the air as a result of the operation of an aluminum reduction plant by Reynolds Metals Co. (Reynolds) (D) in the vicinity of Martin's (P) farm. Martin (P) sued for trespass and was awarded $71,500 for damage to the land caused by the compounds' settling on the land making it impossible to raise livestock thereon. He was also awarded $20,000 for the deterioration to his land from the growth of brush and weeds due to lack of grazing. Actions in trespass had a six-year statute of limitations, but actions in nuisance had a two-year statute of limitations. The damages were awarded for the period from August 1951 through 1955. In an attempt to reduce the award, Reynolds (D) argued that the action was one in nuisance, which was governed by the two-year statute of limitations.

ISSUE: Can a trespass result from any intrusion that invades the possessor's protected interest in exclusive possession, whether the intrusion is by visible or invisible pieces of matter or by energy?

HOLDING AND DECISION: (O'Connell, J.) Yes. If one wants to focus on the character of the instrumentality used in making an intrusion upon another's land, it is best to emphasize the object's energy or force rather than its size. Viewed this way, trespass can be defined as any intrusion that invades the possessor's protected interest in exclusive possession, whether that intrusion is by visible or invisible pieces of matter or by energy that can be measured only by the mathematical language of the physicist. It is thus understandable why actual damage is not an essential ingredient in the law of trespass and why the same conduct on the part of a defendant may and often does constitute both a nuisance and a trespass. It is clear that all the requirements for a trespass were met in this case. Affirmed.

▶ ANALYSIS

Care should be taken not to take this court's liberal view of the scope of the trespass action too far. In *Wilson v. Interlake Steel Co.*, 32 Cal.3d 229, 649 P.2d 922 (1982), the court made clear that "intangible intrusions, such as noise, odor, or light alone, are dealt with as nuisance cases, not trespass."

Quicknotes

NUISANCE An unlawful use of property that interferes with the lawful use of another's property.

TRESPASS Unlawful interference with, or damage to, the real or personal property of another.

■■■

Thyroff v. Nationwide Mutual Insurance Co.

Employee (P) v. Employer (D)

N.Y. Ct. App., 8 N.Y.3d 283, 864 N.E.2d 1272 (2007).

NATURE OF CASE: Certified question from a federal appeals court.

FACT SUMMARY: Louis Thyroff (P)'s electronic data was confiscated along with his company-owned computer system when he was fired by Nationwide Mutual Insurance Company (D). He brought an action for conversion.

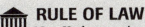

RULE OF LAW
New York recognizes a claim for conversion of electronic data.

FACTS: Louis Thyroff (P) was an insurance agent employed by Nationwide Mutual Insurance Company (Nationwide) (D). Thyroff (P) used a company computer, and he stored personal information on it in addition to using it for work. Every day, Nationwide (D) automatically uploaded all of the information on his system. In September 2000, Thyroff (P) received a letter from Nationwide (D) terminating his employment. Nationwide (D) repossessed its system the next day and denied Thyroff (P) further access to the computer and electronic records and data. Thyroff (P) was therefore unable to retrieve his customer information and other personal information that was stored. He filed an action against Nationwide (D) in federal district court that included a claim for conversion of his business and personal information stored on the hard drive. The court held that the complaint failed to state a cause of action for conversion. Thyroff (P) appealed to the federal appeals court seeking reinstatement of his conversion cause of action, and Nationwide argued that the conversion claim cannot be based on the misappropriation of electronic records and that because New York does not recognize a cause of action for the conversion of intangible property.

ISSUE: Does New York recognize a claim for conversion of electronic data?

HOLDING AND DECISION: (Graffeo, J.) Yes. New York recognizes a claim for conversion of electronic data. The Restatement (Second) of Torts defines conversion as an intentional act of "dominion or control over a chattel which so seriously interferes with the right of another to control it that the actor may justly be required to pay the other the full value of the chattel." At common law, conversion actions were aimed against interferences with tangible personal property, and it normally did not apply to intangible property because there is no physical item that can be misappropriated. Some courts have determined that there really was no good reason for keeping up that distinction, and substituted a theory of conversion that covered things represented by valuable papers, like stock certificates. This led to recognition that an intangible property right can be united—or merged—with a tangible object for conversion purposes, such as conversion of an intangible property right to a musical performance by misappropriating a master recording. While New York courts have not had occasion to consider whether the common law should permit conversion for intangible property interests that do not merge with tangible items of property, some other courts have. There is, in fact, no compelling reason to prohibit conversion for redress of a misappropriation of intangible property. And whereas the merger rule reflected the concept that intangible property interests could be converted only by exercising dominion over the paper document that represented that interest, it is now customary that stock ownership exists only in electronic format. It is anathema to hold that burning a paper stock certificate is conversion, but hacking into a company's mainframe and deleting its data would not. In addition, it's not usually the physical nature of a document that has intrinsic value, but the information memorialized in it. A manuscript of a novel has the same value whether saved on paper on in a computer. The information that Thyroff (P) allegedly stored on his leased computers has value to him regardless of the format was tangible or intangible, and the protections of the law should apply equally to both forms (unless there is a significant difference in the value). So the tort of conversion should keep up with widespread computer use, and the type of data that Nationwide (D) allegedly took is subject to a claim of conversion in New York. Affirmed.

ANALYSIS

Thyroff likely represents the future of conversion law in this country, despite the Restatement (Second) of Torts, which adheres to the merger doctrine, and some jurisdictions that still strictly apply the merger doctrine (see, e.g., *Northeast Coating Technologies Inc. v. Vacuum Metallurgical Co. Ltd.*, 684 A.2d 1322, 1324 (Maine 1996)). In *Kremen v. Cohen*, 337 F.3d 1024, 1031 (9th Cir. 2003), the court held that California "does not follow the Restatement's strict merger requirement" in upholding a conversion claim for the intangible property right in the domain name, "sex .com," a profitable porn site. Several other courts have assumed that computer data are subject to a claim for conversion without reference to the tangible/intangible property distinction.

Continued on next page.

Quicknotes

CONVERSION The act of depriving an owner of his property without permission or justification.

Hart v. Geysel

Estate administrator (P) v. Prize fighter (D)

Wash. Sup. Ct., 159 Wash. 632, 294 P. 570 (1930).

NATURE OF CASE: Action to recover damages for wrongful death.

FACT SUMMARY: Hart (P) sued as administrator of the estate of one who died fighting Geysel (D) in a prize fight in which the deceased voluntarily engaged.

🏛 RULE OF LAW
When one voluntarily engages in unlawful conduct that will cause injury, such as a fight, the privilege of consent can be asserted to defend any civil action the plaintiff may bring.

FACTS: Geysel (D) and the deceased, whom Hart (P) represented as administrator, engaged themselves in a fight. This combat was not the result of violence or anger intended to cause injury but was entered into by the mutual consent of the parties.

ISSUE: Is there a privilege of consent when both parties voluntarily enter a fight that is not sanctioned by law?

HOLDING AND DECISION: (Main, J.) Yes. When one voluntarily engages in unlawful conduct that will cause injury, such as a fight, the privilege of consent can be asserted to defend any civil action the plaintiff may bring. A privilege of consent exists even in the case of unlawful behavior, such as physical attacks, as long as both parties voluntarily entered the foray. To allow the plaintiff to recover when he had of his own free choice engaged in unlawful conduct would mean that the tort law would be sanctioning unlawful behavior. It would be allowing an individual who breaks the law recovery in a civil suit so that the wrongdoer would be profiting from his own wrong. Affirmed.

▶ ANALYSIS

There are two distinct viewpoints on the issue of consent to a criminal action. One view, the majority, is that one can never consent to a crime and, thus, such consent is no defense in a civil action. The other view, the minority recognized by eight states and the Restatement (Second) of Torts, is the rule of this case that one who takes part voluntarily in an unlawful act has consented to it and its consequences.

Quicknotes

CONSENT A voluntary and willful agreement by an individual possessing sufficient mental capacity to undertake an action suggested by another.

PRIVILEGE A benefit or right conferred upon a person or entity beyond those conferred upon the general public.

WRONGFUL DEATH An action brought by the beneficiaries of a deceased person, claiming that the deceased's death was the result of wrongful conduct by the defendant.

Courvoisier v. Raymond

Shop owner (D) v. Sheriff (P)

Colo. Sup. Ct., 23 Colo. 113, 47 P. 284 (1896).

NATURE OF CASE: Appeal from award of damages.

FACT SUMMARY: Courvoisier (D) believed that Raymond (P), a policeman, was one of the rioters outside of his home and shot him as he approached.

🏛 RULE OF LAW
An action of force is justified by self-defense whenever the circumstances are such as to cause a reasonable man to believe that his life is in danger, or that he is in danger of receiving great bodily harm and that it is necessary to use such force for protection.

FACTS: On June 12, 1892, Courvoisier (D) was asleep in a room he occupied over his jewelry store when two men invaded his house. Presuming these men to be burglars, he took his revolver and ejected them. Outside, though, these men were joined by others who assaulted Courvoisier (D) with stones. In order to frighten these men away, Courvoisier (D) fired several shots in the air. These shots, also, attracted the attention of deputy sheriff, Raymond (P), and two other deputy sheriffs. As the other two officers approached the men in the street, Raymond (P), approached Courvoisier (D) from the direction of the rioting men. As Raymond (P) approached, Courvoisier (D) shot him. Thereafter, Raymond (P) sued Courvoisier (D) for damages. As a defense, Courvoisier (D) claimed that he believed that his life was in danger, that Raymond (P) was one of the rioters, and that the shooting was necessary for his self-defense. After a verdict for Raymond (P) for the sum of $3,143, this appeal followed.

ISSUE: Can a person justify the use of force as self-defense only if he was "actually" in danger of being killed or seriously injured?

HOLDING AND DECISION: (Hayt, C.J.) No. An act of force is justified by self-defense whenever the circumstances are such as to cause a reasonable man to believe that his life is in danger, or that he is in danger of receiving great bodily harm and that it is necessary to use such force for protection. Under this rule, a person using force does not actually have to be in danger as long as he reasonably believes that he is and that force is necessary for his self-defense. Here, though, the trial court instructed the jury that the shooting was only justified if Raymond (P) was actually attacking Courvoisier (D). Since this instruction was in error, the judgment must be reversed.

► ANALYSIS

This case illustrates the general view. Note, also, that under the general rule there is no duty to retreat, rather than use force, whenever a person reasonably believes that he is in danger and that force is necessary for self-defense. Under the minority view, though, a person must retreat rather than use deadly force, unless (1) retreating would be dangerous to himself or a third person, (2) he is in his own home; or (3) he is attempting a "valid arrest." Note, finally, that there is no privilege of self-defense when the danger has passed or when excessive force is used.

Quicknotes

MISTAKE An act or failure to perform due to a lack of knowledge or a misconception as to a law or fact.

SELF-DEFENSE A justification doctrine that permits a plaintiff to respond to a threatened injury with a corresponding degree of physical force, while negating any corresponding legal consequence for the results of his defensive act.

Katko v. Briney

Trespasser (P) v. Property owner (D)

Iowa Sup. Ct., 183 N.W.2d 657 (1971).

NATURE OF CASE: Appeal from damage award to plaintiff for compensatory and punitive damages due to physical injury caused by the firing of a spring gun set up by Briney (D).

FACT SUMMARY: In order to protect an uninhabited house, Briney (D) installed a mechanical spring gun whose fire was triggered by the opening of a door; Katko (P) opened the door, and the gun fired, severely injuring him.

RULE OF LAW
No privilege exists to maintain a mechanical device that defends property by automatically inflicting serious bodily injury on those intruders who stimulate the firing mechanism.

FACTS: To guard an unoccupied, isolated house, which had been entered unlawfully on previous occasions, against future unlawful entries, Briney (D) took several precautions such as boarding up the house, posting no trespass signs, and setting up a shotgun trap. There was no warning of the spring gun device that was rigged so that it would fire when a door was opened. When Katko (P), a trespasser, opened the door the gun blast seriously wounded him, blowing away a substantial portion of his leg. The wound left Katko (P) permanently disfigured with a shortened leg.

ISSUE: Does the landowner possess the privilege to install, for the purpose of protecting his property against unlawful intrusions, a mechanism whose sole function is the infliction of death or serious harm upon the intruders?

HOLDING AND DECISION: (Moore, C.J.) No. The fact that an intruder is acting unlawfully does not justify the maintenance of a mechanical device to protect property that can cause great physical injury. Such a man-killing mechanical device is only permissible if the intruder is committing a violent felony, endangering the lives of the occupants. Affirmed.

DISSENT: (Larson, J.) There was reversible error in the court's instructions that the issue of intent in placing the spring gun was not clearly presented to the jury, and that as to punitive damages should not have presented to the jury. I would reverse and remand.

ANALYSIS

The use of a mechanical device cannot expand the privilege to use physical violence in defense of property. There is a severe limitation on this privilege, for there is no right whether by mechanical means or by the landowner's hand to use force that may be lethal. This privilege to use physical force exists only after the landowner's mild methods of expulsion (verbal requests or constrained physical acts) have been met with resistance or when the violence directed at the land is redirected at its occupants. The amount of force that may be utilized cannot exceed the apparent necessities of protecting the land in possession. The necessities are those that would be perceived by a reasonable individual in the property owner's position.

Quicknotes

DEFENSE OF PROPERTY An affirmative defense to criminal liability for the use of force in the protection of one's property.

FELONY A criminal offense of greater seriousness than a misdemeanor; felonies are generally defined pursuant to statute as any crime that is punishable by death or by a term of imprisonment exceeding one year.

PRIVILEGE A benefit or right conferred upon a person or entity beyond those conferred upon the general public.

Vincent v. Lake Erie Transportation Co.

Wharf owner (P) v. Transportation company (D)

Minn. Sup. Ct., 109 Minn. 456, 124 N.W. 221 (1910).

NATURE OF CASE: Appeal from damage award to plaintiff for injury to property.

FACT SUMMARY: Vincent (P) sued for damages to its wharf, caused by Lake Erie Transportation Co. (D) negligently keeping its boat tied to the wharf.

🏛 RULE OF LAW
Public necessity may require the taking of private property for public purposes, but our system of jurisprudence requires that compensation be made.

FACTS: Lake Erie Transportation Co. (D) moored their boat to Vincent's (P) wharf at the place and in the manner designated by Vincent (P). Cargo consigned to Vincent (P) was unloaded. By the time the cargo was unloaded a storm had arisen which prevented the boat from leaving the wharf. Vincent (P) sued for damages caused to the wharf by the boat's hitting it during the storm. The trial court rendered a judgment for Vincent (P). The defendant appealed.

ISSUE: May public necessity, require the taking of private property for public purposes?

HOLDING AND DECISION: (O'Brien, J.) Yes. Public necessity may require the taking of private property for public purposes, but our system of jurisprudence requires that compensation be made. The ship's master was required to use ordinary prudence and care. The evidence showed that it would have been imprudent for the ship's master to have attempted to leave the dock. However, this was not a case in which, because of an act of God or an unavoidable accident, the infliction of injury was beyond the control of the defendant. Here, the defendant prudently and advisedly availed itself of the plaintiff's property for the purpose of preserving its own more valuable property. Having thus preserved the ship at the expense of the dock, the defendants must compensate the owner of the dock for the injury inflicted. The judgment for the plaintiff is affirmed.

DISSENT: (Lewis, J.) The damage was caused by an unavoidable accident. Therefore, the defendant is not liable for damages.

▶ ANALYSIS

The few cases in this area appear to agree with *Vincent*. The same liability apparently attaches to the infliction of personal injury in cases of private necessity. The Restatement (Second) of Torts combines the principles of *Ploof v. Putnam*, 71 A. 188 (Vt. 1908) and *Vincent* in § 197, and

creates a privilege in favor of an actor to enter the land of another in order to avoid serious harm, coupled with an obligation on the part of the actor to pay for whatever he damages.

Quicknotes

NEGLIGENCE Conduct falling below the standard of care that a reasonable person would demonstrate under similar conditions.

PRIVILEGE A benefit or right conferred upon a person or entity beyond those conferred upon the general public.

PUBLIC NECESSITY The defense of necessity, alleging that the harm caused by the defendant was less than the harm sought to be prevented against the public; since the public interest is involved, the defendant is not required to pay for any damage caused.

Quick Reference Rules of Law

14. *Khawar v. Globe International, Inc.* Where a finding of actual malice is based on the republication of a third party's defamatory falsehoods, actual malice may be found where there were obvious reasons to doubt the veracity of the informant or the accuracy of his reports and the re-publisher failed to interview obvious witnesses or consult relevant documentary sources.

Romaine v. Kallinger

Alleged friend of "junkie" (P) v. Author (D)

N.J. Sup. Ct., 109 N.J. 282, 537 A.2d 284 (1988).

NATURE OF CASE: Appeal of dismissal of libel action.

FACT SUMMARY: Romaine (P) sued Kallinger (D) for authoring a book in which it was stated that Romaine "knew a junkie."

RULE OF LAW

A passage in a writing saying a person "knew a junkie" and nothing more is, per se, not libel.

FACTS: Kallinger (D) wrote a book that contained a section concerning one Fasching, an acquaintance of Romaine (P). At one point in the book it was stated that Fasching asked Romaine (P) about a junkie they both knew. Romaine (P) sued for libel, contending that the passage was untrue and defamatory. The trial court dismissed, holding it nondefamatory as a matter of law. The appellate division affirmed, and the state supreme court granted review.

ISSUE: Is a passage in a writing saying a person "knew a junkie" and nothing more, per se, libel?

HOLDING AND DECISION: (Handler, J.) No. A passage in a writing saying a person "knew a junkie" and nothing more is, per se, not libel. The threshold issue in any defamation case is whether a statement is reasonably susceptible of a defamatory meaning; if it is not, it is not defamatory. If it may be, it is a jury question. If it clearly is, then it will be held defamatory as a matter of law. Here, the courts below correctly held the passage in question to be nondefamatory as a matter of law. Contrary to Romaine's (P) assertions, the passage does not imply criminal or illicit conduct on Romaine's (P) part. At most, it says that she knows someone who uses drugs, which is not a crime or illicit activity. Only an unrealistic reading of this section can infer any bad image to Romaine (P). For this reason, the section was, as a matter of law, not defamatory. Affirmed.

DISSENT: (O'Hern, J.) The instant passage was ambiguous and reasonably susceptible of a defamatory meaning and therefore presented a jury question on the issue.

ANALYSIS

Generally speaking, whether a statement is defamatory is a mixed question of law and fact. As such, it is a question for both the court and jury. A court will act as a filter, and only let reasonably questionable passages go to the jury. Passages incapable of differing interpretation will not go to a jury.

Quicknotes

DEFAMATION An intentional false publication, communicated publicly in either oral or written form, subjecting a person to scorn, hatred or ridicule, or injuring him or her in relation to his or her occupation or business.

LIBEL A false or malicious publication subjecting a person to scorn, hatred or ridicule, or injuring him or her in relation to his or her occupation or business.

Davis v. Boeheim

Alleged victim of sexual assault (P) v. Alleged defamer (D)

N.Y. Ct. App. (highest court), 24 N.Y.3d 262, 22 N.E.3d 999, 998 N.Y.S.2d 131 (2015).

NATURE OF CASE: Appeal from affirmance of pre-answer dismissal of defamation action.

FACT SUMMARY: Davis (P) and Lang (P) contended that their defamation action against Boeheim (D) and Syracuse University (University) (D) should not have been dismissed as a matter of law because their complaint sufficiently pleaded a defamation cause of action by asserting that Boeheim (D) made statements that were either defamatory facts, or, alternatively, mixed opinion.

RULE OF LAW
A defamation cause of action may not be dismissed pre-answer where the contested statements are reasonably susceptible of a defamatory connotation.

FACTS: Davis (P) and Lang (P) had alleged that from the time they were children in the 1980s, Fine, an associate head coach at Syracuse University (University) (D), had lured them with opportunities to attend games and assist the team as ball boys, and had sexually molested them in various venues. Davis (P) had made his claims known between 2002 and 2005 to the police, a local newspaper, and the University (D), but none of these entities took any action. These claims became public in 2011 after unrelated but very similar allegations of sexual abuse surfaced against Penn State University's assistant football coach, Jerry Sandusky. In that case, Joe Paterno, the head football coach, was alleged to have covered up the abuse. Within two weeks of the initial coverage of the Penn State story, ESPN issued a news report about the allegations against Fine. That report included Davis's (P) statement that Boeheim (D), the University's (D) head basketball coach and Fine's longtime friend, had seen Davis (P) lying on Fine's hotel room bed during a college tournament in 1987, the NCAA Final Four. The day after the ESPN story, the University (D) released a statement describing a four-month investigation it had made in 2005 into Davis's allegations, and stating that it was unable to corroborate the claims. The day the ESPN story was released, and prior to the University's (D) statement, Boeheim (D) issued a statement in which he stated that: the University (D) had conducted an investigation and had concluded Davis's (P) allegations were unfounded; Fine had his support; and that he had "never seen or witnessed anything to suggest that [Fine] would be involved in any of the activities alleged." In additional statements he made to reporters, which were quoted in print and online, he called Davis (P) and Lang (P) liars, and stated that their allegations were financially motivated. Davis (P) and Lang (P) brought a defamation action against Boeheim (D) and the University (D), claiming that Boeheim's (D) statements to the reporters were false and defamatory, and had caused them economic, emotional, and reputational harm. Boeheim (D) made the following statements on which the action was based: "I know [Davis is] lying about me seeing him in his hotel room. That's a lie. If he's going to tell one lie, I'm sure there's a few more of them." "The Penn State thing came out and the kid behind this is trying to get money. He's tried before. And now he's trying again. . . . That's what this is about. Money." "It is a bunch of a thousand lies that [Davis] has told. . . . He supplied four names to the university that would corroborate his story. None of them did . . . there is only one side to this story. He is lying." "I believe they saw what happened at Penn State, and they are using ESPN to get money. That is what I believe." "You don't think it is a little funny that his cousin (relative) is coming forward?" Boeheim (D) also stated that the timing of Lang's (P) decision to speak out about his abuse seemed "a little suspicious." Boeheim (D) and the University (D) moved to dismiss on the grounds that the statements were not defamatory as a matter of law because they were opinion, not facts. The trial court granted the motion, concluding that a reasonable reader would conclude that Boeheim's (D) statements were a biased personal opinion, and not fact. The state's intermediate appellate court affirmed, concluding that although Boeheim's (D) statements that Davis (P) fabricated allegations and was motivated by financial gain had certain factual elements, based on the content of the communication as a whole, as well as its tone and apparent purpose, and the over-all context in which the assertions were made, a reasonable reader would have believed that the challenged statements were conveying opinion and not facts. A dissenting opinion concluded that dismissal on a pre-answer motion to dismiss was error because Boeheim's (D) statements that Davis (P) was lying about Fine to get money, and that he had done so in the past, constituted opinion that implied a basis in facts not disclosed to the reader or listener, and thus constituted actionable "mixed opinion." The state's highest court granted review.

ISSUE: May a defamation cause of action be dismissed pre-answer where the contested statements are reasonably susceptible of a defamatory connotation?

HOLDING AND DECISION: (Rivera, J.) No. A defamation cause of action may not be dismissed pre-answer where the contested statements are reasonably susceptible of a defamatory connotation. The standard that

Continued on next page.

must be met by the plaintiff is minimal, and if upon any reasonable view of the facts a plaintiff would be entitled to recovery for defamation, the complaint must not be dismissed. There must be a showing of a false statement that tends to expose a person to public contempt, hatred, ridicule, aversion or disgrace. Because only facts are capable of being proven false, only statements alleging facts can support a defamation action. A "pure opinion," no matter how offensive, is not actionable. A pure opinion may take one of two forms. It may be a statement of opinion that is accompanied by a recitation of the facts upon which it is based, or it may be an opinion not accompanied by such a factual recitation so long as it does not imply that it is based upon undisclosed facts. However, an opinion that implies that it is based on facts that justify the opinion but are unknown to those reading or hearing it is a "mixed opinion" and is actionable. Such a mixed opinion implies that the speaker knows certain facts that are unknown to the audience, which support the speaker's opinion and are detrimental to person about whom the statements are being made. Distinguishing between fact and opinion is a question of law left to the courts, which must determine whether a reasonable reader, or average person, could have concluded that the statements were conveying facts about the plaintiff. In turn, three factors are used to determine how the reasonable reader would have interpreted the contested statements. These are the factors: (1) whether the specific language in issue has a precise meaning which is readily understood; (2) whether the statements are capable of being proven true or false; and (3) whether either the full context of the communication in which the statement appears or the broader social context and surrounding circumstances are such as to signal readers or listeners that what is being read or heard is likely to be opinion, not fact. As to the third factor, the court looks at the overall context in which the statements were made. Here, the alleged defamatory statements made by Boeheim (D) were that Davis (P) and Lang (P) were liars seeking money. With respect to the first factor, which weighs in favor of finding that the statements were factual assertions, Boeheim (D) used specific, easily understood language to communicate that Davis (P) and Lang (P) lied, their motive was financial gain, and Davis (P) had made prior similar statements for the same reason. The second factor also weighs in favor of finding that the statements made factual assertions, because the statements are capable of being proven true or false, as they concern whether the plaintiffs made false sexual abuse allegations against Fine in order to get money, and whether Davis (P) had made false statements in the past. The third, and key, factor is one that the parties vigorously dispute. The defendants contend that the context in which the statements were made leads inexorably to the conclusion that Boeheim's (D) statements are nonactionable pure opinion. They argue that a reader would consider the statements as an obvious and transparent effort to defend his longtime close friend and colleague against allegations of sexual abuse, as well as an effort to defend against

suggestions that he knew about the alleged abuse and did nothing. While this interpretation might ultimately prevail, on a motion to dismiss it must be considered whether any reading of the complaint supports the defamation claim, and whether the statement's words, taken in their ordinary meaning and in context, are susceptible to a defamatory connotation. Boeheim's (D) assertions that Davis (P) previously made the same claims, for the same purpose, communicated that Boeheim (D) was relying on undisclosed facts that would justify Boeheim's (D) statements that Davis (P) and Lang (P) were neither credible nor victims of sexual abuse. In context, a reasonable reader could view his statements as supported by undisclosed facts despite any denials he made of not knowing anything. The context further suggests to the reader that Boeheim (D) spoke with authority, and that his statements were based on facts. He was a well-respected member of the University (D) and the community-at-large, and as head coach of the team appeared well placed to have information about the charges. His initial statement, which contained information about the University's (D) investigation, was released on the school's website, confirming his status within the University (D). His statement contained information about Davis's (P) allegations and the University's (D) investigation, which a reader could understand was based on Boeheim's (D) access to factual details unavailable to the public that supported his assertions about Davis (P) and his motive. That Boeheim's (D) statement was issued prior to the University's (D) first public statement about the investigation, further suggests that he had access to otherwise confidential information. Moreover, Boeheim (D) worked with Fine for many years and claimed to "know" Davis (P) from when Davis (P) was a child assisting the team and serving as a babysitter, further suggesting that Boeheim had particular details upon which he relied in asserting that the allegations were untrue. Finally, Boeheim (D) knowingly made these statements to reporters during the media investigation and coverage of the plaintiffs' allegations. These statements could not be viewed as opinion-driven op-eds or letters to the editor, but instead, under the circumstances, they encouraged the reasonable reader to be less skeptical and more willing to conclude that they stated or implied facts. For these reasons, at this stage of the proceedings, it cannot be stated that, as a matter of law, the statements were pure opinion. There is a reasonable view of the claims upon which Davis (P) and Lang (P) would be entitled to recover for defamation; therefore the complaint must be deemed to sufficiently state a cause of action. Reversed; motion to dismiss the complaint is denied.

▌ANALYSIS

The court applied a minimal standard, where if upon any reasonable view of the stated facts the plaintiffs would be

Continued on next page.

entitled to recovery for defamation, the complaint would be deemed to sufficiently state a cause of action. The court applied this liberal standard fully aware that permitting litigation to proceed to discovery would carry the risk of potentially chilling free speech, but it did so because it recognized as well the plaintiffs' right to seek redress, and not have the courthouse doors closed at the very inception of the action, if the pleading met the minimal standard necessary to resist dismissal of the complaint.

━━

Quicknotes

CAUSE OF ACTION A fact or set of facts the occurrence of which entitles a party to seek judicial relief.

DEFAMATION An intentional false publication, communicated publicly in either oral or written form, subjecting a person to scorn, hatred or ridicule, or injuring him in relation to his occupation or business.

MOTION TO DISMISS Motion to terminate an action based on the adequacy of the pleadings, improper service or venue, etc.

━━

Liberman v. Gelstein

Landlord (P) v. Tenant (D)

N.Y. Ct. App., 80 N.Y.2d 429, 605 N.E.2d 344 (1992).

NATURE OF CASE: Appeal from dismissal of action for slander.

FACT SUMMARY: Liberman (P), a landlord, brought an action for slander against Gelstein (D) on the basis that the alleged statements tended to injure his business, trade or profession.

⚖ RULE OF LAW

Slander is not actionable without a showing of special damages unless a plaintiff can prove the defamatory statement falls within one of the four exceptions known collectively as slander per se.

FACTS: Gelstein (D) allegedly made defamatory statements about Liberman (P), a landlord, on two occasions: first, to a fellow member of the building's tenants' board of governors, and second, in the presence of building employees. Liberman (P) brought an action for slander. The lawsuit's second cause of action alleged that Gelstein (D) made an accusation that Liberman (P) routinely paid police officers so that they would not issue parking tickets to cars parked in front of the building. The fifth cause of action stated that Gelstein (D) made a statement in front of employees of the building alleging that Liberman (P) had thrown a punch at him, screamed insults at his family, and threatened to kill him and his family. Gelstein (D) moved to dismiss the complaint, stating that he was privileged to make an inquiry to a fellow board member for the purpose of determining if there was any wrongdoing by Liberman (P) and that the statements regarding his family were either true, not defamatory, or never made. The lower court dismissed both causes of action and the appellate division affirmed.

ISSUE: Does an action for slander exist if the plaintiff does not prove either that the defamatory statement falls within one of the four exceptions known collectively as slander per se or show special damages?

HOLDING AND DECISION: (Kaye, J.) No. Slander is not actionable without a showing of special damages unless a plaintiff can prove the defamatory statement falls within one of the four exceptions known collectively as slander per se. Liberman (P) must show either special damages or that Gelstein's (D) remarks fall into one of the four exceptions known as slander per se. The four categories of statements are: (1) charging the plaintiff with a serious crime; (2) tending to injure the profession, trade, or business of another; (3) imputing unchastity to a woman; and (4) imputing a loathsome or infectious disease. Liberman (P) argued that both sets of

statements were slanderous per se because they charged him with criminal conduct. However, not every allegation of criminal behavior is slanderous, such as a traffic ticket, and only serious offenses are actionable without a showing of special damages. Therefore, the second cause of action, allegations that Liberman (P) bribed a police officer, is actionable under this exception, but the fifth cause of action, that Gelstein (D) falsely attributed the crime of harassment to Liberman (P), is not. Liberman's (P) alternative argument that the statements in the fifth cause of action tended to injure his business, trade or profession does not apply either, because a showing must be made that the remarks were made for a specific purpose, and not just as a general insult. However, both causes of action were properly dismissed. The fifth was properly dismissed because there was no serious crime or business injury involved. The second cause of action was properly dismissed, even though it did involve a serious crime, because Gelstein's (D) argument that he was privileged in making an inquiry to a fellow member of the tenants' board of governors for the purpose of uncovering wrongdoing by a landlord has not been disproved by Liberman (P). Affirmed.

▶ ANALYSIS

Special damages for slander are defined as damages to the plaintiff's reputation in the community as a direct result of the injurious statements. Furthermore, these damages must be measurable pecuniary losses; psychological distress is not sufficient. In contrast to the requirements for bringing an action for slander, to recover for libel, which is essentially written slander, the majority of jurisdictions do not require special damages to be proven.

Quicknotes

DEFAMATION An intentional false publication, communicated publicly in either oral or written form, subjecting a person to scorn, hatred or ridicule, or injuring him or her in relation to his or her occupation or business.

SLANDER Defamatory statement communicated orally.

SPECIAL DAMAGES Damages caused by a specific act that are not the usual consequence of that act and which must be specifically pled and proven.

Yonaty v. Mincolla

Non-homosexual man (P) v. Alleged slanderer (D)

N.Y. App. Div., 945 N.Y.S.2d 774 (2012).

NATURE OF CASE: Cross-appeals from denial of dismissal of slander action.

FACT SUMMARY: Mincolla (D) and a third-party defendant contended that Yonaty's (P) slander action and Mincolla's (D) third-party action seeking indemnification should be dismissed because, despite prior case law to the contrary, statements falsely imputing homosexuality should not constitute defamation per se.

🏛 RULE OF LAW
Statements falsely describing a person as lesbian, gay, or bisexual are not defamatory per se.

FACTS: Someone told Mincolla (D) that Yonaty (P) was gay or bisexual, and Mincolla (D) conveyed that information to a third party (third-party defendant), a close family friend of Yonaty's (P) girlfriend, with the hope that the girlfriend would be told—and she was. Yonaty (P), claiming that Mincolla's (D) actions caused the deterioration and ultimate termination of his relationship with his girlfriend, brought suit against Mincolla (D) for, inter alia, slander. Yonaty (P) did not plead special damages. Mincolla (D) in turn commenced suit against the third-party defendant, seeking indemnification based on the re-publication of the statements. The trial court concluded that it was bound to follow prior appellate case law holding that statements falsely imputing homosexuality constitute defamation per se and, thus, Yonaty's (P) slander claim need not be dismissed despite his failure to allege special damages. The parties cross-appealed, and the state's intermediate appellate court granted review.

ISSUE: Are statements falsely describing a person as lesbian, gay, or bisexual defamatory per se?

HOLDING AND DECISION: (Mercure, J.) No. Statements falsely describing a person as lesbian, gay, or bisexual are not defamatory per se. Whether a particular statement is susceptible of defamatory meaning is a question of law. Only if the contested statements are reasonably susceptible of a defamatory connotation does it become the jury's function to say whether that was the sense in which the words were likely to be understood by the ordinary and average person. Whether a statement has defamatory connotation depends on contemporary public opinion. Generally, a plaintiff asserting a cause of action sounding in slander must allege special damages contemplating the loss of something having economic or pecuniary value. If, as here, the plaintiff has not pleaded such damages, the action must be dismissed, unless challenged statements constitute "slander per se"—those categories of statements

that are commonly recognized as injurious by their nature, and so noxious that the law presumes that pecuniary damages will result. The appellate courts in this state have hitherto recognized statements falsely imputing homosexuality as a per se category. Those decisions are inconsistent with public policy and should no longer be followed, since it is no longer shameful or disgraceful to be described as lesbian, gay, or bisexual. The United State Supreme Court, in *Lawrence v. Texas*, 539 U.S. 558 (2003), stated that homosexuals "are entitled to respect for their private lives," but "[w]hen homosexual conduct is made criminal by the law of the State, that declaration in and of itself is an invitation to subject homosexual persons to discrimination in both the public and in the private spheres." These statements of the Supreme Court simply cannot be reconciled with the prior line of appellate cases concluding that being described as lesbian, gay or bisexual is so self-evidently injurious that the law will presume that pecuniary damages have resulted. Legislation within the state also prohibits discrimination based on sexual orientation, and the state has given same-sex couples the right to marry, with all attendant benefits of marriage. The most recent appellate case to consider this issue in depth was decided nearly 30 years ago. At that point in time, the court concluded that it was constrained to hold that a statement imputing homosexuality was defamatory per se in light of the then-existing "social opprobrium of homosexuality" and legal sanctions imposed upon homosexuals in areas ranging from immigration to military service. In light of the tremendous evolution in social attitudes regarding homosexuality since that case was decided, it cannot be said that current public opinion supports a rule that would equate statements imputing homosexuality with accusations of serious criminal conduct or insinuations that an individual has a loathsome disease (two of the other per se categories). For these reasons, the disputed statements in this case are not slanderous per se and, thus, Yonaty's (P) failure to allege special damages requires that his cause of action for slander be dismissed. Accordingly, the complaint and third-party complaint should be dismissed in their entirety.

▶ ANALYSIS

This case illustrates the relationship between categories of slander per se and evolving social norms and values. As the court points out, a statement that is "harmless in one age . . . may be highly damaging to reputation at another time," and vice versa. Thus, these categories are susceptible to change over time, and also may differ from state to

Continued on next page.

state. Other per se categories in New York are: statements (1) charging a plaintiff with a serious crime; (2) that tend to injure another in his or her trade, business or profession; (3) that a plaintiff has a loathsome disease; or (4) imputing unchastity to a woman.

Quicknotes

DEFAMATION PER SE An intentional false publication of words which, standing alone without proof, communicated publicly in either oral or written form, subject a person to scorn, hatred or ridicule.

SPECIAL DAMAGES Damages caused by a specific act that are not the usual consequence of that act and which must be specifically pled and proven.

Liberman v. Gelstein

Landlord (P) v. Tenant (D)

NY Ct. App., 80 N.Y.2d 429, 605 N.E.2d 344 (1992).

NATURE OF CASE: Appeal from dismissal of action for slander.

FACT SUMMARY: Liberman (P), a landlord, brought an action for slander against Gelstein (D) on the basis that the alleged statements tended to injure his business, trade, or profession.

🏛 RULE OF LAW
A qualified privilege to communicate regarding a common interest may be dissolved if a plaintiff can demonstrate that the statements were defamatory and the defendant spoke with malice.

FACTS: Gelstein (D) allegedly made defamatory statements about Liberman (P), a landlord, on two occasions: first, to Kohler, a fellow member of the building's tenants' board of governors, and second, in the presence of building employees. Liberman (P) brought an action for slander. The lawsuit's second cause of action alleged that Gelstein (D) made an accusation that Liberman (P) routinely paid police officers so that they would not issue parking tickets to cars parked in front of the building. Gelstein (D) moved to dismiss the complaint stating that he had a qualified "common interest" privilege to make an inquiry to a fellow board member for the purpose of determining if there was any wrongdoing by Liberman (P). The lower court dismissed the second cause of action finding that Gelstein (D) did have a qualified privilege and that Liberman (P) had failed to raise the issue of malice. The appellate division affirmed. Liberman (P) appealed.

ISSUE: Can a qualified privilege to communicate regarding a common interest be dissolved if a plaintiff can demonstrate that the statements were defamatory and the defendant spoke with malice?

HOLDING AND DECISION: (Kaye, J.) Yes. A qualified privilege to communicate regarding a common interest may be dissolved if a plaintiff can demonstrate that the statements were defamatory and the defendant spoke with malice. The privilege is only conditional and a finding of malice will dissolve it. Furthermore, courts have used two definitions of malice, and a finding of either one will suffice. The common-law definitions of malice is spite or ill will, while the Supreme Court standard for certain First Amendment cases is defined as "knowledge that the statement was false or reckless disregard of whether it was false or not." However, there is insufficient evidence in this case to support a finding of malice of either type. The common-law definition of ill will refers not to Gelstein's (D) personal feelings but to the motivation for making the statement.

Because of Gelstein's (D) and Kohler's common interest in the building, it cannot be proven that this was not his motivation. Under the Supreme Court definition, it also cannot be proven that Gelstein (D) knew that the statement was false. Although Gelstein (D) admitted that he did not know if the bribery charge was true, this is not the same as knowing for certain that it is false. In further support that malice was not proven, Gelstein (D) is supported by the fact that he made the statements only to Kohler and not the entire board of governors. Therefore, although a finding of malice can dissolve a privilege based on common interest, there is no basis for finding Gelstein (D) acted with malice based on the evidence presented. The appellate division properly upheld the dismissal of the slander action. Affirmed.

DISSENT: (Smith, J.) The evidence indicated that Liberman (P) might have been able to prove one of the definitions of malice, so the second cause of action should have been reinstated.

▶ ANALYSIS

There are two types of privileges that serve as defenses for defamation: absolute privilege and qualified privilege. Absolute privilege provides a complete defense and includes communications between spouses, statements made by public officials acting in their official capacity, and statements made by the parties in the course of a judicial proceeding. As discussed in this case, a qualified privilege may be restricted by a showing of malice. Other types of qualified privilege include employee references, credit reports, and statements made in defense of the speaker's interests.

■■■

Quicknotes

ABSOLUTE PRIVILEGE Complete immunity from liability for the communication of libelous or slanderous statements.

DEFAMATORY Subjecting to hatred, ridicule or injuring one in his occupation or business.

QUALIFIED PRIVILEGE Immunity from liability for libelous or slanderous statements communicated in the execution of a political, judicial, social or personal obligation, unless it is demonstrated that the statement was made with actual malice and knowledge of its falsity.

SLANDER Defamatory statement communicated orally.

■■■

Medico v. Time, Inc.

Alleged mob member (P) v. News magazine (D)

643 F.2d 134 (3d Cir.), *cert. denied*, 454 U.S. 836 (1981).

NATURE OF CASE: Appeal from summary judgment denial of damages for defamation.

FACT SUMMARY: In Medico's (P) action against Time, Inc. (D) for defamation, Medico (P) argued that Time's (D) publication, which described Medico (P) as a member of an organized crime "family," was not privileged under Pennsylvania law.

RULE OF LAW

The publication of defamatory matter concerning another in a report of official action or proceeding or meeting open to the public that deals with a matter of public concern is privileged if the report is accurate and complete or a fair abridgement of the occurrence reported.

FACTS: Time, Inc. (D) published an article that summarized FBI documents identifying Medico (P) as a member of an organized crime "family." Medico (P) sued Time (D) for defamation and contended that Time's (D) publication was not privileged under Pennsylvania law. Time (D) moved for summary judgment based on the substantial truth of its publication. The district court granted Time's (D) motion, but not on the basis of the truth defense. The court concluded that the Time (D) article represented a fair and accurate account of the FBI documents, and that Time's (D) publication was privileged within the common-law privilege given the press to report on official proceedings. Medico (P) appealed.

ISSUE: Is the publication of defamatory matter concerning another in a report of an official action or proceeding or meeting open to the public that deals with a matter of public concern privileged if the report is accurate and complete or a fair abridgement of the occurrence reported?

HOLDING AND DECISION: (Adams, J.) Yes. The fair report privilege allows the publication of defamatory matter concerning another in a report of an official action or proceeding or meeting open to the public that deals with a matter of public concern privileged if the report is accurate and complete or a fair abridgement of the occurrence reported. Here, Medico (P) contends that the FBI documents should not be deemed "official" because they express only tentative and preliminary conclusions that the FBI has never adopted as accurate. Also, because the FBI's information concerning Medico (P) never led to arrest or prosecution, the FBI materials may be thought to stem from such an early stage of official proceedings that the fair report privilege does not attach.

However, because the FBI documents concerning Medico (P) were compiled by government agents acting in their official capacities, the documents may be considered "official" and privileged. Nothing in the record suggests that the Time (D) article unfairly or inaccurately reported on the FBI materials. Therefore, the fair report privilege applies to the Time (D) article. Affirmed.

ANALYSIS

The privilege of "fair comment," developed in English law and adopted by American law, states that criticism, regardless of merit, is privileged if made honestly, with honesty measured by the accuracy of the critic's descriptive observations. The fair comment privilege parallels a general principle that only expressions of fact, not opinion, may be defamatory. Thus, for example, epithets alone are not actionable.

Quicknotes

DEFAMATION An intentional false publication, communicated publicly in either oral or written form, subjecting a person to scorn, hatred or ridicule, or injuring him or her in relation to his or her occupation or business.

LIBEL A false or malicious publication subjecting a person to scorn, hatred or ridicule, or injuring him or her in relation to his or her occupation or business.

Burnett v. National Enquirer, Inc.

Actress (P) v. Tabloid newspaper (D)

Cal. Ct. App., 144 Cal. App. 3d 991, 193 Cal. Rptr. 206 (1983).

NATURE OF CASE: Appeal of award of damages for defamation.

FACT SUMMARY: National Enquirer, Inc. (D) contended that by printing a retraction it was immune from general punitive damages for a defamatory article it carried in its weekly tabloid.

🏛 RULE OF LAW
A retraction will not shield a supermarket tabloid from general and punitive damages for defamatory material.

FACTS: National Enquirer, Inc. (D) published a weekly tabloid called "The National Enquirer." The content of the publication, which was commonly categorized within a generic class called "supermarket tabloids," tended not to include news, but rather how-to articles, stories of unusual events, and gossip columns. In one column, it was alleged that Burnett (P), a well-known actress and comedienne, had a drunken encounter with former Secretary of State Henry Kissinger, a well-known political figure. Burnett (P) demanded and received a retraction, but sued for defamation nonetheless. A jury awarded $300,000 compensatory and $1.3 million punitive damages, which the trial court remitted to $50,000 and $750,000, respectively. National Enquirer (D) appealed, contending that the retraction shielded it from all but special damages.

ISSUE: Will a retraction shield a supermarket tabloid from general and punitive damages for defamatory material?

HOLDING AND DECISION: (Roth, J.) No. A retraction will not shield a supermarket tabloid from general and punitive damages for defamatory material. Civil Code § 48a provides that a retraction will limit damages recoverable against a "newspaper" to special damages. While National Enquirer (D) calls its publication a newspaper, a look at its content reveals the case to be otherwise. The tabloid, like most supermarket tabloids, contains very little of the current events that legitimately can be called news. Its content tends toward personality and instruction. Such content cannot be legitimately classified as news, so § 48a is not available in this instance. [The court, on other grounds, further remitted the punitive damages to $150,000.] Affirmed as modified.

▶ ANALYSIS

The court here did not deal with the validity of the reaction itself. A retraction can be vague, ambiguous, or otherwise somewhat waffling. Another problem with retractions is the classic scenario of a newspaper's retraction to a head-line buried on page 24 of section D. Consequently, a retraction often does little to alleviate the effects of the initial defamation.

■==■

Quicknotes

DEFAMATION An intentional false publication, communicated publicly in either oral or written form, subjecting a person to scorn, hatred or ridicule, or injuring him or her in relation to his or her occupation or business.

LIBEL A false or malicious publication subjecting a person to scorn, hatred or ridicule, or injuring him or her in relation to his or her occupation or business.

PUNITIVE DAMAGES Damages exceeding the actual injury suffered for the purposes of punishment, deterrence and comfort to plaintiff.

■==■

Carafano v. Metrosplash.com, Inc.

Defamed actress (P) v. Computer dating service (D)

339 F.3d 1119 (9th Cir. 2003).

NATURE OF CASE: Appeal from summary judgment for defendant.

FACT SUMMARY: When Metrosplash.com Inc. (Metrosplash) (D) permitted an unknown person to post sexually explicit and personal information about the popular actress Christianne Carafano (P) on its computer dating website without her consent or knowledge, by pretending actually to be the actress, the latter sued Metrosplash (D) for defamation and other claims. Metrosplash (D) argued statutory immunity under 47 U.S.C. § 230(c)(1).

RULE OF LAW
By virtue of 47 U.S.C. § 230(c)(1), a computer match making service is statutorily immune from liability for false content in a dating profile provided by someone posing as another person.

FACTS: An unknown person using a computer in Berlin posted a bogus personal profile of the popular actress Christianne Carafano (P) in the Los Angeles section of "Matchmaker," a computer match making service operated by Metrosplash.com Inc. (Metrosplash) (D). The posting, which was sexually explicit, was made without the consent or even knowledge of Carafano (P). The bogus site also included her address and phone number. As a result, Carafano (P) received sexually explicit mail, phone calls, and had to leave her home for long periods of time for fear of her life and that of her son. Carafano (P) sued Metrosplash (D) for defamation and other claims. The federal district court granted Metrosplash's (D) motion for summary judgment, inter alia, providing immunity for the defamation claim under 47 U.S.C. § 230(c)(1) which states that no provider or user of an interactive computer service may be treated as the publisher or speaker of any information provided by another information content provider. Carafano (P) appealed.

ISSUE: By virtue of 47 U.S.C. § 230(c)(1), is a computer match making service statutorily immune from liability for false content in a dating profile provided by someone posing as another person?

HOLDING AND DECISION: (Thomas, J.) Yes. By virtue of 47 U.S.C. § 230(c)(1), a computer match making service is statutorily immune from liability for false content in a dating profile provided by someone posing as another person. 47 U.S.C. § 230(c)(1) was enacted by Congress to promote the free exchange of information and ideas over the internet and to encourage voluntary monitoring for offensive or obscene material.

Interactive computer services have flourished, to the benefit of all Americans, with a minimum of government regulation. Increasingly Americans are relying on interactive media for a variety of political, educational, cultural, and entertainment services. In view of these legislatively expressed goals, reviewing courts have treated § 230(c) immunity as quite robust, adopting a relatively expansive definition of information content provider. Under the statutory scheme, an interactive computer service, as here, qualifies for the statutory immunity so long as it does not also function as an information content provider for the portion of the statement or publication at issue. In the instant case, it does not since the selection of the content used by the unknown person from the Berlin computer was left exclusively to the user. Furthermore, the fact that some of the content was formulated in response to Metrosplash's (D) questionnaire does not alter this court's conclusion since the actual section of the content was left exclusively to the user. Affirmed.

ANALYSIS

In *Carafano*, the court noted that, even assuming arguendo, that the computer match making service could be considered an information content publisher, the statute precludes treatment as a publisher or speaker for any information provided by another information content provider.

■■■■

Quicknotes

DEFAMATION An intentional false publication, communicated publicly in either oral or written form, subjecting a person to scorn, hatred or ridicule, or injuring him in relation to his occupation or business.

PUBLICATION The communicating of a defamatory statement to a third party.

SUMMARY JUDGMENT Judgment rendered by a court in response to a motion made by one of the parties, claiming that the lack of a question of material fact in respect to an issue warrants disposition of the issue without consideration by the jury.

■■■■

New York Times Co. v. Sullivan

Police commissioner (P) v. Newspaper publisher (D)

376 U.S. 254 (1964).

NATURE OF CASE: Civil action for damages for libel.

FACT SUMMARY: The New York Times (D) published a full-page advertisement critical of the manner in which the Montgomery, Alabama, police, under Commissioner Sullivan (P), responded to civil rights demonstrations.

🏛 RULE OF LAW
A public official may not recover damages for a defamatory falsehood concerning his official conduct unless he can prove that the statement was made with actual malice.

FACTS: On March 29, 1960, the New York Times (D) carried a full-page advertisement entitled "Heed Their Rising Voices," placed by several black clergymen of Alabama. The advertisement charged that southern black students engaged in nonviolent demonstrations were "being met by an unprecedented wave of terror by those who would deny and negate" the United States Constitution and Bill of Rights. The advertisement went on to describe certain alleged events in support of this charge, including various actions taken by the police of Montgomery, Alabama. Sullivan (P), the Police Commissioner of Montgomery, brought a civil libel action against the New York Times (D), claiming that although the advertisement did not mention him by name, it attributed policy misconduct to him by inference. The trial judge instructed the jury that the advertisement was "libelous per se," leaving the New York Times (D) with no defense other than proving the statement true in all respects. Some of the statements were found to be inaccurate descriptions of events that had occurred in Montgomery, and Sullivan (P) was awarded $500,000. The Supreme Court of Alabama affirmed, and the New York Times (D) appealed on grounds of constitutional protection of speech and press.

ISSUE: Does the First Amendment limit the power of a state to award damages in a civil libel action brought by a public official against critics of his official conduct?

HOLDING AND DECISION: (Brennan, J.) Yes. If criticism of a public official's conduct is published without actual malice—that is, without knowledge that it was false and without reckless disregard of whether or not it was false—it is protected by the constitutional guarantees of freedom of speech and press. This qualified privilege to publish defamation of a public office is not limited to comment or opinion, but extends as well to false statements of fact, providing there was no actual malice. Behind this decision is a "profound national commitment to the principle that

debate on public issues should be uninhibited, robust and wide-open," and that "right conclusions are more likely to be gathered out of a multitude of tongues, than through any kind of authoritative selection." There would be a pall of fear and timidity imposed upon those who would give voice to pure criticism by any rule that would compel such a critic of official conduct to guarantee the truth of all his factual assertions. In addition, any attempt to transmute criticism of government to personal criticism, and hence potential libel of the officials of whom the government is composed, would be unconstitutional. Reversed and remanded.

CONCURRENCE: (Black, J.) The First and Fourteenth Amendments do not merely "delimit" a state's power to award damages to "public officials against critics of their official conduct" but completely prohibit the state from exercising such power.

CONCURRENCE: (Goldberg, J.) The First and Fourteenth Amendments afford the right to an absolute, unconditional privilege to criticize official conduct.

▶ ANALYSIS

Prior to the *Sullivan* case, there was a general recognition, at common law, of a qualified privilege known as "fair comment." Criticism of public officials' conduct and qualifications was allowed to be published as a matter of public concern—this much was undisputed. But sharp disagreement existed between state courts: the majority holding that the privilege of public discussion was limited to opinion and comment, and a vigorous minority insisting that even false statements of fact were privileged, if made for the public benefit with an honest belief in their truth. The Supreme Court of Alabama was thus following the majority position in the instant case, and the holding of the Supreme Court came as something of a bombshell, termed by tort law scholar Professor Prosser as "unquestionably the greatest victory won by the defendants in the modern history of the law of torts." Since *Sullivan*, the rule has been applied to criminal, as well as civil, libel and has been extended to all public officers and employees, no matter how inferior their position.

■━━■

Quicknotes

ACTUAL MALICE The issuance of a publication with knowledge of its falsity or with reckless disregard as to its truth.

Continued on next page.

LIBELOUS PER SE A false or malicious publication that subjects a person to scorn, hatred or ridicule, or that injures him in relation to his occupation or business of such an extreme nature that the law will presume that the person has suffered such injury.

Gertz v. Robert Welch, Inc.

Attorney (P) v. Publisher (D)

418 U.S. 323 (1974).

NATURE OF CASE: Action to recover damages for libel.

FACT SUMMARY: In an article written by a regular contributor to a magazine, published by Robert Welch, Inc. (D), it was falsely stated that Gertz (P), the attorney who had represented the family of a youth killed by a Chicago policeman, had participated in "framing" the officer, that he had a long police record, and that he was involved in communist groups.

> ## RULE OF LAW
> As long as they do not impose liability without fault, the states may define for themselves the appropriate standard of liability for a publisher or broadcaster of a defamatory falsehood injurious to a private individual, but they may not permit recovery of presumed or punitive damages if liability is not based on a showing of knowledge of falsity or reckless disregard for the truth.

FACTS: Gertz (P) was not well known to the general public, but he was a lawyer of repute who had participated in certain community and professional affairs. He represented the family of a youth, who had been killed by a Chicago policeman, at the coroner's inquest and in an action for damages, but played no part in the widely publicized criminal proceeding against the policeman for second-degree murder. The John Birch Society, in the name of Robert Welch, Inc. (D), published a monthly magazine for its views that was making an effort to alert the public to an alleged nationwide conspiracy to discredit local police. A regular contributor to the magazine had his article published concerning the aforementioned incident in Chicago, the editor making no effort to confirm or verify the charges made in the article claiming to have no reason to have doubted them. In that article, it was falsely stated that Gertz (P) was a "major architect" of a plot to frame the policeman, that he had a long police record, that he was an official of the Marxist League for Industrial Democracy, and that he was a "Leninist" and a "Communist-fronter." In his libel suit, Gertz (P) was awarded $50,000 by the jury. At first, the trial judge ruled that Robert Welch (D) had no defense because Gertz (P) was not a public official or a public figure, but subsequently the judge decided that the article had involved a matter of public concern. That, he determined, made applicable the "actual malice" standard of *New York Times v. Sullivan* Co., 376 U.S. 254 (1964), that case holding that defamation of a public official did not subject one to liability unless "actual malice" could be shown, meaning that the statement was made with the

knowledge that it was false or with a reckless disregard for whether or not it was false. Noting that *St. Amantv v. Thompson*, 390 U.S. 727 (1968), had held that failure to investigate, without more, could not establish reckless disregard for truth, the judge therefore, granted judgment notwithstanding the verdict to Robert Welch (D), and Gertz (P) appealed. Gertz (P) continued to contend that he was not a public person and that the "actual malice" standard should not, therefore, be applied in his case, while Robert Welch (D) contended that Gertz (P) was a public person and that even if he were not, the "actual malice" standard should apply because the case involved comment on an issue of public concern.

ISSUE: Is it up to the states to determine the appropriate standard of liability for a publisher or broadcaster of defamatory falsehood injurious to a private individual, as long as they do not impose liability without fault?

HOLDING AND DECISION: (Powell, J.) Yes. As long as they do not impose liability without fault, it is up to the states to determine the appropriate standard of liability for a publisher or broadcaster of defamatory falsehood injurious to a private individual. When a private party is defamed, he is less able to gain access to media to rebut the falsehoods, he has not chosen to give up some of his privacy for interaction in public affairs, and the legitimate interest in redressing his injury is greater in relation to the public concern for a vigorous and uninhibited press than when the defamed party is a public official or a public figure. Such public people are, generally, voluntarily in a public position, so they have chosen to hold themselves open to more attention by the public and the press. It does not make sense to simply extend the "actual malice" standard to cases where nonpublic parties are defamed because the state interest in compensating injury to the reputation of private individuals requires that a different rule should obtain with respect to them. Extending the "actual malice" rule to private individuals would necessitate each judge deciding on an ad hoc basis which publications addressed issues of "general or public interest," and that is not the ideal solution. It is better to let each state establish a workable and uniform standard for liability. So, as long as liability is not imposed in the absence of fault, each state can determine for itself the appropriate standard for liability in defamation actions involving private individuals. However, recovery of presumed or punitive damages may not be allowed when liability is not based on the "actual malice" standard, as juries have wide discretion in assessing such tolls and that could lead to recoveries which would

Continued on next page.

engender a type of media self-censorship. Inasmuch as Gertz (P) never became a public person by injecting himself into a public controversy or occupying a position whereby he was what is commonly considered to be a public official, this case clearly is involving defamation of an individual. Thus, insistence that the "actual malice" be used in this case was incorrect. Furthermore, a new trial is necessary because the jury was allowed to impose liability without fault and to presume damages without proof of injury. Reversed and remanded.

CONCURRENCE: (Blackmun, J.) Because there is a need for a final and clear position with regard to defamation, I concur. Otherwise I would hold to my opinion in *Rosenbloom v. Metromedia*, 409 U.S. 29 (1971).

DISSENT: (Burger, C.J.) The important public policy which underlies the tradition of right of counsel would be gravely jeopardized if every lawyer who takes an "unpopular" case, civil or criminal, would automatically become fair game for irresponsible reporters and editors who might, for example, describe the lawyer as a "mob mouthpiece" for representing a client with a serious prior criminal record, or as an "ambulance chaser" for representing a claimant in a personal injury action.

DISSENT: (Douglas, J.) This decision will permit states to adopt even a negligence standard for defamation, which will impose damages on a publisher for not acting as a "reasonable man," whose best course under such circumstances would be simply not to speak at all. I would affirm the judgment below, considering the First and Fourteenth Amendments to prohibit the imposition of damages for such a discussion of public affairs as occurred in this case.

DISSENT: (Brennan, J.) The *Times's* "actual malice" standard should be applied in cases such as this, judges being perfectly capable of exercising the type of judgment needed to determine what is and what is not an issue of "general or public interest." They already make that type of decision daily.

DISSENT: (White, J.) In essence, this decision shifts the burden of published falsehoods to the innocent victim, which is unnecessary since it has not been proven that holding a publisher responsible for his libel of a private person has hampered the press in publishing the truth.

▌ ANALYSIS

It has been held that punitive damages are permitted when liability is predicated on a standard of "actual malice." *Maheu v. Highs Tool Co.*, 569 F.2d 459 (9th Cir. 1978). However, some state courts have absolutely prohibited the imposition of such damages in defamation cases, expressing a concern about the tendency to create self-censorship among the media.

Quicknotes

ACTUAL MALICE The issuance of a publication with knowledge of its falsity or with reckless disregard as to its truth.

DEFAMATION An intentional false publication, communicated publicly in either oral or written form, subjecting a person to scorn, hatred or ridicule, or injuring him or her in relation to his or her occupation or business.

LIBEL A false or malicious publication subjecting a person to scorn, hatred or ridicule, or injuring him or her in relation to his or her occupation or business.

NEGLIGENCE Conduct falling below the standard of care that a reasonable person would demonstrate under similar conditions.

STRICT LIABILITY Liability for all injuries proximately caused by a party's conducting of certain inherently dangerous activities without regard to negligence or fault.

Wells v. Liddy

Defamed secretary (P) v. Alleged defamer (D)

186 F.3d 505 (4th Cir. 1999).

NATURE OF CASE: Appeal of dismissal of defamation claims.

FACT SUMMARY: Wells (P) alleged that Liddy (D) had made defamatory remarks about her role in the break-in at the Democratic National Committee offices in the Watergate building complex.

🏛 **RULE OF LAW**
To prove that a plaintiff is an involuntary public figure, the defendant must demonstrate that the plaintiff has become a central figure in a significant public controversy and the allegedly defamatory statement has arisen in the course of discourse regarding the public matter.

FACTS: Wells (P) was secretary to the Executive Director of the Association of State Democratic Chairmen, whose phone was tapped at the time the office of Democratic National Committee, located in the Watergate building complex, was broken into in 1972. Liddy (D) was counsel to the Committee to Reelect the President (Nixon) and was convicted of various charges and served 52 months in jail. In 1991 Liddy (D) began repeating information published in a book in 1984 mentioning the possibility that the break-in was tied to an investigation into prostitution, and that a book with names had been locked in Wells's (P) drawer. When Wells (P) sued for defamation, Liddy (D) successfully maintained that Wells (P) was an involuntary public figure and therefore had to prove actual malice in order to succeed in her defamation suit. The district court concluded that Wells (P) was an involuntary public figure and dismissed all charges. Wells (P) appealed.

ISSUE: To prove that a plaintiff is an involuntary public figure, must the defendant demonstrate that the plaintiff has become a central figure in a significant public controversy and the allegedly defamatory statement has arisen in the course of discourse regarding the public matter?

HOLDING AND DECISION: (Williams, J.) Yes. To prove that a plaintiff is an involuntary public figure, the defendant must demonstrate that the plaintiff has become a central figure in a significant public controversy and the allegedly defamatory statement has arisen in the course of discourse regarding the public matter. Liddy (D) failed to show that Wells (P) had voluntarily assumed a role of special prominence in a public controversy, so she could not be a limited-purpose public figure. Nor can Wells (P) be considered an involuntary public figure. Wells (P) has not been a central figure in media reports on Watergate.

Wells (P) is a private figure, and she need not prove actual malice to recover compensatory damages. Reversed and remanded.

▶ **ANALYSIS**

The court reviewed all recent cases in defamation law. The actual malice standard applies only to public figures. The level of fault to be proved by private figures to recover compensatory damages in defamation suits is now a matter of state law.

━━■■■━━

Quicknotes

ACTUAL MALICE The issuance of a publication with knowledge of its falsity or with reckless disregard as to its truth.

COMPENSATORY DAMAGES Measure of damages necessary to compensate victim for actual injuries suffered.

DEFAMATION An intentional false publication, communicated publicly in either oral or written form, subjecting a person to scorn, hatred or ridicule, or injuring him or her in relation to his or her occupation or business.

PRIVATE FIGURES/CITIZENS An individual who does not hold a public office or that is not a member of the armed forces.

PUBLIC FIGURE Any person who is generally known in the community.

Milkovich v. Lorain Journal Co.

High school coach (P) v. Publisher (D) and Columnist (D)

497 U.S. 1 (1990).

NATURE OF CASE: Review of order dismissing libel action.

FACT SUMMARY: Diadiun (D) contended that allegedly libelous passages he had written could not be so because they were assertions of opinion, not fact.

🏛 **RULE OF LAW**
An expression of opinion may be actionable defamation.

FACTS: Milkovich (P) was the coach of a high school wrestling team. After a fight broke out with an opposing team and Milkovich (P) was found to have instigated it, he was censured and the team put on probation by local authorities. Parents of some team members filed a lawsuit to enjoin the sanctions. Milkovich (P) testified at the hearing. A judge issued a restraining order against the authorities. Subsequent to this, Diadiun (D), a sports journalist, published an article in a local newspaper published by Lorain Journal Co. (D). In the article, Diadiun (D) essentially made the point that successful sports figures, such as Milkovich (P), could get out of trouble by lying their way out, as Milkovich (P) had done at the court hearing. Milkovich (P) sued for libel, contending that Diadiun (D) had accused him of perjury. After a lengthy pretrial process, the trial court dismissed on the grounds that the article constituted assertions of opinion, not fact. The state court of appeals affirmed, and the state supreme court denied review. The United States Supreme Court granted certiorari.

ISSUE: May an expression of opinion be actionable defamation?

HOLDING AND DECISION: (Rehnquist, C.J.) Yes. An expression of opinion may be actionable defamation. To hold otherwise would ignore the fact that expressions of opinion often imply the assertion of an objective fact. For instance, to say "in my opinion Jones is a liar" is to imply that facts indicating that Jones is a liar exist. Either mode of expression can be equally damaging to one's reputation. As a matter of constitutional protection of speech, the First Amendment already requires that a public figure prove actual malice, which is to say, knowledge of falsity or reckless disregard for the truth. To add another layer of analysis regarding whether a statement is one of opinion or fact is neither necessary nor appropriate. In this instance, the assertions made by Diadiun (D) are capable of being inferred by a reader as saying that Milkovich (P) had committed perjury, and therefore the issue should go to a jury. Reversed and remanded.

DISSENT: (Brennan, J.) The Court's analytical framework is correct. In this case, however, the issue should not go to the jury, because Diadiun's (D) statements are not capable of being interpreted as either stating or implying defamatory facts about Milkovich (P).

▶ **ANALYSIS**

In every defamation action a court must make the threshold determination of whether the statements at issue are capable of defamatory interpretation. This legal conclusion is necessary before a case goes to a jury. Here, the Court did rule on this issue. Also, where a public official is involved, the court must make a determination of malice. The Supreme Court did not reach this issue here.

━━━

Quicknotes

ACTUAL MALICE The issuance of a publication with knowledge of its falsity or with reckless disregard as to its truth.

DEFAMATION An intentional false publication, communicated publicly in either oral or written form, subjecting a person to scorn, hatred or ridicule, or injuring him or her in relation to his or her occupation or business.

LIBEL A false or malicious publication subjecting a person to scorn, hatred or ridicule, or injuring him or her in relation to his or her occupation or business.

━━━

Flamm v. American Association of University Women

Defamed attorney (P) v. Alleged defamer (D)

201 F.3d 144 (2d Cir. 2000).

NATURE OF CASE: Review of dismissal of defamation suit.

FACT SUMMARY: Flamm (P) alleged that the American Association of University Women (AAUW) (D) had defamed him when they listed him in a directory as an "ambulance chaser."

RULE OF LAW

In a suit by a private plaintiff involving a matter of public concern, the allegedly defamatory statements must be provably false, and the plaintiff must bear the burden of proving falsity.

FACTS: The American Association of University Women (AAUW) (D) published a directory listing attorneys who handle gender discrimination cases and distributed it to its members. Flamm (P) was the only attorney with negative comments next to his name. He was said to be an "ambulance chaser" with interest only in "slam dunk cases." When Flamm (P) sued for libel per se, the district court dismissed because the statement challenged by Flamm (P) could not reasonably be construed as a statement of objective fact. Flamm (P) appealed.

ISSUE: In a suit by a private plaintiff involving a matter of public concern, must the allegedly defamatory statements be provably false, and must the plaintiff bear the burden of proving falsity?

HOLDING AND DECISION: (Meskill, J.) Yes. In a suit by a private plaintiff involving a matter of public concern, the allegedly defamatory statements must be provably false, and the plaintiff must bear the burden of proving falsity. A reasonable person could find that the challenged statement alleged or implied a provably false fact. The term "ambulance chaser" reasonably implied that Flamm (P) had engaged in unethical solicitation, and was reasonably susceptible to the defamatory meaning imputed to it. Reversed.

▶ ANALYSIS

The AAUW (D) tried to argue that the language was mere hyperbole. Rhetorical hyperbole may not be actionable. It was sufficient to show that the challenged statement reasonably implied the defamatory meaning to withstand a motion to dismiss.

Quicknotes

COMPENSATORY DAMAGES Measure of damages necessary to compensate victim for actual injuries suffered.

DEFAMATION An intentional false publication, communicated publicly in either oral or written form, subjecting a person to scorn, hatred or ridicule, or injuring him or her in relation to his or her occupation or business.

LIBEL PER SE A false or malicious publication that subjects a person to scorn, hatred or ridicule, or that injures him in relation to his occupation or business of such an extreme nature that the law will presume that the person has suffered such injury.

PUNITIVE DAMAGES Damages exceeding the actual injury suffered for the purposes of punishment, deterrence and comfort to plaintiff.

Khawar v. Globe International, Inc.

Defamed photographer (P) v. Alleged defamer (D)

Cal. Sup. Ct., 19 Cal. 4th 254, 965 P.2d 696 (1998), cert. denied, 526 U.S. 1114 (1999).

NATURE OF CASE: Appeal from damages award in defamation suit.

FACT SUMMARY: Khawar (P) alleged that Globe International, Inc. (D) had defamed him by publishing a photograph and an uncritical book review of a book that claimed he had killed Robert Kennedy.

> ## RULE OF LAW
> Where a finding of actual malice is based on the republication of a third party's defamatory falsehoods, actual malice may be found where there were obvious reasons to doubt the veracity of the informant or the accuracy of his reports and the republisher failed to interview obvious witnesses or consult relevant documentary sources.

FACTS: Khawar (P) was a photographer working near the scene when Robert Kennedy was assassinated in 1968. Globe International Inc. (Globe) (D) published a weekly tabloid and in one 1989 issue published a book review of a book claiming that Khawar (P) had killed Kennedy. Khawar (P) successfully sued for damages for defamation. The judgment was affirmed on appeal and Globe (D) petitioned for review. The state supreme court granted review.

ISSUE: Where a finding of actual malice is based on the republication of a third party's defamatory falsehoods, may actual malice be found where there were obvious reasons to doubt the veracity of the informant or the accuracy of his reports and the re-publisher failed to interview obvious witnesses or consult relevant documentary sources?

HOLDING AND DECISION: (Kennard, J.) Yes. Where a finding of actual malice is based on the republication of a third party's defamatory falsehoods, actual malice may be found where there were obvious reasons to doubt the veracity of the informant or the accuracy of his reports and the re-publisher failed to interview obvious witnesses or consult relevant documentary sources. Because there were obvious reasons to doubt the accuracy of the book's accusation that Khawar (P) had killed Kennedy, and because that claim was an inherently defamatory accusation against Khawar (P), the jury could properly conclude that Globe (D) acted with actual malice in republishing the claim if it also found that Globe (D) failed to use readily available means to verify the accuracy of the claim. Affirmed.

▶ ANALYSIS

The court found there was clear and convincing evidence to support the jury's finding. Clear and convincing evi-

dence is a higher standard that must be met in cases where actual malice is the test. The court also determined that Khawar (P) was not a public figure.

Quicknotes

ACTUAL MALICE The issuance of a publication with knowledge of its falsity or with reckless disregard as to its truth.

COMPENSATORY DAMAGES Measure of damages necessary to compensate victim for actual injuries suffered.

DEFAMATION An intentional false publication, communicated publicly in either oral or written form, subjecting a person to scorn, hatred or ridicule, or injuring him or her in relation to his or her occupation or business.

PRIVATE FIGURES/CITIZENS An individual that does not hold a public office or that is not a member of the armed forces.

PUBLIC FIGURE Any person who is generally known in the community.

PUNITIVE DAMAGES Damages exceeding the actual injury suffered for the purposes of punishment, deterrence and comfort to plaintiff.

▓▓▓

▓▓▓

CHAPTER 15

Protecting Privacy

Quick Reference Rules of Law

Haynes v. Alfred A. Knopf, Inc.

Subject of book (P) v. Publisher (D)

8 F.3d 1222 (7th Cir. 1993).

NATURE OF CASE: Appeal from dismissal of right to privacy claim.

FACT SUMMARY: Haynes (P), whose personal life was discussed by his former wife in a book published by Alfred A. Knopf, Inc. (Knopf) (D), brought a claim for invasion of privacy against Knopf (D) and the book's author.

🏛 **RULE OF LAW**
To recover for invasion of privacy, a plaintiff must show that the private facts disclosed were of the type that would make a reasonable person deeply offended and in which the public has no legitimate interest.

FACTS: Nicholas Lemann (D) wrote a book about the social, political, and economic effects of the movement of blacks from the rural south to the cities of the north between 1940 and 1970. To illustrate these themes and to add a personal dimension, he used the life of Ruby Lee Daniels, who had moved from Mississippi to Chicago during the same time period. She offered stories on all aspects of her life, including her relationship with her former husband, Luther Haynes (P). She described him as a man who drank too much, neglected his family, and could not hold down a job. Daniels stated that Haynes (P) was unfaithful and eventually left her for another woman. Haynes (P) sued publisher Alfred A. Knopf, Inc. (Knopf) (D) and author Lemann (D) for libel and invasion of privacy. Although he admitted that many of the incidents in the book were true, he argued that they had occurred more than twenty-five years earlier and he was now a reformed man. The trial court dismissed the claim, stating that, on the facts, no reasonable jury could render a verdict for Haynes (P). Haynes (P) appealed.

ISSUE: To recover for invasion of privacy, must a plaintiff show that the private facts disclosed were of the type that would make a reasonable person deeply offended and in which the public has no legitimate interest?

HOLDING AND DECISION: (Posner, C.J.) Yes. To recover for invasion of privacy, a plaintiff must show that the private facts disclosed were of the type that would make a reasonable person deeply offended and in which the public has no legitimate interest. The type of information must be of a type that has no element of newsworthiness other than catering to voyeurism. The details contained in the book about Haynes (P) do not fall into this category. Although Haynes's (P) claims that embarrassing and intimate details were disclosed, this is simply untrue. There

was no sexual act described, only foreplay, and references to adultery and heavy drinking Haynes (P) admitted to be true. All of the details revealed were relevant to the story that Lemann (D) was telling. The tone of the book is serious and it addresses real social and political issues. In fact, the book has received high praise from many distinguished black scholars. Furthermore, Haynes's (P) suggestion that pseudonyms should have been used is not a solution because he still could have sued if the descriptions in the book unmistakably identified him. Although questions of fact are usually decided by a jury, the trial court was justified in granting summary judgment for Knopf (D) and Lemann (D) since there was no evidence upon which a jury could have reached a verdict for Haynes (P). Affirmed.

▶ **ANALYSIS**

The court distinguished this case from that of a former prostitute acquitted of murder who was successful in her invasion of privacy claim. She had been living a quiet life in a new neighborhood until a movie about the murder used her maiden name, and all of her friends and neighbors learned of the past she had tried to leave behind. See *Melvin v. Reid*, 297 P. 91 (1931). Although there was some similarity to Haynes's (P) claim, the court was probably justified in dismissing his case as the details were far less revealing and shocking, and the format in which they appeared, a book about social and historical themes, was not as likely to be sensationalized as a movie.

▄▬▬▄

Quicknotes

LIBEL A false or malicious publication subjecting a person to scorn, hatred or ridicule, or injuring him or her in relation to his or her occupation or business.

▄▬▬▄

The Florida Star v. B.J.F.

Publisher (D) v. Rape victim (P)

491 U.S. 524 (1989).

NATURE OF CASE: Review of award of damages for invasion of privacy.

FACT SUMMARY: B.J.F. (P), an alleged rape victim, sued The Florida Star (D) under a state statute prohibiting the publication of rape victims' names.

🏛 **RULE OF LAW**
A statute that prohibits the publication of a rape victim's name in any instrument of mass communication is unconstitutional.

FACTS: B.J.F. (P) filed a police report that she had been robbed and raped. The report was typed and left in the press room. A reporter from The Florida Star (D), a weekly newspaper, picked up the report. It was included in the paper's "Police Reports" section. B.J.F. (P) was identified by name. Subsequent to this, B.J.F. (P) brought an action for damages under Florida Statutes § 794.03, which prohibited the publication of a rape victim's name in any "instrument of mass communication." A jury awarded $100,000 in damages. The state court of appeals affirmed, and the state supreme court denied review. The United States Supreme Court accepted review.

ISSUE: Is a statute that prohibits the publication of a rape victim's name in any instrument of mass communication constitutional?

HOLDING AND DECISION: (Marshall, J.) No. A statute that prohibits the publication of a rape victim's name in any instrument of mass communication is unconstitutional. A natural tension exists between the First Amendment's freedom of the press and state laws protecting privacy. Previous decisions of this Court regarding publication of truthful material can be synthesized as follows: A state may punish publication of truthful material lawfully obtained only to further a state interest of the highest order. This standard adequately protects the competing interests of the First Amendment and privacy. First, since only lawfully obtained information is included in the standard, the state may protect its interests by not disseminating the information. Second, punishing an informant of mass communication for disseminating information that is already public is unlikely to advance state interests. Finally, to deny such protection would result in media timidity inconsistent with the First Amendment. Applying this standard to the law at issue, it appears clearly that § 794.03 is constitutionally infirm. First, the information was lawfully obtained. The question then becomes whether § 794.03 serves a government interest of the highest order. It does not. First, The Florida Star obtained the record from the state itself. Second, § 794.03 imposes liability per se without a case-by-case analysis of what facts have been made available. Finally, the section is underinclusive in that it prohibits dissemination by "instruments of mass communication" only. If the state's interest in nondisclosure was of the highest order, other sources would need to be included in its ambit as well. Based on these considerations, the conclusion must be that § 794.03, violates the Constitution. Reversed.

CONCURRENCE: (Scalia, J.) The underinclusiveness of the statute, standing alone, justifies holding it unconstitutional.

DISSENT: (White, J.) Florida's release of the information was inadvertent and not a matter of policy. Consequently, a major justification for holding no high state interest to be served by § 794.03, the fact that the information was made public, is inappropriate. To protect rape victims from further public exposure is such an interest.

▶ **ANALYSIS**

The standard articulated here appears to be very deferential to the press. Exactly what sort of state interest would justify a law like § 794.03, is difficult to envision. Justice Marshall suggested information related to troop movements in time of war. Whether anything less compelling could meet the test, here, remains to be seen.

━━━

Quicknotes

FIRST AMENDMENT Prohibits Congress from enacting any law respecting an establishment of religion, prohibiting the free exercise of religion, abridging freedom of speech or the press, the right of peaceful assembly and the right to petition for a redress of grievances.

NEGLIGENCE Conduct falling below the standard of care that a reasonable person would demonstrate under similar conditions.

━━━

Cantrell v. Forest City Publishing Co.

Wife of accident victim (P) v. Publisher (D)

419 U.S. 245 (1974).

NATURE OF CASE: Action for damages for invasion of privacy.

FACT SUMMARY: Eszterhas (D), a reporter, did a follow-up story on the effects of a bridge collapse on the survivors of those who had died.

🏛 RULE OF LAW

A reckless disregard of the truth will expose a publisher to liability in an action for invasion of privacy.

FACTS: Cantrell's (P) husband died in a bridge collapse. Forest City Publishing Co. (D) decided to do a follow-up story on the disaster. Eszterhas (D), a reporter, decided to interview the Cantrells (P) to determine the effect that her husband's death had on the family. Eszterhas (D) went to the Cantrells' (P) home and interviewed and took pictures of the children. Mrs. Cantrell (P) was not at home. The story, when published, contained many inaccuracies including a so-called interview with and description of Mrs. Cantrell (P). Mrs. Cantrell (P) sued for invasion of privacy in that she and her children were cast in a false light and were exposed to ridicule and pity. The court dismissed the punitive damage issue on the basis that there was no showing of actual malice. It declined to dismiss the entire action and instructed the jury that liability could be found for reckless disregard of the truth. The jury found for Cantrell (P), but was reversed by the appellate court. It felt that the district court's dismissal of the punitive damage issue through a showing of no actual malice was dispositive of the issue since this was necessary for recovery.

ISSUE: Will a reckless disregard of the truth expose a publisher to liability for invasion of privacy?

HOLDING AND DECISION: (Stewart, J.) Yes. It is obvious from the facts that the district court was using "malice" in its common-law meaning when the punitive damage issue was dismissed. The jury was properly instructed that they could find liability for a reckless falsehood or a knowing disregard of the truth. The record contains adequate facts upon which to find that Eszterhas (P) knew that a portion of his story was false and published it in reckless disregard of the truth. For this, both he and Forest City Publishing (D) are liable. Reversed and remanded.

DISSENT: (Douglas, J.) The Cantrells (P) were cast into the public eye. First Amendment guarantees require that, absent a showing of actual malice, publications should be immune from defamation actions.

▶ ANALYSIS

This case should be compared with *Gobin v. Globe Publishing Co.*, 649 P.2d 1239 (Kan. 1982), and *Cox Broadcasting Corp. v. Cohn*, 420 U.S. 469 (1975). In *Cantrell*, the newsworthy value and interest in the story were stale. The embellishments in the story were knowingly false. They were included to make the feature more interesting. Such knowingly false attempts to sensationalize a story abrogate the conditional privilege to inform the public. It would appear that simple negligence would not be sufficient to establish liability. Malice is necessary.

Quicknotes

ACTUAL MALICE The issuance of a publication with knowledge of its falsity or with reckless disregard as to its truth.

DEFAMATION An intentional false publication, communicated publicly in either oral or written form, subjecting a person to scorn, hatred or ridicule, or injuring him or her in relation to his or her occupation or business.

PUNITIVE DAMAGES Damages exceeding the actual injury suffered for the purposes of punishment, deterrence and comfort to plaintiff.

Nader v. General Motors Corp.

Consumer advocate (P) v. Automobile manufacturer (D)

N.Y. Ct. App., 25 N.Y.2d 560, 255 N.E.2d 765 (1970).

NATURE OF CASE: Appeal from denial of dismissal in action in damages for invasion of privacy.

FACT SUMMARY: Nader (P) alleged that his telephone had been tapped and he had been followed in public places.

🏛 RULE OF LAW
A party has the right to privacy, even when out in public, if the conduct is overly intrusive and the information sought would not be available through normal inquires.

FACTS: Nader (P) was writing a book exposing the automobile industry. In an attempt to prevent publication, General Motors Corp. (D) allegedly tapped Nader's (P) telephone, engaged in public harassment and kept him under surveillance while he was in public places. Nader (P) alleged that he had been accosted on the street by women who publicly propositioned him; that he had calls at odd hours; that his friends were contacted by General Motors' (D) agents who asked personal questions concerning Nader; that agents followed him to his bank and attempted to ascertain the denomination of bills he had received. General Motors (D) filed a motion to dismiss alleging that the acts charged did not constitute an invasion of privacy, but it was denied by the trial court and affirmed by the Appellate Division.

ISSUE: Does a party have a right to privacy while in public if conduct is overly intrusive and the information sought would not be available through normal inquires?

HOLDING AND DECISION: (Fuld, C.J.) Yes. A party has the right to privacy, even when out in public, if the conduct is overly intrusive and the information sought would not be available through normal inquires. Normally the right to privacy does not extend to activities done in public. Everyone must accept a limited invasion on his or her right to privacy while out in public. However, if the intrusion is unreasonable and the information sought would not otherwise be available through normal inquiry an action for invasion of privacy will lie. Nader's (P) allegations concerning the contacting of friends concerning him does not involve an invasion of privacy since the information would not be private since it was known to others. The alleged propositions on the street or harassing phone calls also fail to constitute an invasion of privacy. They may be annoying, but they are not actionable as invasions of privacy. The electronic surveillance and the telephone taps however do constitute an invasion of privacy since one has a right to expect that one's conversations will not be intercepted by others. The actions of General Motors' (D) agents at the bank may also constitute an invasion of privacy—a party, even in public, has some rights to privacy. If surveillance is overly intrusive and the information sought would not otherwise be available, an action would lie. If Nader (P) acted in a manner to prevent the general public from ascertaining the denomination of the bills he received, a cause of action may lie. All of the activities, taken together, are relevant to a cause of action for intentional infliction of emotional distress. Affirmed.

CONCURRENCE: (Breitel, J.) The court goes well beyond an analysis of whether the causes of action for invasion of privacy should be dismissed. Rather it appears to be rendering an advisory opinion on the merits and the law in general. This was well beyond the scope of the motion that should merely have been denied.

▌ ANALYSIS

Professor Prosser analyzes invasion of privacy as four torts: intrusion, public disclosure of private facts, making one appear in a false light in the public eye, and appropriation of one's likeness or name. The *Nader* case involves intrusion. Intrusion occurs if there is a prying into the plaintiff's privacy that would be offensive or objectionable to a reasonable man. The thing pried into or intruded upon must be private and entitled to privacy. The tort fills the gaps left by trespass, nuisance, and whatever remedies there may be for the invasion of constitutional rights.

Quicknotes

INTENTIONAL INFLICTION OF EMOTIONAL DISTRESS Intentional and extreme behavior on the part of the wrongdoer with the intent to cause the victim to suffer from severe emotional distress, or with reckless indifference, resulting in the victim's suffering from severe emotional distress.

Galella v. Onassis

Photographer (P) v. Widow of ex-President (D)

487 F.2d 986 (2d Cir. 1973).

NATURE OF CASE: Appeal of injunction restraining harassment.

FACT SUMMARY: Galella (P), self-ordained photographer of celebrity Onassis (D), contended that the First Amendment prohibited a court from restraining him from following her.

> ## RULE OF LAW
> The First Amendment does not prohibit a court from issuing a restraining order against a photographer.

FACTS: Galella (P) considered himself a "paparazzo" with respect to Onassis (D), wife of a wealthy industrialist and widow of President John F. Kennedy. Pursuant to this calling, Galella (P) engaged in a pattern of "tailing" Onassis (D) and her children. His activities included interrupting recreational activities, bribing apartment and restaurant doormen, and driving a power boat uncomfortably close to Onassis (D) when she swam in the lake. At Onassis's (D) behest, Galella (P) was arrested by the Secret Service. He sued for malicious prosecution. Onassis counterclaimed for an injunction against Galella's (P) harassment. The district court dismissed Galella's (P) action and issued an order restraining Galella (P) from approaching within 100 yards of the Onassis home, 75 yards of Onassis (D), or 50 yards of her children. Galella (P) appealed.

ISSUE: Does the First Amendment prohibit a court from issuing a restraining order against a photographer?

HOLDING AND DECISION: (Smith, J.) No. The First Amendment does not prohibit a court from issuing a restraining order against a photographer. A photographer or newsgatherer is not shielded by the First Amendment from state laws; crimes and torts committed while gathering news are not protected. Here, there is no question but that Galella (P) violated New York privacy laws in his pattern of following Onassis (D) and her children. The fact that Onassis (D) is a public figure gave Galella (P) no special rights in this context. Consequently, the district court was justified in entering the order restraining Galella (P). [The court then modified the district court's order decreasing the prohibited distances to twenty-five feet of Onassis (D) and thirty feet of her children.] Affirmed as modified.

▶ ANALYSIS

The rule of Onassis's (D) being a public figure is not entirely certain in the context of this case. It seems clear from the opinion that a photographer may not with impunity tail a public figure. The fact that the injunction was modified may imply some limited right, but the court did not render itself explicit on this point. Whether a modification would have been effected if a nonpublic individual had been involved is unclear.

■=■

Quicknotes

FIRST AMENDMENT Prohibits Congress from enacting any law respecting an establishment of religion, prohibiting the free exercise of religion, abridging freedom of speech or the press, the right of peaceful assembly and the right to petition for a redress of grievances.

PUBLIC FIGURE Any person who is generally known in the community.

■=■

Desnick v. American Broadcasting Companies, Inc.

Physicians (P) v. Broadcaster (D)

44 F.3d 1345 (7th Cir. 1995).

NATURE OF CASE: Appeal from dismissal of claims for trespass and invasion of privacy.

FACT SUMMARY: Doctors from the Desnick Eye Center (P) filed suit against American Broadcasting Companies, Inc. (ABC) (D) for sending reporters equipped with hidden video cameras pretending to be patients to the eye clinics.

RULE OF LAW
No invasion of privacy or trespass occurs when an individual posing as a patient, for investigative purposes, visits a doctor and secretly videotapes the consultation.

FACTS: Producers and reporters of the American Broadcasting Companies, Inc. (ABC) (D) program Prime-Time Live prepared to run a story on the Desnick Eye Center (P) in which they would allege that Dr. Desnick was performing unnecessary cataract surgeries. ABC (D) had contacted Desnick, asking if they could tape a surgery at his office and stating that they would not conduct an ambush-type interview. Desnick consented. In addition to this taping, however, ABC (D) sent individuals posing as patients to other Desnick Eye Clinic (P) locations and equipped them with hidden cameras. Two doctors (P) at those clinics filed a suit against ABC (D), alleging that the methods used in sending undercover patients to the clinics constituted a trespass, invasion of privacy, fraud, and a violation of electronic surveillance statutes. The lower court dismissed these claims and the doctors (P) appealed.

ISSUE: Is an individual who poses as a patient for investigative purposes, visits a doctor, and secretly videotapes the consultation liable for invasion of privacy or trespass?

HOLDING AND DECISION: (Posner, C.J.) No. No invasion of privacy or trespass occurs when an individual posing as a patient, for investigative purposes, visits a doctor and secretly videotapes the consultation. There was no invasion of privacy because the test patients visited the Desnick Eye Clinics (P) during regular business hours, just like others there for eye examinations did, and did not disrupt the daily office activities. ABC's (D) test patients were similar to individuals who pose as prospective home buyers to gather evidence of discrimination. No intimate or personal facts were revealed, and no other conversations were recorded other than the ones between the doctors and the test patients. There has been no trespass or trespass by fraud because the entry onto the property was not an interference with ownership or possession. The fact is that

ABC's (D) test patients were there to get eye exams, even if only for the purpose of uncovering any tampering with medical records or malpractice. State and federal wiretapping statutes permit a party to record a conversation as long as their purposes are not to commit a crime or tort, and it has been determined that the activities of the test patients do not fall into those categories. Although tabloid reporting of the type used by ABC (D) can be very aggressive, the First Amendment still protects it. If the broadcast itself does not contain actionable defamation, and no other crimes are committed in the process of creating the program, then the target of the story does not have a claim in tort even if the investigative tactics used by reporters and producers were surreptitious, confrontational, or even unscrupulous. Affirmed in part, reversed in part, and remanded.

ANALYSIS

The tort of intrusion upon privacy can be very similar to trespass. While often a claim will be brought on both grounds, courts will not grant damages on both claims. The court here, in dismissing both claims, makes note of the fact that ABC (D) went to Desnick's place of business, which was open to the general public, rather than his personal residence. However, another court has held that a trespass occurred when a camera crew went into a crowded restaurant during lunch time with the lights on and the camera rolling, causing some patrons to duck under tables and others to leave without paying, *Le Mistral, Inc. v. Columbia Broadcasting System*, 61 A.D.2d 491, 402 N.Y.S.2d 815 (1978).

Quicknotes

DEFAMATION An intentional false publication, communicated publicly in either oral or written form, subjecting a person to scorn, hatred or ridicule, or injuring him or her in relation to his or her occupation or business.

TRESPASS Unlawful interference with, or damage to, the real or personal property of another.

Shulman v. Group W Productions, Inc.

Injured patient (P) v. Media (D)

Cal. Sup. Ct., 18 Cal. 4th 200, 955 P.2d 469 (1998).

NATURE OF CASE: Appeal from reversal of dismissal of claims of intrusion.

FACT SUMMARY: Shulman (P) alleged that Group W Productions, Inc. (D) had invaded her privacy by filming her helicopter rescue following an auto accident.

RULE OF LAW

One who intentionally intrudes, physically or otherwise, upon the solitude or seclusion of another or his private affairs or concerns, is subject to liability to the other for invasion of his privacy, if the intrusion would be highly offensive to a reasonable person.

FACTS: Shulman (P) was pinned in the wreckage when the car she was riding in overturned, tumbled down an embankment and came to rest upside down in a ditch. A Mercy Air rescue helicopter was dispatched to the scene and a video cameraman employed by Group W Productions, Inc. (Group W) (D) was recording the events for later broadcasting. The entire rescue operation was recorded and later shown on television. Shulman (P) was left a paraplegic as a result of the accident and sued Group W (D) for invasion of privacy, both for intrusion, and for public disclosure of private facts. The district court dismissed all claims. The court of appeals found triable issues existed as whether Group W (D) invaded Shulman's (P) privacy. Group W (D) appealed.

ISSUE: Is one who intentionally intrudes, physically or otherwise, upon the solitude or seclusion of another or his private affairs or concerns, subject to liability to the other for invasion of his privacy, if the intrusion would be highly offensive to a reasonable person?

HOLDING AND DECISION: (Werdegar, J.) Yes. One who intentionally intrudes, physically or otherwise, upon the solitude or seclusion of another or his private affairs or concerns, is subject to liability to the other for invasion of his privacy, if the intrusion would be highly offensive to a reasonable person. Triable issues also exist as to whether Group W (D) tortiously intruded by listening to Shulman's (P) confidential conversations with the nurse without her consent. There was no constitutional privilege protecting Group W's (D) intrusion on Shulman's (P) seclusion and private communications. Affirmed in part, reversed in part, and remanded.

CONCURRENCE AND DISSENT: (Chin, J.) As to the intrusion on Shulman's (P) privacy part of the complaint, Group W's (D) conduct did not meet the standard of "highly offensive to a reasonable person."

ANALYSIS

The plurality found that a jury could find the recording of Shulman's (P) communications to be highly offensive to a reasonable person. Group W's (D) motive was to gather newsworthy material and it was not found to be privileged in this instance. In general, newsgathering activities enjoy no immunity or exemption from laws.

Quicknotes

FIRST AMENDMENT Prohibits Congress from enacting any law respecting an establishment of religion, prohibiting the free exercise of religion, abridging freedom of speech or the press, the right of peaceful assembly and the right to petition for a redress of grievances.

INTRUSION For purposes of an invasion of privacy claim, constitutes an intrusion into an actionable individual's seclusion.

INVASION OF PRIVACY The violation of an individual's right to be protected against unwarranted interference in his personal affairs, falling into one of four categories: (1) appropriating the individual's likeness or name for commercial benefit; (2) intrusion into the individual's seclusion; (3) public disclosure of private facts regarding the individual; and (4) disclosure of facts placing the individual in a false light.

Bartnicki v. Vopper

Wiretapped individual (P) v. Radio commentator (D)

532 U.S. 514 (2001).

NATURE OF CASE: Appeal from a defense summary judgment in a suit for publication by a third party of an illegally obtained wiretap conversation.

FACT SUMMARY: When Bartnicki (P) sued Vopper (D), a radio commentator, for playing on the air a tape of Bartnicki's (P) telephone conversation which had been obtained by the illegal interception by an unknown person, Vopper (D) defended on the grounds of First Amendment free speech.

> ### 🏛 RULE OF LAW
> The disclosure of the contents of an illegally intercepted telephonic communication by a party who did not participate in the disclosure is not actionable.

FACTS: During 1992 and 1993, a teachers' union was engaged in highly contentious negotiations with its school board. At one point, Bartnicki (P), the union's chief negotiator, used her cell phone to speak with Kane, the president of her union. Their remarks were highly inflammatory as to their proposed strike and as to what the union might do. An unidentified person illegally intercepted and recorded the call, then turned the tape over to Vopper (D), a radio commentator highly critical of the union, who played the tape on the air. Bartnicki (P) and Kane (P) sued Vopper (D) for damages for publishing the contents of the illegally obtained tape conversation of the call, relying on both federal and state statutes making unauthorized phone tap a crime. The federal court of appeals concluded that the statutes were invalid because they deterred more speech than necessary to protect the privacy interests at stake. Bartnicki (P) appealed.

ISSUE: Is the disclosure of the contents of an illegally intercepted telephonic communication by a party who did not participate in the disclosure actionable?

HOLDING AND DECISION: (Stevens, J.) No. The disclosure of the contents of an illegally intercepted telephonic communication by a party who did not participate in the disclosure is not actionable. Here, Vopper (D) played no part in the illegal interception. Rather, he found out about the interception only after it occurred, and in fact never learned the identity of the person who made the interception. Vopper's (D) access to the information on the tape was obtained lawfully even though the information itself was intercepted unlawfully by someone else. Furthermore, the subject of the communication was a matter of public concern. If the statements about the labor negotiations had been made in a public arena, during a bargaining session for example, they would have been newsworthy.

This would also be true if a third party had inadvertently overheard Bartnicki (P) making the same statements to Kane (P) when the two thought they were alone. It would be quite remarkable to hold that speech by a law-abiding possessor of information can be suppressed in order to deter conduct by a non-law-abiding third party, as here. There is no basis for assuming that imposing sanctions upon Vopper (D) will deter the unidentified wire tapper (or scanner) from continuing to engage in surreptitious interceptions. Affirmed.

CONCURRENCE: (Breyer, J.) The broadcasters in the instant case engaged in no unlawful activity other than the ultimate publication of the information another had previously obtained. They neither encouraged nor participated directly or indirectly in the interception.

DISSENT: (Rehnquist, C.J.) The transmission of the intercepted communication from the eavesdropper to the third party is itself illegal; where, as here, the third party then knowingly discloses that communication, another illegal act has been committed. The third party in this situation cannot be likened to the reporters in cases who lawfully obtained their information through consensual interviews or public documents.

▶ *ANALYSIS*

In its *Bartnicki* decision, the United States Supreme Court specifically stated that on the facts of the particular case, "privacy concerns give way" when balanced against the interest in publishing matters of public importance. The Court thus made clear that a stranger's illegal conduct does not suffice to remove the First Amendment shield from speech about a matter of public concern.

■▬▬■

Quicknotes

EXPECTATION OF PRIVACY Requirement that in order to invoke the Fourth Amendment's protection against unreasonable searches and seizures, the individual must have a reasonable expectation of privacy in respect to the location searched or thing seized.

FIRST AMENDMENT Prohibits Congress from enacting any law respecting an establishment of religion, prohibiting the free exercise of religion, abridging freedom of speech or the press, the right of peaceful assembly and the right to petition for a redress of grievances.

Continued on next page.

PUBLIC INTEREST Something in which the public has either a monetary or legal interest.

WIRETAP A means of acquiring the content of a communication through an electronic or other device.

Zacchini v. Scripps-Howard Broadcasting Co.

Performer (P) v. Broadcaster (D)

433 U.S. 562 (1977).

NATURE OF CASE: Appeal from dismissal of action for commercial appropriation.

FACT SUMMARY: Zacchini (P), who performed a human cannonball act, sued Scripps-Howard Broadcasting Co. (D) for commercial appropriation after they filmed his act and broadcast it on the 11 o'clock news.

🏛 RULE OF LAW
The First and Fourteenth Amendments do not immunize the media from liability for commercial appropriation when they broadcast a performer's entire act without his consent, thereby posing a substantial threat to his or her ability to earn a living.

FACTS: Zacchini (P) was performing his human cannonball act, which lasted 15 seconds, at a fair in Ohio. The area in which he performed was a fenced area surrounded by grandstands, and anyone attending the fair could observe his act without paying a separate admission. Zacchini (P) noticed a reporter for Scripps-Howard Broadcasting Co. (Scripps-Howard) (D) carrying a small movie camera and asked him not to film the performance. The reporter did not film Zacchini (P) on that day, but returned the next day on the instructions of his producer, and filmed the entire act, which was later broadcast on the 11 o'clock news. Zacchini (P) brought an action for damages on the basis that Scripps-Howard (D) had commercially appropriated his act without his consent. The trial court granted summary judgment for Scripps-Howard (D), and the Ohio Supreme Court affirmed based on the First and Fourteenth Amendments.

ISSUE: Do the First and Fourteenth Amendments immunize the media from liability for commercial appropriation when they broadcast a performer's entire act without his consent, thereby posing a substantial threat to his or her ability to earn a living?

HOLDING AND DECISION: (White, J.) No. The First and Fourteenth Amendments do not immunize the media from liability for commercial appropriation when they broadcast a performer's entire act without his consent, thereby posing a substantial threat to his or her ability to earn a living. The Ohio court incorrectly relied on the First and Fourteenth Amendments to deny Zacchini (P) recovery for commercial appropriation. Although the media does have a right to report newsworthy events, it does not have a "right of publicity" as the Ohio court stated. While they are permitted to broadcast the footage, the right of publicity belongs to Zacchini (P). His 15 second act is his livelihood, similar to a copyrighted play,

and Scripps-Howard (D) broadcast of footage deprives Zacchini (P) of his ability to earn a living. The doctrine of commercial appropriation requires that Zacchini (P) be compensated for the loss of income he will suffer because fewer people will attend his act in person. Reversed.

DISSENT: (Powell, J.) The majority's interpretation of what the First Amendment requires is incorrect. The broadcast of Zacchini's (P) act is not comparable to the unauthorized commercial use broadcast of sporting events or a copyrighted play. Scripps-Howard (D) did not use the film to make a profit, only as a segment of a news broadcast.

DISSENT: (Stevens, J.) Because the record fails to indicate whether the Ohio Supreme Court relied on federal constitutional issues in deciding the instant case, I would remand the matter for clarification of its holding before deciding the federal constitutional issue.

▌ ANALYSIS

The dissent's argument is convincing in that allowing Zacchini (P) to recover could create endless liability when similar human-interest type stories are broadcast. In fact, other plaintiffs since *Zacchini* have had less success when attempting similar arguments if they did not have a copyright or contract to back up the claim. Most entertainers who perform live now, however, know now more about protecting their interests, especially since video recording devices are commonplace on most cellphones.

━■━

Quicknotes

FIRST AMENDMENT Prohibits Congress from enacting any law respecting an establishment of religion, prohibiting the free exercise of religion, abridging freedom of speech or the press, the right of peaceful assembly and the right to petition for a redress of grievances.

FOURTEENTH AMENDMENT No person shall be deprived of life, liberty, or property, without the due process of law.

RIGHT OF PUBLICITY The right of a person to control the commercial exploitation of his name or likeness.

COPYRIGHT Refers to the exclusive rights granted to an artist pursuant to Article I, section 8, clause 8 of the United States Constitution over the reproduction, display, performance, distribution, and adaptation of his work for a period prescribed by statute.

━■━

Winter v. DC Comics

Celebrities (P) v. Comic book publisher (D)

Cal. Sup. Ct., 30 Cal. 4th 881, 69 P.3d 473 (2003).

NATURE OF CASE: Appeal from the refusal to grant a defense motion for summary judgment in a suit for the wrongful appropriation of a celebrity's likeness.

FACT SUMMARY: When DC Comics (D) parodied Johnny and Edgar Winter (P), well-known performing and recording musicians. Johnny and Edgar Winter (P) sued DC Comics (D) for wrongful appropriation of their likeness.

🏛 **RULE OF LAW**

A work containing significant creative elements that transform it into something more than a mere celebrity likeness is entitled to First Amendment protection.

FACTS: Johnny and Edgar Winter (P), well-known performing and recording musicians, were parodied in DC Comics (D), which used a somewhat similar likeness them in lampooning them. The Winter brothers (P) sued DC Comics (D) for several causes of action, including the wrongful misappropriation of their name or likeness under a California statutory provision. DC Comics (D) moved for a summary judgment on First Amendment grounds. The trial court granted the motion on some of the counts, concluding however, that triable issues existed as to the count for statutory misappropriation of a celebrity's name or likeness. DC Comics (D) appealed.

ISSUE: Is a work containing significant creative elements that transform it into something more than a mere celebrity likeness entitled to First Amendment protection?

HOLDING AND DECISION: (Chin, J.) Yes. A work containing significant creative elements that transform it into something more than a mere celebrity likeness is entitled to First Amendment protection. Although celebrities have a state statutory right by which they can prohibit others from using their likeness, the constitutional right to First Amendment free speech may, as here, trump the statutory right of publicity. Applying a balancing test to the instant case, the comic books published by DC Comics (D) contain "significant creative elements that transform them into something more than a mere likeness" of the performers Johnny and Edgar Winter (P). The comic book depictions of the latter were drawn in a highly stylized and distorted form to parody the performers rather than to trade on their economic success and public image. When artistic expression takes the form of a literal depiction of a celebrity for commercial gain, the state law interest in protecting the fruits of artistic labor outweighs the expressive interest of the imitative artist. On the other hand, where, as here, the extreme parody of

Winter (P) which was created by DC Comics (D), did not generally threaten any of the former's markets for celebrity memorabilia or otherwise, hence constitutes constitutionally protected speech. Furthermore, in determining whether the work is transformative, courts are not to be concerned with the quality of the artistic contribution; in this regard, even vulgar forms of expression, as here, fully qualify for First Amendment protection. Reversed and remanded.

📎 **ANALYSIS**

As made clear by the court in the *Winter* decision, the right of publicity derived from public prominence does not confer a shield to ward off caricature, parody, and satire.

■━■

Quicknotes

APPROPRIATION (OF LIKENESS) The act of making something one's own or making use of something to serve one's own interest.

FIRST AMENDMENT Prohibits Congress from enacting any law respecting an establishment of religion, prohibiting the free exercise of religion, abridging freedom of speech or the press, the right of peaceful assembly and the right to petition for a redress of grievances.

MISAPPROPRIATION The unlawful use of another's property or funds.

PARODY Affirmative defense to an action for copyright infringement under the fair use doctrine the infringer's use of the copyrighted material was permissible for the purpose of criticism or satire.

RIGHT OF PUBLICITY The right of a person to control the commercial exploitation of his name or likeness.

TRANSFORMATIVE TEST In right to publicity action, defense that the work is protected by the First Amendment if it contains significant transformative elements or the value of the work does not derive primarily from a celebrity's fame.

Intentional Economic Harm

Quick Reference Rules of Law

Ollerman v. O'Rourke Co., Inc.

Buyer (P) v. Seller (D)

Wis. Sup. Ct., 94 Wis. 2d 17, 288 N.W.2d 95 (1980).

NATURE OF CASE: Appeal from order overruling motion to dismiss for failure to state a claim.

FACT SUMMARY: Ollerman (P), who bought a vacant lot on which he planned to build a house, discovered a well while excavating and brought suit against seller O'Rourke Co., Inc. (D) for misrepresentation.

🏛 RULE OF LAW
A subdivider-vendor of a residential lot has a duty to a non-commercial purchaser to disclose facts that are known to the vendor, material to the transaction, and not readily discernible to the purchaser.

FACTS: Ollerman (P) bought a vacant lot in a subdivided residential area with the intent of building his home on the property. The seller of the property was O'Rourke Co., Inc. (D), a corporation engaged in the business of developing and selling real estate. After beginning excavation of the land for the construction of the house, a well was uncapped and water released. Ollerman (P) brought suit for misrepresentation alleging that O'Rourke (D) had failed to disclose the well, thereby inducing Ollerman (P) to purchase the land. Ollerman (P) stated that O'Rourke knew (D) that Ollerman (P) was unfamiliar with the area in which the land was located and with real estate transactions as a whole. Ollerman (P) further alleged that the property was worth significantly less with a well beneath it and that constructing a house on the land was far more costly. O'Rourke (D) made a motion to dismiss the complaint for failure to state a claim upon which relief could be granted, the motion was overruled by the circuit court, and O'Rourke (D) appealed.

ISSUE: Does a subdivider-vendor of a residential lot have a duty to a non-commercial purchaser to disclose facts that are known to the vendor, material to the transaction, and not readily discernible to the purchaser?

HOLDING AND DECISION: (Abrahamson, J.) Yes. A subdivider-vendor of a residential lot has a duty to a noncommercial purchaser to disclose facts that are known to the vendor, material to the transaction, not readily discernible to the purchaser. Although the traditional legal rule is that there is no duty to disclose in an arm's length transaction, there is a trend toward finding exceptions to this rule. Where the vendor is in the real estate business and skilled and knowledgeable and the purchaser is not, the purchaser is in a poor position to discover a condition that is not readily discernible. Material facts are those to which a reasonable purchaser would attach importance in determining whether or not to go ahead with a transaction. Therefore, if the facts not disclosed were material, Ollerman (P) may be justified in his reliance on the knowledge, skill, and representations of O'Rourke (D). These are issues that need to be decided at trial, so the motion to dismiss was properly overruled. Affirmed.

▶ ANALYSIS
The court's holding that a duty to disclose may exist is a strong trend. Using a similar rationale, another court has held that a residential developer and real estate broker had a duty to disclose to prospective buyers the fact that a landfill was located nearby. See *Strawn v. Caruso*, 657 A.2d 420 (1995). On the other hand, although considerations of fairness and ethics in business transactions are significant, it is not one party's job to do the other side's research.

■■■

Quicknotes

DUTY TO DISCLOSE The duty owed by a fiduciary to reveal those facts that have a material effect on the interests of the party that must be informed.

MISREPRESENTATION A statement or conduct by one party to another that constitutes a false representation of fact.

■■■

Imperial Ice Co. v. Rossier

Ice provider (P) v. Competing ice provider (D)

Cal. Sup. Ct., 18 Cal. 2d 33, 112 P.2d 631 (1941).

NATURE OF CASE: An action for damages for inducing breach of contract.

FACT SUMMARY: In violation of a covenant not to compete with Imperial Ice Co.'s (P) business, Coker began selling ice supplied to him by Rossier (D). Imperial Ice Co. (P) alleged that Rossier (D) induced Coker to violate his covenant.

🏛 RULE OF LAW
A person may not intentionally induce the breach of a contract for the reason that he is in competition with one of the parties to the contract and seeks to further his own economic advantage at the expense of the other.

FACTS: Coker sold an ice distributing company to California Consumers Company. In the purchase agreement Coker agreed that he would not engage in the business of ice distributing or selling in that area "so long as the purchasers, or anyone deriving title to the good will of said business from said purchasers, shall be engaged in a like business therein." Imperial Ice Co. (P) acquired the company from California Consumers Company, including the right to enforce the covenant not to compete. Coker subsequently began selling, in the area, ice supplied to him by Rossier (D). Imperial Ice Co. (P) alleged that Rossier (D) induced Coker to violate his covenant not to compete so that Rossier (D) might sell ice to him at a profit.

ISSUE: May an action be maintained against a defendant who has induced another to violate a contract with the plaintiff because the defendant is in competition with the plaintiff and seeks to further his own economic advantage at the expense of the plaintiff's?

HOLDING AND DECISION: (Traynor, J.) Yes. Most jurisdictions hold that an action will lie for inducing a breach of contract by the use of moral, social or economic pressures, unless there is sufficient justification for such inducement. Such justification exists when a person induces a breach of contract to protect an interest that has greater social value than insuring the stability of the contract. Examples are inducing breaches of contract that would be injurious to health, safety, or good morals. However, a person is not justified in inducing a breach of contract simply because he is in competition with one of the parties to the contract and seeks to further his own economic advantage at the expense of the other. In this case the contract gave Imperial Ice Co. (P) the right to sell ice in the area free from competition by Coker. Rossier (D), by virtue of his interest in the sale of ice in the area,

was in competition with Imperial (P). By inducing Coker to violate his contract, as alleged in the complaint, he sought to further his own advantage at Imperial's (P) expense. Such conduct is not justified. Reversed.

▶ ANALYSIS

A person may induce a third party to forsake another competitor if no contractual relationship exists between the latter two. Also if two parties have separate contracts with a third, each may resort to any legitimate means to secure performance of his contract even though the necessary result will be to cause a breach of the other contract.

━■━

Quicknotes

BREACH OF CONTRACT Unlawful failure by a party to perform its obligations pursuant to contract.

━■━

Della Penna v. Toyota Motor Sales, U.S.A., Inc.

Automobile wholesaler (P) v. Automobile manufacturer (D)

Cal. Sup. Ct., 11 Cal. 4th 376, 902 P.2d 740 (1995).

NATURE OF CASE: Appeal from reversal of verdict for defendant in claim for interference with prospective economic advantage.

FACT SUMMARY: Della Penna (P), an auto wholesaler who exported cars to Japan for resale, brought action against Toyota Motor Sales, U.S.A., Inc. (D) when it took steps to prevent him from conducting his business.

🏛 RULE OF LAW
A plaintiff seeking to recover for interference with prospective economic advantage has the burden of proving that the defendant's interference was wrongful by some measure beyond the fact of the interference itself.

FACTS: Della Penna (P) had a lucrative business in which he bought Lexus cars from U.S. retailers at near retail prices and then exported them to Japan for resale. Toyota Motor Sales, U.S.A., Inc. (Toyota) (D), the maker of Lexus, wanted to prevent imported U.S. Lexus cars from being re-exported to Japan. To try to curb this practice, Toyota (D) compiled a list of offending auto brokers and warned its dealers that those who did business with them faced possible sanctions. As a result, Della Penna's (P) supply of cars dried up. Della Penna (P) brought suit for interference of prospective economic advantage. The judge gave the jury instructions that Della Penna (P) had the burden of showing that Toyota's (D) interference was wrongful "by some measure beyond the fact of the interference itself." The jury returned a verdict for Toyota (D), but the court of appeals reversed, finding that the judge erred in placing the burden on Della Penna (P). The Supreme Court of California granted review.

ISSUE: Is it unfair to charge a plaintiff seeking to recover for interference with prospective economic advantage with the burden of proving that the defendant's interference was wrongful by "some measure beyond the fact of the interference itself?"

HOLDING AND DECISION: (Arabian, J.) No. A plaintiff seeking to recover for interference with prospective economic advantage has the burden of proving that the defendant's interference was wrongful by some measure beyond the fact of the interference itself. There is an important distinction between the disruption of an existing contract and the interference with a prospective contract or economic relationship. Courts should firmly distinguish these differences and acknowledge that relationships short of a contract have inherent risks. Della Penna's (P) busi-

ness, although lucrative, was inherently risky because it was entirely speculative. Della Penna (P) did not have contracts with the dealers he bought from. Therefore, the instruction given by the trial court, that Della Penna (P) had the burden of proving that Toyota's (D) actions were wrongful beyond the fact of the interference, was proper under the circumstances. The judgment of the court of appeals should be reversed, and the trial court's judgment for Toyota (D) should be reinstated. Reversed and remanded.

CONCURRENCE: (Mosk, J.) The majority's reversal of the court of appeals was correct although the rationale was not. The tort of interference with prospective economic advantage can be proven by showing other tortious conduct such as defamation, fraud, or deceit. The majority was wrong in accepting that the instruction given to the jury by the trial court was proper. The formulation of an instruction should not include any reference to motive. However, this error was not prejudicial.

▶ ANALYSIS
Courts faced with cases of interference with prospective economic advantage have developed numerous formulas and tests for determining liability. The Restatement (Second) of Torts § 766B identified a seven-factor balancing test that the California court declined to apply. These factors include: (1) the nature of the actor's conduct; (2) the actor's motive; (3) the interests of the other with which the actor's conduct interferes; (4) the interests sought to be advanced by the actor; (5) the social interests in protecting the freedom of action of the actor and the contractual interests of the other; (6) the proximity or remoteness of the actor's conduct to the interference; and (7) the relations between the parties.

Quicknotes

BURDEN OF PROOF The duty of a party to introduce evidence to support a fact that is in dispute in an action.

INTERFERENCE WITH PROSPECTIVE ADVANTAGE An intentional tort whereby a defendant intentionally interferes with a valid business expectancy, resulting in the termination of the expectancy and damages.

All-Tech Telecom, Inc. v. Amway Corp.

Distributor (P) v. Producer (D)

174 F.3d 862 (7th Cir. 1999).

NATURE OF CASE: Appeal from dismissal of claims of intentional and negligent misrepresentation.

FACT SUMMARY: All-Tech Telecom, Inc. (P) alleged that Amway Corp. (D) had misrepresented a new product, and sued for damages in tort and for breach of warranty.

🏛 RULE OF LAW
Where there are well-developed contract remedies, there is no need to provide tort remedies for misrepresentation.

FACTS: Amway Corp. (D) contracted with All-Tech Telecom, Inc. (All-Tech) (P) and others to distribute a new telephone service. When the new service proved unprofitable, All-Tech (P) sued Amway (D) for misrepresentations it had allegedly made at a trade meeting. The district court threw out all of All-Tech's (P) claims of misrepresentation on the basis of the economic loss doctrine. A jury found a breach of warranty, but no damages were awarded on that claim. All-Tech (P) appealed.

ISSUE: Where there are well-developed contract remedies, is there a need to provide tort remedies for misrepresentation?

HOLDING AND DECISION: (Posner, C.J.) No. Where there are well-developed contract remedies, there is no need to provide tort remedies for misrepresentation. Tort remedies would duplicate the contract remedies, adding unnecessary complexity to the law. The representations allegedly made by Amway (D) were in fact statements made by independent contractors who worked as Amway (D) distributors. Amway (D) was therefore not legally responsible for the statements. Other alleged misrepresentations were mere puffing or sales patter. Affirmed.

▶ ANALYSIS

The court also dismissed claims based on promissory estoppel. It found that promissory estoppel would not apply since there was an express contract. Promissory estoppel is not a doctrine designed to give a party a second bite at the apple in the event it fails to prove breach of contract.

▬▬▬

Quicknotes

BREACH OF WARRANTY The breach of a promise made by one party to a contract that the other party may rely on a fact, relieving that party from the obligation of determining whether the fact is true and indemnifying the other party from liability if that fact is shown to be false.

INDEPENDENT CONTRACTOR A party undertaking a particular assignment for another who retains control over the manner in which it is executed.

INTENTIONAL MISREPRESENTATION A statement or conduct by one party to another that constitutes a false representation of fact.

NEGLIGENT MISREPRESENTATION A misrepresentation that is made pursuant to a business relationship, in violation of an obligation owed, upon which the plaintiff relies to his detriment.

PROMISSORY ESTOPPEL A promise that is enforceable if the promisor should reasonably expect that it will induce action or forbearance on the part of the promisee, and does in fact cause such action or forbearance, and it is the only means of avoiding injustice.

▬▬▬

Glossary

Common Latin Words and Phrases Encountered in the Law

A FORTIORI: Because one fact exists or has been proven, therefore a second fact that is related to the first fact must also exist.

A PRIORI: From the cause to the effect. A term of logic used to denote that when one generally accepted truth is shown to be a cause, another particular effect must necessarily follow.

AB INITIO: From the beginning; a condition which has existed throughout, as in a marriage which was void ab initio.

ACTUS REUS: The wrongful act; in criminal law, such action sufficient to trigger criminal liability.

AD VALOREM: According to value; an ad valorem tax is imposed upon an item located within the taxing jurisdiction calculated by the value of such item.

AMICUS CURIAE: Friend of the court. Its most common usage takes the form of an amicus curiae brief, filed by a person who is not a party to an action but is nonetheless allowed to offer an argument supporting his legal interests.

ARGUENDO: In arguing. A statement, possibly hypothetical, made for the purpose of argument, is one made arguendo.

BILL QUIA TIMET: A bill to quiet title (establish ownership) to real property.

BONA FIDE: True, honest, or genuine. May refer to a person's legal position based on good faith or lacking notice of fraud (such as a bona fide purchaser for value) or to the authenticity of a particular document (such as a bona fide last will and testament).

CAUSA MORTIS: With approaching death in mind. A gift causa mortis is a gift given by a party who feels certain that death is imminent.

CAVEAT EMPTOR: Let the buyer beware. This maxim is reflected in the rule of law that a buyer purchases at his own risk because it is his responsibility to examine, judge, test, and otherwise inspect what he is buying.

CERTIORARI: A writ of review. Petitions for review of a case by the United States Supreme Court are most often done by means of a writ of certiorari.

CONTRA: On the other hand. Opposite. Contrary to.

CORAM NOBIS: Before us; writs of error directed to the court that originally rendered the judgment.

CORAM VOBIS: Before you; writs of error directed by an appellate court to a lower court to correct a factual error.

CORPUS DELICTI: The body of the crime; the requisite elements of a crime amounting to objective proof that a crime has been committed.

CUM TESTAMENTO ANNEXO, ADMINISTRATOR (ADMINISTRATOR C.T.A.): With will annexed; an administrator c.t.a. settles an estate pursuant to a will in which he is not appointed.

DE BONIS NON, ADMINISTRATOR (ADMINISTRATOR D.B.N.): Of goods not administered; an administrator d.b.n. settles a partially settled estate.

DE FACTO: In fact; in reality; actually. Existing in fact but not officially approved or engendered.

DE JURE: By right; lawful. Describes a condition that is legitimate "as a matter of law," in contrast to the term "de facto," which connotes something existing in fact but not legally sanctioned or authorized. For example, de facto segregation refers to segregation brought about by housing patterns, etc., whereas de jure segregation refers to segregation created by law.

DE MINIMIS: Of minimal importance; insignificant; a trifle; not worth bothering about.

DE NOVO: Anew; a second time; afresh. A trial de novo is a new trial held at the appellate level as if the case originated there and the trial at a lower level had not taken place.

DICTA: Generally used as an abbreviated form of obiter dicta, a term describing those portions of a judicial opinion incidental or not necessary to resolution of the specific question before the court. Such nonessential statements and remarks are not considered to be binding precedent.

DUCES TECUM: Refers to a particular type of writ or subpoena requesting a party or organization to produce certain documents in their possession.

EN BANC: Full bench. Where a court sits with all justices present rather than the usual quorum.

EX PARTE: For one side or one party only. An ex parte proceeding is one undertaken for the benefit of only one party, without notice to, or an appearance by, an adverse party.

EX POST FACTO: After the fact. An ex post facto law is a law that retroactively changes the consequences of a prior act.

EX REL.: Abbreviated form of the term "ex relatione," meaning upon relation or information. When the state brings an action in which it has no interest against an individual at the instigation of one who has a private interest in the matter.

FORUM NON CONVENIENS: Inconvenient forum. Although a court may have jurisdiction over the case, the action should be tried in a more conveniently located court, one to which parties and witnesses may more easily travel, for example.

GUARDIAN AD LITEM: A guardian of an infant as to litigation, appointed to represent the infant and pursue his/her rights.

HABEAS CORPUS: You have the body. The modern writ of habeas corpus is a writ directing that a person (body) being detained (such as a prisoner) be brought before the court so that the legality of his detention can be judicially ascertained.

IN CAMERA: In private, in chambers. When a hearing is held before a judge in his chambers or when all spectators are excluded from the courtroom.

IN FORMA PAUPERIS: In the manner of a pauper. A party who proceeds in forma pauperis because of his poverty is one who is allowed to bring suit without liability for costs.

INFRA: Below, under. A word referring the reader to a later part of a book. (The opposite of supra.)

IN LOCO PARENTIS: In the place of a parent.

IN PARI DELICTO: Equally wrong; a court of equity will not grant requested relief to an applicant who is in pari delicto, or as much at fault in the transactions giving rise to the controversy as is the opponent of the applicant.

IN PARI MATERIA: On like subject matter or upon the same matter. Statutes relating to the same person or things are said to be in pari materia. It is a general rule of statutory construction that such statutes should be construed together, i.e., looked at as if they together constituted one law.

IN PERSONAM: Against the person. Jurisdiction over the person of an individual.

IN RE: In the matter of. Used to designate a proceeding involving an estate or other property.

IN REM: A term that signifies an action against the res, or thing. An action in rem is basically one that is taken directly against property, as distinguished from an action in personam, i.e., against the person.

INTER ALIA: Among other things. Used to show that the whole of a statement, pleading, list, statute, etc., has not been set forth in its entirety.

INTER PARTES: Between the parties. May refer to contracts, conveyances or other transactions having legal significance.

INTER VIVOS: Between the living. An inter vivos gift is a gift made by a living grantor, as distinguished from bequests contained in a will, which pass upon the death of the testator.

IPSO FACTO: By the mere fact itself.

JUS: Law or the entire body of law.

LEX LOCI: The law of the place; the notion that the rights of parties to a legal proceeding are governed by the law of the place where those rights arose.

MALUM IN SE: Evil or wrong in and of itself; inherently wrong. This term describes an act that is wrong by its very nature, as opposed to one which would not be wrong but for the fact that there is a specific legal prohibition against it (malum prohibitum).

MALUM PROHIBITUM: Wrong because prohibited, but not inherently evil. Used to describe something that is wrong because it is expressly forbidden by law but that is not in and of itself evil, e.g., speeding.

MANDAMUS: We command. A writ directing an official to take a certain action.

MENS REA: A guilty mind; a criminal intent. A term used to signify the mental state that accompanies a crime or other prohibited act. Some crimes require only a general mens rea (general intent to do the prohibited act), but others, like assault with intent to murder, require the existence of a specific mens rea.

MODUS OPERANDI: Method of operating; generally refers to the manner or style of a criminal in committing crimes, admissible in appropriate cases as evidence of the identity of a defendant.

NEXUS: A connection to.

NISI PRIUS: A court of first impression. A nisi prius court is one where issues of fact are tried before a judge or jury.

N.O.V. (NON OBSTANTE VEREDICTO): Notwithstanding the verdict. A judgment n.o.v. is a judgment given in favor of one party despite the fact that a verdict was returned in favor of the other party, the justification being that the verdict either had no reasonable support in fact or was contrary to law.

NUNC PRO TUNC: Now for then. This phrase refers to actions that may be taken and will then have full retroactive effect.

PENDENTE LITE: Pending the suit; pending litigation under way.

PER CAPITA: By head; beneficiaries of an estate, if they take in equal shares, take per capita.

PER CURIAM: By the court; signifies an opinion ostensibly written "by the whole court" and with no identified author.

PER SE: By itself, in itself; inherently.

PER STIRPES: By representation. Used primarily in the law of wills to describe the method of distribution where a person, generally because of death, is unable to take that which is left to him by the will of another, and therefore his heirs divide such property between them rather than take under the will individually.

PRIMA FACIE: On its face, at first sight. A prima facie case is one that is sufficient on its face, meaning that the evidence supporting it is adequate to establish the case until contradicted or overcome by other evidence.

PRO TANTO: For so much; as far as it goes. Often used in eminent domain cases when a property owner receives partial payment for his land without prejudice to his right to bring suit for the full amount he claims his land to be worth.

QUANTUM MERUIT: As much as he deserves. Refers to recovery based on the doctrine of unjust enrichment in those cases in which a party has rendered valuable services or furnished materials that were accepted and enjoyed by another under circumstances that would reasonably notify the recipient that the rendering party expected to be paid. In essence, the law implies a contract to pay the reasonable value of the services or materials furnished.

QUASI: Almost like; as if; nearly. This term is essentially used to signify that one subject or thing is almost analogous to another but that material differences between them do exist. For example, a quasi-criminal proceeding is one that is not strictly criminal but shares enough of the same characteristics to require some of the same safeguards (e.g., procedural due process must be followed in a parole hearing).

QUID PRO QUO: Something for something. In contract law, the consideration, something of value, passed between the parties to render the contract binding.

RES GESTAE: Things done; in evidence law, this principle justifies the admission of a statement that would otherwise be hearsay when it is made so closely to the event in question as to be said to be a part of it, or with such spontaneity as not to have the possibility of falsehood.

RES IPSA LOQUITUR: The thing speaks for itself. This doctrine gives rise to a rebuttable presumption of negligence when the instrumentality causing the injury was within the exclusive control of the defendant, and the injury was one that does not normally occur unless a person has been negligent.

RES JUDICATA: A matter adjudged. Doctrine which provides that once a court of competent jurisdiction has rendered a final judgment or decree on the merits, that judgment or decree is conclusive upon the parties to the case and prevents them from engaging in any other litigation on the points and issues determined therein.

RESPONDEAT SUPERIOR: Let the master reply. This doctrine holds the master liable for the wrongful acts of his servant (or the principal for his agent) in those cases in which the servant (or agent) was acting within the scope of his authority at the time of the injury.

STARE DECISIS: To stand by or adhere to that which has been decided. The common law doctrine of stare decisis attempts to give security and certainty to the law by following the policy that once a principle of law as applicable to a certain set of facts has been set forth in a decision, it forms a precedent which will subsequently be followed, even though a different decision might be made were it the first time the question had arisen. Of course, stare decisis is not an inviolable principle and is departed from in instances where there is good cause (e.g., considerations of public policy led the Supreme Court to disregard prior decisions sanctioning segregation).

SUPRA: Above. A word referring a reader to an earlier part of a book.

ULTRA VIRES: Beyond the power. This phrase is most commonly used to refer to actions taken by a corporation that are beyond the power or legal authority of the corporation.

Addendum of French Derivatives

IN PAIS: Not pursuant to legal proceedings.

CHATTEL: Tangible personal property.

CY PRES: Doctrine permitting courts to apply trust funds to purposes not expressed in the trust but necessary to carry out the settlor's intent.

PER AUTRE VIE: For another's life; during another's life. In property law, an estate may be granted that will terminate upon the death of someone other than the grantee.

PROFIT A PRENDRE: A license to remove minerals or other produce from land.

VOIR DIRE: Process of questioning jurors as to their predispositions about the case or parties to a proceeding in order to identify those jurors displaying bias or prejudice.